CIVIL WAR BLUNDERS

CIVIL WAR BLUNDERS

Clint Johnson

JOHN F. BLAIR, PUBLISHER
WINSTON-SALEM, NORTH CAROLINA

The paper in this book meets the guidelines
for permanence and durability of the
Committee on Production Guidelines for
Book Longevity of the Council on Library Resources.

Design: Liza Langrall

Cover art: Soldiers playing football, an engraving by
Winslow Homer originally appearing in Harper's
Weekly, July 15, 1865.

Library of Congress Cataloging-in-Publication Data
Johnson, Clint, 1953–
    Civil War blunders / Clint Johnson.
        p.   cm.
    Includes bibliographical references and index.
    ISBN 0-89587-163-7 (alk. paper)
    1. United States—History—Civil War, 1861–
1865—Anecdotes. 2. United States—History—Civil
War, 1861–1865—Campaigns—Anecdotes.
3. Errors—History—19th century—Anecdotes.
I. Title.
E655.J674 1997
973.7—dc21   97-7289

To my mother, **LAURA HARTSFIELD JOHNSON**, *a teacher for more than forty years who still misses it, and my mother-in-law,* **LAVERNE BROZOVICH GEDEMER**, *who gave me my wife, Barbara*

CONTENTS

1 8 6 3

1864

1865

Nothing was funny about the Civil War. More than 620,000 Americans and their allies died on battlefields, in camps, on marches, and aboard ships from New Mexico to France. And that does not count the thousands of civilians, mostly Southerners of all races, who suffered early death due to the hunger, disease, and stress associated with the Union's calculated destruction of the Confederacy's farms, crops, livestock, factories, warehouses, and urban infrastructure.

No, nothing was funny, but it was finding humor amidst the devastation that kept soldiers marching forward into the face of the enemy. When a soldier saw the shallow graves of comrades or mounds of dead artillery horses, he reacted by making jokes about his situation. Confederates made fun of their officers and the men of other states, singing songs about the "Georgia militia eating goober peas." Northerners sang about their fleeting bravery with lyrics like "to the rear I quickly flew." Some real battles and incidents were given amusing names, such as "the Buckland Races" and "Kilpatrick's Shirttail Skedaddle." Even so sober a figure as Robert E. Lee had a sense of humor. When Lee saw Union soldiers scurrying in retreat from the woods near Fredericksburg, Virginia, just minutes after they had charged, he turned and said to another general, "It is well that war is so terrible—we should grow too fond of it."

So the Civil War did have its amusing side. Many of those moments came when someone, usually a general or an admiral, blundered. Those high in the command chain proved themselves very good at making major, sometimes catastrophic, mistakes. Many of the men the two governments selected as their military leaders were drunkards, didn't know a cannon's breech from its muzzle, couldn't ride a horse, didn't have the slightest idea what a general was supposed to do on a battlefield, or couldn't speak English. Some were cowards. Others were foolishly brave. Some had inflated egos that got them and their men into precarious positions. Some simply died by being in the wrong place at the wrong time. Others escaped injury time and time again for no reason other than luck.

This book does not attempt to record all the serious military mistakes made during the Civil War, not even those some historians consider obvious, such as that of the Union general who pulled his division out of line at the Battle of Chickamauga under orders he knew he should ignore. Every battle had its mistakes, its generals who should have gone left instead of right. And accounts of all those mistakes can be countered by other historians who claim that the so-called errors were not that at all, but just maneuvers that didn't work out.

What this book does is try to describe Civil War blunders that had something funny about them. Not everyone will find all these stories amusing. The death of Union major general John Sedgwick at Spotsylvania Court House was certainly more tragic than entertaining, but I hope even serious-minded readers will admit the black humor and irony of a general's confidently announcing that Confederate sharpshooters "can't hit an elephant at this distance" just before taking a round.

Though I am descended from Floridians, Georgians, and Alabamans, I have tried to be bipartisan. For every story I tell of bad Union generals like Brigadier General James H. Ledlie, who blew the heads off his own men with misplaced artillery fire, I tell stories of bad Confederate generals like Brigadier General Nathan Evans, who shelled his own men because he apparently forgot they were in the positions where he had ordered them.

The book is organized chronologically starting with mistakes that occurred before the war even erupted. If I've missed any of your favorites, or if you know stories that have not been told outside your local area, please write me in care of the publisher. Maybe we can collect enough to publish a second volume of Civil War blunders.

Even if you do not send them to me, put those stories in writing and do everything you can to preserve the Civil War history of your community. There is an almost imperceptible movement to erase the war from the nation's consciousness. Witness the casually announced plan late in 1996 to remove the Civil War exhibits from the Museum of American History in Washington and the scattered attempts around the South to remove Confederate statues and historical markers. This movement would just as soon there be no South, no North, no East, no West—just one country with one accent and one history. Such a country would be much easier to sell to, much easier to govern, much easier to control.

Those of us who care about history should not give in to suggestions that "the Late Unpleasantness" be wiped from the nation's consciousness as a means of healing divisions. Forgetting the war and destroying memories of the Confederacy, the Confederate flag, and the millions who fought on both sides will not help people understand each other any better. In my view, a much better approach is to examine the accomplishments—and the blunders—on both sides. When you can appreciate the brilliance of your enemies and laugh at the blunders of your heroes, you have truly grown.

ACKNOWLEDGMENTS

I want to thank Mark L. Jenkins of Westerville, Ohio, for information on John Ericsson and for alerting me to the Battle of the Head of the Passes on the Mississippi River. I also wish to thank Arthur W. Bergeron, Jr., of Chester, Virginia, for sending me details on the Confederates who caught grenades on blankets at the Battle of Port Hudson, Louisiana. I've never met these two gentlemen, but their electronically mailed suggestions found their way into the book. Thanks also goes to Spessard Stone of Wauchula, Florida, for compiling details on some little-known Florida engagements.

Thanks goes to Anne Holcomb, publicity manager at John F. Blair, Publisher, for suggesting the idea for this book. After reading in my *Touring the Carolinas' Civil War Sites* about how naked Confederates defeated clothed Federals at the Battle of Boone's Mill, North Carolina, in July 1863, she asked me if I knew any more "funny but true" stories from the war. This book is my attempt to answer that question.

Thanks also goes to Blair employees Steve Kirk for his editing; Liza Langrall for her book design; Anne Schultz for her sales efforts; and

Carolyn Sakowski, president, for taking on another oddball Civil War book. The other Blair employees—Lisa Wagoner, Margaret Couch, Debbie Hampton, Sue Clark, Andrew Waters, and Heath Simpson—all contributed to the production and sale of the book.

Once again, I thank my Green Bay Packer–fan, Racine-native wife, Barbara, for 13 years of marriage to a man who is often fighting reenactments on distant Civil War battlefields in his role of private with the 26th North Carolina or the 24th Michigan Regiments. She is only the second Yankee in my 270-year-old Southern family. Barbara has always been there when I needed her and always will be. She has put up with Civil War books, snoring, inside-out underwear, muddy reenacting clothes, hardheadedness, black-powder stains on the carpet, and a variety of other habits that make up my character. She is something special.

Finally, I want to thank the teachers in Arcadia, DeSoto County, Florida, for educating me. Miss Francis Pooser, my fourth-grade teacher at Memorial Grammar, got me interested in the Civil War with a thrilling story about the Battle of Natural Bridge, Florida. I've been hooked on reading about the war ever since. Later, in junior high, Sam McDowell taught me composition and Joy Barnard taught me English, though I still confess problems diagraming sentences, conjugating verbs, recognizing dangling participles, and remembering other fine points. In high school, Miss Sydney Anderson taught me everything I needed to get started in journalism, a twenty-two-year career that still puts food on the table. Of the dozens of teachers over my twelve years in school, I can't think of one who didn't teach me something valuable. Teachers helped me get interested in something early in my life that has brought me pleasure and a career.

1 8 6 1

"It is true *that your men*

are green, but so are the

Confederates. You are all

green together."

–ABRAHAM LINCOLN

$\boxed{1861}$

A PERFUMED LETTER
ALMOST STARTS THE WAR

As a settled land, Florida had an ancient history by the time the Civil War started. But as a state, it was one of the most undeveloped in the nation. The addition of Florida as a territory and state came almost as an afterthought to throwing the Spanish out of the eastern United States. Named a state in 1845, Florida was little more than a frontier at the start of the war. It ranked thirty-first in population among the thirty-five states, dead last among the Southern states. The next-smallest Southern state, Arkansas, had four times the number of residents Florida did. Only fourteen thousand Floridians voted in the 1860 election, an indication both of how few white men of voting age were in the state and how scattered they were in rural counties where national politics rarely reached.

Abraham Lincoln, with his suspicious platform of letting slavery exist where it already did but not allowing it to spread to the Western territories, did not win the vote of a single person in the state. When Lincoln was victorious in the four-way race, Florida's politicians, most of them slave owners, joined others throughout the South in drawing up plans to leave the Union. Florida seceded on January 11, 1861, just one day after Alabama.

Not everyone agreed it was a good idea. "You have opened the gates of Hell, from which shall flow the curses of the damned to sink you to perdition," cried former governor Richard Keith Call. He proved a perceptive man.

The war might have started in Pensacola months before it erupted in Charleston if not for polite Confederates who allowed a lady's letter to pass through their lines.

Secessionists around Pensacola were hoping to prevent the delivery of orders from Washington to the Federal lieutenant at Fort Barrancas. On January 9, 1861, the orders arrived in a pink, scented envelope addressed by a female hand. Southern gentlemen do not read ladies' love letters, so they let the mash note go through.

By order of the Union's secretary of war, the lieutenant was to abandon Fort Barrancas on the mainland, occupy Fort Pickens in Pensacola Harbor, and take any means necessary to prevent the capture of the latter fort. The lieutenant made plans to transfer his command to Fort Pickens and destroy any Federal property that might aid the secessionists.

Had the Confederates intercepted the orders, they likely would have tried to capture Fort Barrancas, a hostile act that could only have been taken as the opening of warfare. They also would have probably occupied Fort Pickens. Instead, they let the Union men make the move to Fort Pickens unmolested.

In September 1861, an attempt was made to capture Fort Pickens by night assault. Confederate forces were sneaking up on the fort when they stumbled into a camp of Federal soldiers outside. Shooting erupted and the fort was alerted. The Confederates retreated.

In retaliation, the Federals in Fort Pickens decided to bombard the Confederates in Fort McRee on the mainland. For two days, the two forts traded shots. More than five thousand cannonballs and explosive shells were fired. Only eight soldiers were killed, a small number for such tonnage of iron flying through the air.

"I had been complimenting the captain of one of our guns for the accuracy of his aim when a shell from Confederate Fort McRee bounded through our bulwarks and took the poor fellow's head square off. His brains and blood were scattered all over my face, blinding my eyes and making my head reel," wrote a sailor on a Union ship that took part in the bombardment.

The bombardment had a positive side. Thousands of fish, stunned by the concussion of the cannons, floated to the surface of Pensacola Bay. Barely waiting for the firing to cease, hundreds of civilians and soldiers on both sides rushed into the water to retrieve this unexpected bounty from the sea.

The parallels between Charleston and Pensacola are striking. Much as Federal forces were ordered to abandon mainland Fort Moultrie and occupy Fort Sumter in Charleston Harbor, they were instructed to abandon mainland Fort Barrancas and occupy Fort Pickens in Pensacola Harbor. And the first shots of the coming war rang out in Pensacola just a day after Confederate cannon rounds were fired at the *Star of the West* as it tried to resupply Fort Sumter in Charleston. The Florida action occurred when secessionists fired musket rounds at Union navy men escaping Fort McRee (then held by the Federals) after an intramural dispute that saw the navy men dump several thousand pounds of Federal army gunpowder into the ocean.

If not for a perfumed letter, the Civil War might have begun in Florida. As it was, no Federal forts in the state fell permanently into Confederate hands. Indeed, unfinished Fort Clinch in Fernandina was ordered abandoned by a new Confederate general assigned to examine Florida's chances of surviving an invasion. His name was Robert E. Lee.

GENERAL DAVID TWIGGS AND THE "OLD WOMAN WITH A BROOMSTICK"

Old soldiers never die. They just join other armies. And if they happen to bring along all the men, weapons, and supplies under their command, so much the better.

The United States Army learned a valuable lesson from Brigadier General David Emanuel Twiggs. If the commanding officer of one of the nation's most important posts asks in an official letter if he should turn it over to the enemy, it might be time to replace him.

––––––––––

In 1860, Twiggs was one of four generals in the United States Army and the third-oldest man on active duty, surpassed only by Generals Winfield Scott and John Wool. William S. Harney was the fourth general in the army, a youngster at age sixty, compared with Twiggs's seventy-one, Scott's seventy-four, and Wool's seventy-six.

Twiggs, Scott, and Wool had fought together in the War of 1812 against the British. Joined by Harney, they all served prominent roles in the Mexican War, Scott acting as commanding general of the army and Twiggs receiving a promotion to brigadier general and commendations for his role in capturing the key Mexican city of Monterey. Scott, his old friend and boss, ran unsuccessfully for president in 1852 in a campaign built around his war-hero status.

During the 1850s, there was not much for soldiers to do other than fight Indians and the occasional Mormon in Utah. Officers who knew how to do nothing other than be soldiers stayed in the army well past the age when they should have retired. Scott grew to more than 350 pounds, so fat that he rarely climbed atop a horse to review his troops. When he did manage to fit himself into a saddle, he reached it by climbing a stepladder, than lowering himself on the unfortunate horse.

By 1860, Twiggs, too, had packed on a few pounds since he boldly led charges into Mexican cannons in 1846. Pictures of him late in his career show the buttons of his dress uniform gamely holding the stretched fabric in place. Despite—or maybe because of—Twiggs's high rank, he also began to fall out of favor with his men. Twiggs had joined the army as a civilian when West Point was still in its infancy. Now, the junior officers who had come through the academy and earned experience in the Mexican War were beginning to look on Twiggs as an old man past his prime. He was taking up space someone younger could have been filling.

In December 1860, Twiggs was in command of the Department of Texas, based at San Antonio, probably the most important post in the prewar army, as it was the bulwark standing between westward settlement and the warring Indians. While Texas was important to the United States, it was also a cotton-growing state talking of secession in order to preserve its citizens' right to own slaves. Twiggs, born in Georgia in 1790, was unsure what he should do. He was torn between an army he had served for forty-eight years and his loyalty to the South.

In December 1860 and again in January 1861, Twiggs wrote his boss in Washington, General Winfield Scott, asking for instructions on what he should do if Texas seceded. Scott's answer implied that any general in the United States Army knew his duty. In a letter to Twiggs dated December 28, 1860, Scott wrote, "The general [meaning himself] does not see, at this moment, that he can tender you any special advice, but leaves the administration of your command in your hands, with the laws and regulations to guide, in the full confidence that your discretion, firmness, and patriotism will affect all of good that the sad state of the times may permit."

When Twiggs received the letter on January 15, 1861, he immediately wrote back suggesting that he be relieved of command by March 4, the day President Lincoln was to be inaugurated. When Scott received that Twiggs letter, he immediately ordered another officer, a colonel born in New York, to leave another Texas post to replace Twiggs, the Georgian whose loyalties were now showing.

Twiggs was colorful in expressing his final opinion on his responsibilities should Texas secede and demand surrender of his department: "If an old woman with a broomstick should come with full authority from the state of Texas to demand the public property, I would give it to her."

No old woman came, but 500 Texas volunteers did on February 16, 1861, fifteen days after a secession convention voted to take Texas out of the Union. Twiggs formally protested but didn't put up any fight when the leaders of the group, which called itself the Texas Committee on Public Safety, demanded his surrender. In addition to the 160 men who surrendered with Twiggs, nearly 2,500 soldiers were ordered to leave the state. They represented 15 percent of the entire United States Army. Also surrendered were more than $1.2 million worth of horses, saddles, food, muskets, pistols, gunpowder, and all manner of United States government equipment. That equipment was used within months to arm several hundred Texans, who marched on New Mexico and Arizona in the name of the Confederacy.

Scott must have felt sadness for his comrade when he learned of Twiggs's surrender to the Texans. Amid calls for Twiggs's arrest for treason, Scott dismissed his old friend from the army on the grounds of "treachery to the flag of his country." An illustrious military career thus came to an abrupt end.

Twiggs felt insulted by the charge. He challenged outgoing United States president James Buchanan to a duel over his dismissal. The two old men never met on the field of honor. One wonders if a seventy-one-year-old general and a seventy-year-old president would have been able to even see each other at twenty paces, much less hit each other with a pistol ball.

History has not answered some basic questions about the episode. Why did Twiggs so easily surrender a fifty-year career that had only occasionally allowed him to visit his home state? Why did he not honor his sworn oath, at least until war was more certain? Many other Southern soldiers in the United States Army, such as Albert Sidney Johnston, were approached early about resigning from the army. Even after Johnston announced his decision to resign, he stayed at his post until his replacement arrived. Would Twiggs have fought the secessionists had Scott's letter more strongly appealed to his sense of duty, rather than cloaking itself in bureaucratic language? Had he held his command, could his small but professional force have held out against five hundred untrained, poorly armed civilians until help arrived?

We will never know. Twiggs accepted a major general's rank in the Confederate army and command of the District of Louisiana, but he had really been unfit for duty for years. He soon resigned his command and returned to Georgia, where he died in 1862. He never even witnessed the Confederacy fire a shot.

Scott suffered some recriminations for not replacing his old comrade sooner, but his career was on the wane anyway. Within nine months after Twiggs gave up Texas, Scott was forced to retire. He turned over the conduct of the war to those same young officers who had been after him and Twiggs for years.

While Twiggs died a forgotten man early in a war he helped start, Scott lived to see the nation united. Scott had the satisfaction of knowing he was correct in his opinion that the war would be long, bloody, and costly. He also watched the Union follow his "Anaconda Plan" of squeezing the South into submission.

THE SEWARD-MEIGS-PORTER AFFAIR

Before the war even started, President Abraham Lincoln displayed a tendency to get involved in military matters.

What history calls the Seward-Meigs-Porter Affair started in early April 1861 when Secretary of the Navy Gideon Welles began outfitting a fleet to sail to the relief of Fort Sumter. With war so close, Lincoln took a personal interest, even authorizing the ship for the risky mission. He told Welles he could send one of the few warships the United States Navy had, the *Powhatan*.

For reasons still unclear, Lincoln, working with Secretary of State William H. Seward, approved a second mission, to relieve Fort Pickens, just off Pensacola, Florida. Lincoln kept this mission a secret. He did not even tell Welles he was planning to send a navy ship to Florida. More important, he assigned the *Powhatan* to Seward's secret mission, forgetting he had already promised it to Welles.

United States Army captain Montgomery C. Meigs, in charge of outfitting his soldiers for a mission to Fort Sumter, was thoroughly confused.

Was he going to Florida or South Carolina? He telegraphed Seward to settle the issue. Seward reluctantly told Welles about his secret mission.

When Lincoln was confronted by an irate Welles about the secret appropriation of his ship—not to mention its assignment to serve at the same time in two different places more than a thousand miles apart— he caved. The three men agreed that the State Department had no business meddling in War Department affairs. The *Powhatan* was formally assigned to Welles's mission to Fort Sumter.

But mistake still piled on mistake. While the politicians argued in Washington over which mission was more important, impatient United States Navy lieutenant David C. Porter, commanding the *Powhatan*, set sail for Florida. A ship carrying orders for the *Powhatan* to return to New York was sent in pursuit. Though the new orders signed by Welles caught up with him, Porter ignored them. He figured that since he was following an earlier order from the president of the United States, he did not have to abide by orders from a mere secretary of the navy. Porter continued to Fort Pickens.

History shows that Porter did the right thing in sailing to Florida. The arrival of the *Powhatan* reenforced Fort Pickens at a time when the Confederates were close to attacking. The fort stayed in Union hands the remainder of the war. Fort Sumter was never reenforced and fell. It is doubtful that any amount of reenforcement could have kept it from being captured by Confederate forces, since they had ringed the harbor with a system of strong forts—something they didn't have the time, the guns, or the inclination to do in Florida.

Both sides really wanted the fight to come at Fort Sumter. Charleston, one of the South's largest cities, was a much bigger stage than faraway, little-known Pensacola.

What the Seward-Meigs-Porter Affair demonstrated was that Abraham Lincoln would be a hands-on president, and that his cabinet would often bicker over how to win the war.

"Entirely Unfit to Meet the Enemy": Carelessness and Stupidity at Fort Sumter

In four years of war stretching from New Mexico to Vermont, more than 620,000 Americans died. At least a quarter died in violent combat, shot by rifles or pistols, run through by bayonets, or blown apart by cannon fire. These men could at least claim some sort of glory in that they died for their country.

The first men to die on both sides perished by their own stupidity.

The early months of 1861 were spent preparing for what both North and South assumed would be war. Major Robert Anderson and his 90-man Union force that had occupied Fort Sumter in Charleston Harbor on December 26, 1860, mounted cannons and drilled continually for what they knew would be an impossible task. The fort was designed for a garrison of 650 men. Even if all the guns in the fort were mounted, Anderson did not have the men to crew them. But he did have one advantage. His soldiers and officers were all "regular army," meaning they had been trained to fight. They were familiar with the weapons they might have to use in the coming weeks.

By contrast, the Confederates were a collection of fired-up volunteers, most of whom had never even seen the type of huge seacoast cannons aimed at Fort Sumter. One exception was their overall commander, General Pierre Gustave Toutant Beauregard, a regular-army man and a skilled gunnery officer. He and his staff had little confidence in the men they were commanding. For example, when Fort Moultrie's commander, Confederate lieutenant colonel Roswell Ripley, an Ohio-born West Point graduate, was ordered to shift a battery, he replied that he had "219 indifferent artillerymen and 318 helpless infantry recruits, almost without arms, without clothing, and entirely unfit to meet the enemy."

Ripley was dealing with a growing collection of men and boys flowing in from all parts of South Carolina. Eager to get a shot at the Yankees before the fun was over, they had no regard for military training, discipline, or safety. Like any group of rambunctious youths, they played games with each other. One lost, a careless Confederate who was stabbed in the eye with a bayonet while horsing around in the barracks. He has remained nameless to historians, since most war martyrs want to be remembered with a better epitaph than "His mother always warned him about running with sharp objects."

It must have been nerve-racking for the Federals in Fort Sumter to watch the Confederates preparing to blast them out of their harbor fortress. By early April 1861, the small contingent in the fort was facing six thousand Confederates clustered in Fort Moultrie, Fort Johnson, and an armored "floating battery" of four cannons. Every gun facing Fort Sumter was less than a mile away, creating what General Beauregard called a "ring of fire" that could drop explosive shells weighing upwards of forty-two pounds into the Federals' laps.

The Federals knew the Confederates were serious. On January 9, a battery of cannons manned by Citadel cadets on Morris Island had fired three rounds at the *Star of the West*, a ship bearing supplies for Fort Sumter. The first cannonball had whistled across the bow as a warning and the second two had hit the ship. The ship's captain was startled at the good shooting by the rebels. Luckily for him, the range was long for the old smoothbore twenty-four-pounders, so little damage was done, but the captain knew to ship out when the shipping was good. The *Star* turned around and left without delivering any supplies to the besieged fort.

Major Anderson, the commander at Fort Sumter, considered firing on Morris Island to support his relief ship but held his fire. He had no orders from Washington telling him to fire on the Confederates. Besides, he did not want to start the war. He would leave that to Beauregard, one of his best students when Anderson had taught artillery tactics at West Point.

Two months dragged by. Both sides drilled. Both sides watched the other drill.

On March 8, the first Confederate cannon fired on Fort Sumter. A ball screamed across the water, slammed into the wharf, and then ricocheted into the ocean. The soldiers at Fort Sumter rushed to their guns. Officers climbed the parapets to scan the opposing forts to see where the shot had come from. Had the war finally begun?

That first shot was a mistake. Embarrassed Confederate officers quickly climbed into rowboats and pulled over to Fort Sumter to apologize to the Federals and make sure no one had been hurt. Their story was that inexperienced gunners had been practicing with a cannon but had not fired their last live round. After a break in their training, they had simply forgotten the ball was still in the cannon when they went back to firing what they thought were blanks. The battery's inexperienced officers had not checked the cannon's bore to see if it was loaded.

Just over a month later, the Confederates sent more than three thousand shells and balls toward Fort Sumter over a two-day bombardment that started on April 12. Despite all the tonnage of iron that fell on the fort, no one was wounded. Neither were any Confederates hurt—at least by the Federals. One prominent Confederate did almost die, but his blunder had nothing to do with warfare.

Roger Pryor was a former United States congressman from South Carolina who had resigned his seat when the secession crisis reached the boiling point. Legend says he rejected the historic opportunity to fire the first cannon at Fort Sumter, but he did row out to the fort after the bombardment to negotiate surrender terms.

Pryor was sitting in Fort Sumter's hospital chatting with Federal officers when he got thirsty. Rather than dip water from a handy barrel, he poured himself a glass from a bottle on the hospital table, probably thinking that any hospital would keep a ready supply of whiskey—for medicinal purposes, of course. The United States Army doctor rushed the secessionist outside and pumped several ounces of iodine from his stomach. Thanks to a Yankee who was now his enemy, Pryor survived his thirst and became an incompetent Confederate general who was eventually removed from command at the insistence of Robert E. Lee.

The surrender terms for the Federals inside Fort Sumter were generous.

The Confederates would allow them to embark on a ship bound for New York City. They would be able to take their belongings, including their small arms. They would even be allowed to salute the United States flag by firing blank cannon rounds.

On April 14, the day after the fort was surrendered, Major Anderson ordered a hundred-gun salute. Apparently to save time conducting such a large salute, the fort's officers allowed their gunners to pile cloth cartridges filled with black powder beside the cannons. Such a practice was normally against safety procedures.

Exactly what happened next is open to debate. Some sources say the cannoneers got careless and were not properly sponging the barrels with water to kill live sparks. Others say sparks and pieces of flaming cloth were flying back toward the cannons, since the ocean wind was blowing toward the fort. A flaming piece of cloth may have landed on one of the piles of cartridges. One of the guns exploded. Masonry, pieces of cannon, and wooden gun carriages flew like shrapnel. The right arm of Private Daniel Hough, a regular-army artillerist, was blown off. He died within minutes. Another soldier later died in a Charleston hospital despite the best efforts of the Confederates to save him. Four other members of the Fort Sumter garrison suffered minor wounds and were treated in New York.

Carelessness and outright stupidity marked the beginning of the Civil War. Those same traits would crop up throughout the four years of conflict.

THE UNION ABANDONS GOSPORT NAVY YARD

On April 20, 1861, the United States Navy gave the Confederate government twelve hundred heavy seacoast defense cannons, twenty-eight hundred barrels of gunpowder, four ships, including a heavy frigate mounting forty guns, and a dry dock that cost millions of dollars to build.

The gift giver, at least in the eyes of the government, was a sixty-seven-year-old career United States Navy captain. Treason, senility, and drunkenness were all charges flung at the captain. What the members of the United States Senate investigating committee did not make public was that the real blame rested at least as much with the Navy Department for issuing orders not to upset the locals, since Virginia had not yet followed the seven Confederate states out of the Union.

Captain Charles Stewart McCauley was one of the oldest men on active service in the United States armed forces in 1861. Born in Philadelphia in 1793, McCauley had joined the navy as a midshipman at age fifteen. His combat record went all the way back to the War of 1812, when he fought the British on Lake Ontario. For the next forty-nine years, he commanded one important post after another, including heading the Washington Navy Yard during the Mexican War and commanding both the Pacific and the South Atlantic Squadrons after that. By the time the Civil War came around, McCauley had sailed almost all of the world's oceans. He was a sailor's sailor.

He was also old. There is speculation that he might have been confused and unfit for duty. Still, those worries did not stop naval officials from putting McCauley in command of the Gosport Navy Yard in Norfolk. He was, after all, one of the most senior officers in the navy, still on active duty, and loyal to the Union.

Union admiral David Porter, in his postwar history of the Civil War, speculated that this policy of being gentle with Virginia was actually a plot hatched by Southerners still in the navy. "The secession of Virginia had been resolved upon, which was known to these disloyal officers, although not to the Government; for the action of the Secessionists had been delayed and kept secret, so that the blow would be more decisive and enable the conspirators to seize the public property at Norfolk and elsewhere, to help them carry out their designs," he wrote.

Though he did not accuse Union commanding general Winfield Scott of being disloyal, Porter did write that Scott told Welles that he could not spare the troops from Fort Monroe, on the mainland across from Norfolk, to reenforce Gosport.

Scott probably regretted that decision. For thirty years, Gosport had been one of the largest and most important naval facilities in the country. Inside were ship houses, dry docks, sheds for the shaping of masts and the repair of rigging and sails, machine shops for the construction of boilers, even a laboratory where ordnance, chemicals, and guns were tested. Docked at the yard for repair in April 1861 were eleven ships, including the forty-gun steam frigate USS *Merrimac*. A smaller sloop of war, the USS *Cumberland*, was anchored at Gosport. Together, these ships mounted eighty-eight guns and represented a sizable portion of the small United States Navy's strength. Porter estimated the value of the two ships alone at more than two million dollars.

Perhaps most important of all, at least to the cannon-short Confederate government, Gosport was the storage center for more than three thousand cannons. The cream of that crop included more than three hundred nine- and eleven-inch Dahlgren shell guns, cannons designed specifically to send explosive shells into the sides of wooden ships.

By early April 1861, naval officials were growing increasingly nervous about the fate of Gosport. Secession talk was growing louder in Virginia. Welles sent secret orders to McCauley ordering him to quicken repairs on the *Merrimac* and make what preparations he could to destroy the yard. McCauley replied that it would take at least a month to repair the ship, which had put into port for extensive repairs to her boilers and engines.

That was time the Union did not have. Welles detached the navy's chief engineer from other duties and rushed him to Gosport to make the repairs. He accomplished in three days what McCauley had reported would take a month, yet another indication that the old captain no longer fully understood what was happening around him. McCauley might also have been influenced by his officers when he made that report. Many officers at the yard were native Southerners who were stalling for time for Virginia to secede.

The naval engineer and the ship's captain he brought with him quickly threw together a crew of forty-four seamen volunteers and fired up the boilers of the Merrimac on April 18 to sail her out of Norfolk. It was the day after Virginia seceded. There was still time to save one of the most powerful warships in the United States Navy.

McCauley then made another bad decision. He refused to order the Merrimac away. Though he had orders from the secretary of the navy to save the ship, he chose to obey his earlier orders not to upset the locals. The engineer tried to get the ship's captain to defy McCauley, but the man refused to mutiny against an official who had spent nearly fifty years serving his country.

The two officers returned to Washington to report what had happened. Welles immediately sent Captain Hiram Paulding to assess the worsening situation and to replace McCauley if necessary. Paulding was literally an old colleague of McCauley's. He was sixty-four to McCauley's sixty-seven. Paulding had served in the navy since he was fourteen.

It is not known if Paulding's age or friendship with McCauley had any bearing on what happened next, but by the time Paulding arrived, the situation had changed radically from just a week earlier. Paulding could see old hulks being hauled into the bay to be sunk in Norfolk's channels to prevent vessels from leaving or coming. All of the Southern officers had resigned their commissions and left their posts. Many of the mechanics and workers in the yard were refusing to report for work.

There was also a mob of men camped just outside the yard's gates. McCauley, without any orders from Washington, had already scuttled three ships, including the Merrimac, which he had refused permission to sail just two days earlier. Most odd of all his actions, McCauley had also started spiking the cannons in the yard, including the very guns he could have used to blast any secessionists who dared break down the gates.

Looking at all the destruction, Paulding concluded there was nothing he could do but order it completed. Since he had been ordered to save what he could and destroy what he could not, he proceeded to order the entire yard destroyed.

On the night of April 20, 1861, every ship in the yard but the anchored Cumberland was splashed with turpentine, as were all the buildings.

Poor, old, exhausted Captain McCauley went to bed early, assuming that Paulding and his single ship and single regiment were there to help him defend Gosport. He was awakened at midnight, just before his house was set afire, and told that everything was going to burn. According to Porter, the old sailor was "mortified at the idea of abandoning his post without any attempt to defend it."

At two-thirty on the morning of April 21, the Gosport Naval Yard was set afire and the last of the Federal defenders climbed aboard the *Cumberland* and the *Pawnee*, the ship that had brought Paulding. Paulding thought he had accomplished his mission in destroying a facility it had cost the government ten million dollars to build.

He had not. Almost as soon as the Federal soldiers were gone, waiting citizens of Norfolk poured into the yard to put the fires out. Some of the buildings burned, but most did not. The explosive charges at the dry dock and the powder magazine failed to go off. At least a third of the stored cannons were still serviceable. Three ship fires were put out before they could do much damage. The *Merrimac* burned to the waterline, but divers discovered that her hull could be repaired. They also found a gift left by the inefficient Yankees. Inside one of the ship's watertight compartments were more than two thousand ten-pound shells.

The Union navy would see the *Merrimac* again in less than a year. Actually, they would not literally see the same ship, since all that was salvageable was below water. On top of that serviceable hull, the Confederates built the 262-foot-long CSS *Virginia*. She came out to do battle twice, once to smash with ease several wooden ships and the next day to fight the USS *Monitor*. One of the ships the *Virginia* sank on the first day was the *Merrimac*'s old harbor mate, the USS *Cumberland*. The *Virginia* sent one shell crashing through the *Cumberland* before ramming her. The men of the sinking *Cumberland* stayed at their stations, continuing to fire at the *Virginia* until ocean water lapped into their guns' muzzles. More than 120 seamen were killed outright in the attack.

Of all the gifts the Union navy left the Confederacy, none was more valuable than those cannons. They formed the backbone of Confederate fort defenses for the rest of the war.

In the end, however, the North got back those cannons as it slowly but surely captured the forts where the Confederates had sent them. Some were mounted at forts surrounding Norfolk, which was finally abandoned after the *Monitor* fought the *Virginia* to a draw. Some were sent to Forts Clark and Hatteras on North Carolina's Outer Banks, where they were recaptured in August 1861. Some went to the forts around Port Royal, South Carolina, where they were recaptured in November 1861. At least fifty-three went to four forts at Roanoke Island, North Carolina, where they were captured in February 1862. Others were sent to Island Number 10; Fort Donelson and Fort Henry in Tennessee; Vicksburg, Mississippi; and Port Hudson, Louisiana. The farthest any guns went was Arkansas. Though the Federal government recovered almost all of the twelve hundred guns it lost at Norfolk, it came at a cost of thousands of Union soldiers' lives.

The two old Union navy men who failed to destroy the yard suffered more from embarrassment over what happened than any punishment. Perhaps that embarrassment was enough for men who had both spent a half-century otherwise honorably serving their country.

Though he had miserably failed in his mission to destroy the yard, Paulding was not officially censured. Later in the year, he was appointed to serve on the board that reviewed plans to develop and build ironclads to fight the *Virginia*, then taking shape near Norfolk. Paulding, though an old wooden ship man, would champion the idea of building a ship completely out of iron. The ship plans that he liked would become the *Monitor*.

Paulding officially retired from the navy at the end of 1861, though as a civilian he commanded the New York Navy Yard for the rest of the war. Since he did not have to worry about secessionists attacking him in New York Harbor, Paulding proved valuable to the war effort by keeping the ships of the Atlantic Blockading Squadron in good repair. He finally retired from all work in 1870 at age seventy-three. He had been at sea or serving on shore for almost sixty years. He died in 1878 at age eighty-one.

McCauley suffered through a Senate inquiry on the disaster at Norfolk, which found that he had acted irresponsibly in not releasing the Merrimac to sail and abandoning his post before making sure everything was destroyed. What hurt him the most were charges that he was drunk on the last night he spent in Norfolk. His only defense was that he had been following his orders not to do anything that might provoke the people of Norfolk.

McCauley retired in 1862 and went into virtual seclusion at his home in Washington, D.C. After the war was over and passions cooled, someone high in the government remembered the old sailor's service. He was promoted to commodore, retired, in 1867. He died a restored man in 1869 at the age of seventy-six.

What many Union navy men considered the greatest disaster of the Civil War occurred without a shot being fired because one of their officers had been ordered not to hurt the feelings of the civilians of his port city. In the end, however, the navy got back some of its self-respect when the Confederates were forced to abandon Gosport after holding it just over a year. When Union major general George McClellan launched his Peninsula Campaign in the spring of 1862, Norfolk was abandoned by the Confederates. Though the Southerners did a better job of destroying the yard than the Federals had, the Union navy was still able to salvage enough of the facilities to use the rest of the war.

A CRY OF "BOSTON!" AT BIG BETHEL

In the late spring of 1861, the Confederacy was fully formed. North Carolina, the eleventh and last state to leave the Union, voted itself out of the United States on May 20. On May 29, President Jefferson Davis arrived in the newly designated Confederate capital of Richmond saying he was ready to defend the states' constitutional rights.

Within days, the area where armed conflict would first occur was clear. The ground war would start in Virginia. Federal troops had kept control of some bases on the peninsula between the York and James

Rivers. The most important was Fort Monroe, located on the mainland across from Norfolk. It seemed clear to both sides that Federals marching upland from Fort Monroe would meet Confederates marching down from Richmond.

Everyone was spoiling for a fight. Too spoiling, perhaps. When gunfire finally started, Federal soldiers had a hard time figuring out whom they should be shooting. In the first land battle of the war, they shot each other.

By June 6, 1861, the First North Carolina Volunteers arrived at Bethel Church, Virginia, a community below Yorktown, less than fifteen miles from Fort Monroe. The volunteers were eager to start the fighting. Their ranks included some teenagers who had been most recently at the North Carolina Military Academy in Charlotte. In command was Colonel Daniel Harvey Hill, a West Point graduate who had been superintendent of the Charlotte school when the war started.

On June 8, the Confederates saw their first Yankees and fired on them, almost chasing them back to a large camp near Fort Monroe. On June 10, seven regiments of Federals, about forty-four hundred troops, moved out of their camp before dawn, intent on finding the insolent rebels who had fired on them. The Federals knew from talking with Unionist Virginians that the Confederates, numbering about fourteen hundred, were camped at Bethel Church, sometimes called Big Bethel.

The Federal commander, Brigadier General Benjamin Butler, a Massachusetts politician with no military training, liked the numbers. He figured a rousing first land victory in the war might be enough to end it right there. At the very least, a win would make him nationally famous, always nice for a man planning a bigger political future.

Before dawn, the Confederates were awakened by heavy gunfire to the southeast. It was not directed at them, at least not yet. Two of the Federal columns had run into each other in the darkness. When one column's commander shouted the supposed Federal recognition signal of "Boston!" he did not get an answer because the second column's commander had not heard anything about signs and countersigns. Now, each commander assumed he was facing Confederates.

The two columns opened fire. Before the officers realized their mistake and stopped the intramural engagement, at least two Federals were killed and nineteen wounded. And they had not even seen their first Confederate.

Things did not improve when the New York, Vermont, and Massachusetts men finally did find the Confederates. The Federals attacked and were driven off the right flank by artillery directed by Major George Randolph, the grandson of former president Thomas Jefferson. Unsuccessful on the right flank, they tried the left. No luck there either. One of Butler's trusted staff officers was killed, perhaps by a black body servant among the Confederates, a crack shot who had been handed a musket. That officer, Major Theodore Winthrop, started a dubious tradition on both sides that continued throughout the war—smart men doing stupid things. Winthrop was a Yale graduate and a writer who was becoming prominent in New York publishing circles. When he was shot, he was standing high on a fence waving his sword and making a spectacle of himself. He was too good a target to pass up.

After a while, the fighting slackened. Colonel Hill ordered some volunteers into the open between the lines to burn down a farmhouse that had been used as cover by Union sharpshooters. Five North Carolinians ran toward the house. One man, Private Henry Wyatt of Tarboro, North Carolina, fell mortally wounded. The twenty-year-old died that night and was given a hero's funeral in Richmond as the first Confederate to die in the war. (Captain John Marr had been killed by raiding Federal cavalrymen ten days earlier at Fairfax Court House, Virginia, but since Marr was a Virginia militiaman not yet sworn into service of the Confederacy, history does not consider him the first Confederate casualty.)

The Battle of Big Bethel ended soon after this action. The Federals lost eighteen killed, five missing and probably dead, and more than fifty wounded. The Confederates suffered seven wounded. The unfortunate Wyatt was the only Confederate killed.

The Confederates had gone into battle outnumbered more than three to one, so they rejoiced. Southern newspapers trumpeted a great victory. In fact, compared to later battles, Big Bethel was little more than a minor skirmish. But it would lend its name to North Carolina's wartime slogan: "First at Bethel, farthest to the front at Gettysburg and Chickamauga, and last at Appomattox."

The battles would get bigger and the Federals better. Most of them would know the signs and countersigns and shoot each other less often.

First Manassas: "You Are All Green Together"

When the Civil War began, politicians and generals on both sides predicted the other side would give up quickly. One foolish legislator offered to mop up all the blood that would be spilled with his handkerchief.

Even after the June 10, 1861, Battle of Big Bethel, where the Union had eighteen men confirmed killed and the Confederates one killed, the horror of war did not strike home. Neither did it come with the Battle of Rich Mountain on July 11, or Corrick's Ford on July 12, or Blackburn's Ford on July 18. In each of those battles—really nothing more than skirmishes—an increasingly large number of men were engaged and an increasingly large number died or were wounded. It would take the Battle of Manassas, or Bull Run, to finally convince the boastful on both sides that war was hell. In that first major battle, a total of five thousand men on both sides would end up killed, wounded, or missing. It would be a battle rife with blunders. Some would be amusing. Some would be deadly.

Perhaps the largest blunder of all was that the battle even took place that July. Brigadier General Irwin McDowell, who had never commanded more than a few squads in his entire military career before being handed command of the Union army, tried telling President Lincoln that his "army" was nothing more than a mob of raw, undertrained recruits.

Lincoln, anxious to get the war on and over with, told McDowell, "It is true that your men are green, but so are the Confederates. You are all green together."

With that vote of confidence ringing in his ears, McDowell left Washington with his army of thirty-five thousand men on July 16. It took him two days to march less than twenty miles, not an auspicious beginning for an army that liked to chant "On to Richmond" at intervals along the way.

Another problem McDowell faced was just keeping his men in the army on the day before the battle took place. When war was declared after the firing on Fort Sumter, the politicians in Washington had called on patriots all over the North to join the army—for ninety days. No one imagined that it would take longer than three months to bring the wayward Southern states back into the Union. On July 20, when the Union army was poised to strike across Bull Run Creek onto Manassas Junction, Virginia, three Northern units announced that their enlistments were up and they were going home. One regiment graciously—as it pointed out—agreed to stay through the coming battle. The other two, including a battery of badly needed artillery, demanded that they be allowed to go home—now.

The Confederates had their own problems. General P. G. T. Beauregard complained that he did not have enough men and that the commissary general back in Richmond had not supplied enough train cars to transport men to what would soon be the front. An investigation into the charges found forty railroad cars sitting at Manassas Junction. They were loaded with the suitcases and trunks of the wealthiest of the Southern soldiers who had rushed to Manassas to face the Yankees.

Confronted with the railroad cars being used as giant storage trunks, Beauregard actually defended their use: "The Confederate army was filled with generous youth who answered the first call to arms. Many of them came with their baggage and servants."

One side was ready to go home before the fighting even started, and the other was pampering dandies who needed fresh changes of under-wear. It would be a long war.

On the morning of the attack, July 21, one Union regiment was as-signed as skirmishers, soldiers who would advance in front of the rest of the army to find the enemy. While skirmishers are supposed to be highly mobile infantry, this regiment was saddled with a thirty-pounder can-non, a monster of a gun that weighed more than three tons and proved extremely difficult to move up the Virginia hills. The thing was so big that it took up an entire road. Regiments marching behind had to slow down while it was manhandled up each hill.

When the huge cannon fired on Colonel Nathan "Shanks" Evans's men at the stone bridge over Bull Run, it was the signal for the battle to begin. The Federals poured fire into the woods on the other side of the bridge but caught very little back. The Confederates wouldn't play!

Evans, who had only two regiments at that point on the battlefield, refused to fire on the Federals lest he reveal how few men he had. Still, part of his command made its first blunder. Upstream from the stone bridge, two Confederate cavalrymen rode their horses into the shallow middle of Bull Run and verbally challenged the Federals to come across and fight. Colonel William T. Sherman, a professional soldier from Ohio, grinned with pleasure. He had been searching for a shallow ford away from the defended stone bridge. The two Confederate horsemen had un-wittingly shown him the place.

The Federals then committed another mistake. They let their secret attack be seen. A Confederate searching the battlefield with a spyglass noticed a flash of reflected sunlight in the distance. He turned to its source and saw sunlight bouncing off a highly polished brass cannon being pulled to the left of Evans. The officer sent Evans a message that the bulk of the Federals appeared to be moving to a ford north of his position. Evans left four companies to hold the stone bridge and took the bulk of his force to the left.

Finding himself commanding a few hundred men in front of two Fed-eral brigades of several thousand men, he did the only thing that made sense to him. He attacked. Some of his soldiers, ruffians of the First

Louisiana Battalion who called themselves Wheat's Tigers after their colonel, threw down their muskets and, waving their large bowie knives, dashed toward the Federals. The trick had worked against the South American peasants some of the men had fought while acting as soldiers of fortune, and they saw no reason why it wouldn't work on Yankees. They were right. The surprised Federals actually pulled back until their officers noticed how thin the Confederate ranks were.

Now the Federals began to push forward. Coming in behind Evans were twenty-eight hundred men under Confederate brigadier general Barnard Bee and Colonel Francis Bartow. The forces mingled as they slowly fell back up Henry House Hill toward a force of Virginians lying in the grass on the reverse slope.

Bee was puzzled at the actions of the Virginians and their officer, who was wearing an old blue regulation army uniform. Surely, the Virginia general could see that Bee's troops were being cut to ribbons by the larger number of Federals. But the general continued to keep his men in reserve rather than rushing them down to help Bee's men. Bee rode up to the officer and pointedly said that his men were being beaten back. The officer calmly replied, "Then we will give them the bayonet."

Bee rode back to his men, pointed to the Virginians, and noted, "There stands Jackson like a stone wall! Rally 'round the Virginians!" A nickname for the man in the shabby blue coat was thus created, but it might not have been a compliment. Some sources say Bee was complaining about Brigadier General Thomas J. Jackson's holding back his support on Henry House Hill, rather than complimenting the Virginian on how his men were holding steady, waiting for the Federal onslaught to reach them.

All over the battlefield, mistakes were made in identifying troops. Some occurred because the slack wind kept the national flags carried by regiments from being displayed. The Confederate flag, also known as the "Stars and Bars," had a blue field with a ring of seven stars in the upper left corner; alternating bands of red and white covered the rest of the flag. If it hung limp, as it often did that windless day, it could pass for the Stars and Stripes. Generals on both sides spent precious time staring at battle flags and hoping for a puff of wind so they could tell who was who.

And if the similar flags were not confusing enough, there was no standardization of uniforms. Some Wisconsin troops arrived wearing their gray militia uniforms and some Virginia troops wearing their blue militia uniforms. Some regiments yelled to each other asking who they were in order to determine if they should receive an angry volley.

Confederate colonel J. E. B. Stuart, seeing the members of a Zouave regiment facing him, thought they were Alabama Zouaves retreating. Leading his cavalry, he rode forward calling gaily, "Don't run, boys! We are here to protect you!" When he got close enough to discover that they were really New York Fire Zouaves, Stuart ordered a charge. The New Yorkers scattered, and Stuart's men and a following infantry regiment accidentally captured eleven Federal cannons.

There was no mistaking the members of the First Minnesota Regiment, which probably made them curse the man back home who had designed their uniforms. The men of the First Minnesota wore bright red shirts and no coats. They definitely stood out on the field, as their casualty rate later showed.

Still, they were not the most interesting-looking Federal regiment. That was the Seventy-ninth New York Highlanders, Scotsmen who fought wearing kilts (with no underwear, according to witnesses) and glengarry hats with gaily colored ribbons hanging behind. This was the only battle at which the brave New Yorkers got to wear their kilts. The next month, they were ordered to put on long pants. Fortified with whiskey and bored with being assigned to dig ditches, they considered losing their kilts the last straw. The men actually considered mutiny, but their officers and the threat of being shot by pants-wearing Yankees convinced them to trade in their plaids for sky-blue trousers.

A case of mistaken identity probably won Manassas for the Confederates. Late in the morning as the Federals pushed the Confederates back on Henry House Hill, a battery of Federal cannons found itself on the left side of Stonewall Jackson's line. As the Union battery officer ordered his guns loaded with canister to blast down the line, a regiment emerged from the distant woods and started marching toward the guns. The Federal officer swung his cannons toward the regiment and prepared to fire on this new threat. His superior countermanded his order, explaining that the oncoming regiment was his expected artillery support. The battery commander argued that the approaching column was composed of Confederates, not Federals, based on the direction from which they came. The superior insisted they were Union soldiers and refused to approve an order to fire. The battery commander glumly watched as the members of the regiment finally leveled their muskets at him and fired. More than fifty of his battery's horses were killed, as were many men in his gun crews. From that point of the battle, the tide shifted to the Confederates.

The battery officer later found his superior watering his horse in Bull Run. He rode up to him and sarcastically asked if he still thought the regiment was his support troops.

At least one civilian died on the battlefield. That was eighty-year-old Mrs. Henry, a dying invalid who refused to leave her house on the hill that bore her name. She should have listened to her sons, who tried to evacuate her from between the lines. During the battle, a Federal cannon shell exploded in the house, flinging her body outside and to the ground. She would not be the last innocent to die during the four-year war.

The Union army finally broke and ran, right through hundreds of tourists who had come to watch what they assumed would be a Federal victory. As the bluecoats streamed back toward Washington, some Confederates—even President Jefferson Davis—suggested that the South launch an immediate attack on the capital city itself. "Give me 10,000 men and I will be in Washington tomorrow," said Stonewall Jackson, who had a finger shot off by a Federal bullet during the battle, thanks to his curious habit of holding one arm over his head to "balance" his body's blood flow. Despite the loss, he was not dissuaded from throwing his arms into future rains of whistling bullets.

Jackson wanted to attack that night, but Davis favored waiting until daylight, since the Confederates were exhausted and inexperienced in marching—much less fighting—in the dark. He wrote an order that the Confederates launch an expedition toward Washington the next morning, an order that was never acted upon.

July 21 had been oppressively hot and dry, but July 22 opened with a downpour. The several days of rain that followed made the roads impassible. The Confederates decided that the weather and their inexperience made an attack on Washington unwise.

First Manassas (there would be a second, larger, and bloodier battle over the same ground the following year) was a messy, mistake-filled battle. Neither side was proud of the performance of its officers or men. Both looked on it as a training ground for the war to follow.

The next four years would see more battles and more deaths. If this battle did anything positive, it was to create a standard for battlefield uniforms and a Confederate battle flag. From this point, the Federal army would dress in blue, with the exception of Zouaves, who would dress in variations of red, white, and blue based on French Algerian uniforms. Confederates would dress in gray or butternut (varying shades of brown). Confederate regiments would march under a square battle flag made up of a blue cross with thirteen stars on a field of red.

Now the teams could tell each other apart without a scorecard.

SHANKS EVANS AND HIS FELLOW DRUNKEN GENERALS

Drinking on the job will always get an employee fired—unless that employee carries a general's rank in the army. Reports of Civil War generals issuing idiotic commands, running from battles, causing the deaths of hundreds of soldiers, and falling off their horses while under the influence of alcohol were common.

Some generals combined drinking with sheer incompetence to carve their place in Civil War history. Others, like Confederate brigadier general Nathan George "Shanks" Evans, ruined promising careers by finding the bottom of too many whiskey bottles.

Evans was a 1848 graduate of West Point. Because he graduated almost last in his class, he did not get a plum engineering assignment. Instead, he was assigned to the cavalry, where he spent his entire career until resigning his rank of captain in 1861 to return to his home state of South Carolina. He was present at the firing on Fort Sumter. Since he was an experienced field officer, he was sent to the front lines at Manassas as a colonel to oppose the expected Federal attack.

"Shanks" was a West Point nickname that referred to Evans's slim legs. It was probably the most polite name to be found for the man. He was a first-class eccentric said to be one of the worst cursers in the army. More telling, Evans made no secret that he was a heavy drinker. At Manassas, he assigned an aide to do nothing other than carry a small keg of whiskey around the field. Whenever Evans needed a nip, he waved for his "barrelista."

How often Evans called for that keg is not known, but he is credited with saving the young Confederacy at Manassas. He discovered the Federal plan to turn the Confederate left and, without orders, moved most of his command to stop the Union movement. He even ordered his few hundred men to attack the bulk of the Union army to buy time for Confederate reenforcements to come up. The Federals, surprised by the attack, reeled backwards a short distance before they realized how few Confederates there were. Evans had to pull back, but his men had won enough time to save the day.

Later that year, in October 1861, Evans was in overall command of Confederate forces at Ball's Bluff, Virginia. Though he seems to have played a more minor role than he is given credit for, his command drove dozens of Federals off the bluff to their deaths in the Potomac River. It was a disaster that almost resulted in the North's calling for a reevaluation of its willingness to stay in the war. For this victory, Evans was voted the rare "Thanks of Congress" by the Confederate Congress.

Evans was successful in every battle he fought, but his superiors kept watching him tipping the bottle. He was transferred off the front lines to South Carolina, then back to Virginia, then to North Carolina, then back to Virginia again.

On his South Carolina assignment, in June 1862, Evans was in command at the Battle of Secessionville, fought on James Island, east of Charleston. The Federals thought they could sneak up on and capture a Confederate fort in the middle of a swamp. If they could, Charleston lay virtually unprotected just a few miles west. Slowed by the coastal mud flats, the Union attack bogged down, and Evans's men killed hundreds of Federal soldiers, whose bodies sank beneath the swamp water without a trace.

Evans had by now saved the entire Confederate command at Manassas and, twice acting in sole command, won at Ball's Bluff and Secessionville. Still, the Confederate high command had problems with his drinking. Once more transferred from Virginia to the Carolinas, Evans found himself in command at Kinston, North Carolina, in December 1862. There, he faced the approach of Union major general John Foster. Just as at Ball's Bluff and Secessionville, Evans was on his own with little chance that reenforcements could reach him in time.

Evans set up a good defensive line on the south side of the Neuse River, one flank anchored in a swamp and the other on a bend in the river itself. Behind him was a bridge into town. If he had to, he could abandon his lines, run across the bridge, and continue the fight on the other side of the river, burning the bridge after his men crossed.

The plan was working until overwhelming numbers of Federals and artillery fire caved in the Confederate left flank. It retreated, and Evans followed. His center and right flanks stayed behind, unaware that their commanding officer had left that portion of the field. Once on the other side of the river, Evans forgot about his center and right flanks. He ordered the bridge set on fire, which meant he was inadvertently leaving at least four hundred of his own troops without a way to rejoin his command. Worse, Evans ordered artillery fire poured into the old Confederate positions on the center and right. He thought the smoke he saw in the trenches was Federal fire shooting at him. In reality, it was his Confederates still shooting outward at the stalled Federal advance. Shelled by their own guns, the Confederate center and right collapsed. Many of them surrendered, since the bridge they had planned to use was on fire, thanks to their commander. It was for this order that Evans was accused of drunkenness.

From that point, it appears the Confederate high command gave up on Evans. He was tried on separate charges of intoxication and disobedience of orders. He was acquitted both times, perhaps because his friends felt sorry for him, since it was becoming obvious that liquor was diminishing his skills on the battlefield. He was once given another chance, but a fall from his horse incapacitated him. He was never again given command. Evans died just three years after the war at the young age of forty-four.

Evans died a man fallen from his hero status because of his alcoholism. Confederate brigadier general John Dunovant, another alcoholic, died trying to win that hero status.

Dunovant was one of those rare generals who started his military career in the enlisted ranks. Born in South Carolina in 1825, he joined the army during the Mexican War and worked his way up to sergeant. Discharged after being wounded, he was a civilian until the army was expanded in 1855. Dunovant was given the rare honor of being promoted to captain in an army that had few slots open for West Point graduates. He resigned that hard-won commission when South Carolina seceded from the Union in 1860. He was soon named a colonel in the First South Carolina Regulars.

Details on when Dunovant's problems with alcohol started are sketchy, but those problems came to a head in June 1862, when he was accused of being drunk. He was ordered out of the army by direct personal order of President Jefferson Davis that November. This surprising attention of the president to a minor colonel not even serving on an active battlefield is unexplained in the biographies of Dunovant. Davis biographies note that the president often spent time on what his frustrated staff considered trivial matters.

Dunovant, shocked and embarrassed, appealed to his governor, Francis Pickens, for another assignment. He was given colonelcy of the Fifth South Carolina Cavalry. This was a safe assignment away from Virginia, where Davis might run into him again. Dunovant served in South Carolina for more than a year before being transferred to Virginia in March 1864 just in time to help Lee fight Grant in the Wilderness. He was wounded in the hand in May and returned for duty in July with his arm in a sling. By August, the president let bygones be bygones, approving both Dunovant's appointment to brigadier general and his command of a cavalry brigade.

Then, almost as soon as he had won back respect, he lost it again. That September, Dunovant was leading his regiment on a night patrol near Petersburg when he ran into another body of men. Dunovant believed he had stumbled onto Confederate pickets. Challenged by the regiment, Dunovant kept yelling out his name and demanding he be allowed to pass. The general was probably the only man in the darkness who didn't grasp that the two bodies of men were enemies. He ordered one of his captains forward so the "pickets" should see that they were Confederates. The captain tried to persuade Dunovant that they were facing a Federal cavalry regiment. Dunovant would not listen.

"Are you afraid, sir?" Dunovant asked.

The captain, seeing that it was useless to argue, got off his horse and walked forward into the darkness, toward what he knew were Yankees. The captain, a huge man nearly seven feet tall, attracted the undivided attention of the Yankees when they saw him walking toward them.

"Dismount or I will shoot," cried the Yankee who had challenged the Confederates.

"I am dismounted. I am a very tall man and I am leading my horse," replied the captain, who was forced to surrender to prove to his general that they had indeed met a Yankee column. Shrewdly, however, the captain had shifted his direction of travel as he walked up to the Yankees. When they saw he was a Confederate, they fired into the woods from which they had seen him emerge. The remainder of the mounted Confederates were unhurt by the volley, which surprised no one but Dunovant. The Confederates turned and rode their horses to safety, leaving the captured captain seething with anger. Dunovant was more than embarrassed. He knew his mistake would lead to rumors that he was drinking again.

Later, finding Yankees dug in along a road with a broad swamp in front of them, several generals conferred on what to do. Major General Matthew Butler wanted to turn their flank. Most officers agreed it could be done.

Dunovant objected and said so to Butler. "General, let me charge them. We've got them going and let us keep them going."

Butler, knowing that the swampy land offered no cover, replied, "I am afraid I will lose too many men."

Dunovant said, "No, we won't! My men are perfectly enthusiastic and ready to charge. And we've got the Yankees demoralized. One more charge will finish them. Let me charge them!"

Butler, exasperated with Dunovant's persistence, finally said, "Then charge them, sir, if you wish!"

Dunovant rushed from the generals' meeting to his men. He told them about the attack they would lead. The cavalrymen looked across that broad plain and wondered whether their general was crazy or drunk. They did not budge. Again, Dunovant explained how the enemy was demoralized and ready to break and how one more cavalry charge would do it. Finally, reluctantly, they agreed to go.

The South Carolinians charged down the road and toward the swamp where the Yankees were dug in. Dunovant, his arm still in a sling, was at their head. In the first volley, a bullet tore into his chest. He was dead before he hit the ground. His men, now without the leader who had gotten them into this mess, immediately retreated from the killing ground.

Dunovant had gotten a regimental command back and even gotten a promotion to general after being cashiered from the army for drunkenness. But it is doubtful he ever got his reputation back. Even after the man was dead, at least one of his soldiers claimed Dunovant had been drunk while leading his suicidal charge into the face of the Yankees.

No drunken general had a more bizarre military reputation than Union brigadier general Thomas Sweeny, a fiery Irish immigrant. Sweeny came to the country when he was twelve years old and learned how to be a soldier by joining the militia. That led him to serve in the Mexican War, during which he lost his arm. That did not slow him down. He stayed in the army and fought Indians right up until the Civil War.

Wounded at Wilson's Creek, Missouri, during one of the first battles of the Western theater, Sweeny was out of action before returning in January 1862 to accept a colonelcy of an Illinois regiment. He led his men at Fort Donelson and Shiloh, where he was wounded again. By March 1863, he rejoined the army and was promoted to brigadier general.

His frequent absences from the field—albeit for the noble reason of being wounded—put Sweeny far down the promotions list and made him junior to other generals. One man over him was Major General Grenville Mellen Dodge, who was eleven years younger than Sweeny. Dodge, too, had learned his skills in the militia. But he was a Massachusetts Yankee with a civil-engineering degree. To the Irish immigrant Sweeny, who had given his arm to the service of his country, it was obvious what Dodge was—a college boy who had used his political power to get a general's commission. It didn't matter to Sweeny that Dodge had been fighting the Confederates as long as he had, and that Dodge had been wounded at the Battle of Pea Ridge, Arkansas. What mattered was that Dodge had been promoted to major general in reward for repairing some vital railroads in the Western campaigns and had been given a corps command. Sweeny was but a brigadier commanding a division in Dodge's corps.

Sweeny had a hard time getting along with another division commander in Dodge's corps, Brigadier General John Wallace Fuller. As was the case with Dodge, Fuller's only military experience before the war had been leading a militia unit. Though Fuller had a long war record and had participated in one of the early Northern victories, at Island Number 10, Sweeny considered him a political general like Dodge.

Sweeny's resentment of the two men finally came to a head on July 25, 1864, right in the middle of Sherman's campaign for Atlanta. During battle, Dodge, riding along the lines, issued orders directly to some of Sweeny's regiments in violation of the chain of command, which normally would have called for Dodge to tell Sweeny what he wanted done. On top of that, Sweeny had a conflict with Fuller during the battle. Perhaps he was jealous at learning that Fuller had grabbed a regimental battle flag and planted it exactly where he wanted his troops to rally. That sort of bravery led to promotions.

That night, the generals met in Sweeny's tent to celebrate the victory. Sweeny had already been celebrating by himself with a bottle. When Dodge arrived, Sweeny cursed him, called him a coward, then slugged his superior officer. When Fuller tried to intervene, Sweeny grabbed him and wrestled him to the ground. The other officers present must have been shocked at the wonder of a one-armed man fighting two two-armed men. When the combatants were finally pulled apart, Dodge arrested Sweeny and charged him with assault. Sweeny's Civil War career was over.

That did not mean his army career was over. Though the tent was filled with witnesses, a military court acquitted him, probably because of his long career and otherwise brave record. He stayed in the army until 1870. The army even refused to prosecute him in 1866 when he tried to lead a group of Irish-Americans into Canada in an attempt to free that country from British rule. Sweeny died in 1892 at the age of seventy-two with the retired rank of brigadier general.

"A Perfect Stampede If There Ever Was One"

Blunders are a part of warfare, but generally one side makes them and the other takes advantage of them. In one early naval engagement on the Mississippi, neither side could do anything with the mistakes made by the other.

───────────────────────────────

The world's first ironclad was not the CSS *Virginia*, the ship that dueled with the USS *Monitor* in March 1862. The first ironclad had actually appeared six months earlier in the form of the CSS *Manassas*.

And what an ugly form it was. Built on the hull of a New England–launched icebreaker (whose purpose down south at the start of the war remains unknown), the *Manassas* was 143 feet long. Covered with thin iron plates, she mounted a single smoothbore thirty-two-pounder. The *Manassas* looked something like a half-submerged, ungainly cigar with a smokestack on top and a cannon poking out the front. The ironclad was crude, slow, and hard to control, but the Confederates hoped she would be effective in driving the Federals from the "Head of the Passes" of the Mississippi, eighty-five miles south of New Orleans, where the river branched apart into the delta. A four-ship squadron of wooden Federal vessels mounting a total of fifty-one guns guarded it.

The ambitious Confederate plan was to send the ironclad in the dead of night to ram the wooden ships. Following the *Manassas* and a couple of small gunboats would be three "fire rafts," which would be lit and sent downriver in hopes that the current would carry them into contact with the Union ships. With luck—an incredible amount of luck—the wooden ships would go up in flames.

The commander of the Federal fleet had anchored all his ships in the river and had not placed a vessel on patrol. At four o'clock in the morning, the largest ship, the USS *Richmond*, was taking on coal when the crewmen noticed a strange ship bearing down on them. It was the

Manassas, which struck a glancing blow on the coaling schooner before hitting the targeted warship. The ram punched a hole in the *Richmond* two feet below the waterline, the first time an ironclad had ever done damage to a wooden ship.

There were no shouts of celebration inside the *Manassas*. Everyone was choking for breath. When the boat had struck the coaling schooner and the warship, the shock of the impact had knocked the ironclad's engines loose. On top of that, when the *Manassas* was pulling away, a hawser from one of the Union ships caught on the Confederate boat's smokestack and pulled it loose. The stack toppled into the water, leaving only the part that ran inside the ship. Coal smoke filled the *Manassas*, blinding her crew and threatening to asphyxiate them all.

The Union ships did not know this. In the inky blackness, the Federals could not see the *Manassas*. But that did not keep them from firing broadsides in all directions.

Inside the *Manassas*, confusion reigned as the crew struggled to light a signal rocket out an open hatch, the signal for the fire rafts to be lit and cast adrift. The rocket was lit, but it fell back inside the ironclad, creating some fun until it could be doused. A second rocket made it outside the ship, and the fire rafts were sent down the river.

The Union ships panicked, hauled in their anchors, and drifted with the river while their stokers tried desperately to get steam in the boilers. Admiral David Porter, writing about the incident in his postwar history, noted of the Federal ships that "having been sent to the passes to defend them, on the first appearance of an enemy, they deserted their posts and made a most shameful retreat—a retreat from a few river boats that a broadside of either ship would have sent to the bottom in five minutes. It was a perfect stampede if there ever was one."

Both the *Richmond* and the USS *Vincennes* grounded on a sandbar, making them perfect targets for the return of the Confederate ironclad and her accompanying gunboats. While the ironclad was still sorting herself out, her intrepid little consorts moved in for the kill—as much of a kill as six-pounder guns mounted on gunboats could deliver.

That was not much. Most of their shots fell short of the two stranded ships. One shot did make it, however. After the battle, the captain of the *Richmond* went to his cabin to change clothes. Lodged inside one of his bureau drawers was a Confederate cannon bolt (a solid shot in the shape of a bolt).

The tiny, ineffectual display of force by the Confederate gunboats panicked the captain of the *Vincennes*, which mounted ten heavy cannons. He ordered a fuse laid to his ship's magazine, wrapped the vessel's American flag around his body, and abandoned ship without orders. Porter wryly wrote about the captain of the *Vincennes*, "He never reflected that his small 32-pounders might be whisked about in the air and fall upon the decks of the stranded *Richmond*. Captain Handy's reception on board the flagship was not a flattering one."

Handy was ordered back to his ship, which he was surprised to see had not blown up. The mystery was solved when he gingerly climbed aboard. He found that the old sailor instructed to light the fuse to blow the ship had disobeyed orders. Recognizing that Handy had lost his common sense, the old sailor had let the captain abandon his vessel, then thrown the lit fuse overboard.

In the end, nothing much happened at the Battle of the Head of the Passes. The fire rafts grounded well away from the Federal ships. No one on either side was hurt, save probably some Confederates on the *Manassas* whose lungs were scarred by coal smoke.

The *Manassas* would be repaired but was so severely damaged seven months later during the Battle of New Orleans that she was abandoned and allowed to sink into the Mississippi. Both the *Richmond* and the *Vincennes* were refloated. The *Richmond*'s captain did have to buy a new chest of drawers, but he found he would not be needing it on another ship. His request to resign was granted. Porter would have fired him anyway.

Everyone on both sides was embarrassed. Porter wrote, "There is not much more to tell of this painful business—It would have been better to have left out the telling of it, but history cannot be written fairly if that alone is told which is creditable, and if that which smacks of the disgraceful is omitted. There is no excuse for anything that happened in this squadron, and the mistakes made were not redeemed by any after-acts of gallantry."

"Sudden, Bold, Forward, Determined War," Ball's Bluff–Style

Politicians work hard at appearing to be everything to everyone. If the crowd is full of farmers, they ask about the weather. If the crowd is lawyers, they say how tough law school was. A politician with a national reputation has to have personal ties to as many states as possible.

Edward Dickinson Baker, perhaps the archetype of the politician of his day, was exactly that kind of man. Though he was born in London, his wanderlust was such that he could legitimately claim to be from England, Illinois, California, Pennsylvania, and Oregon, depending upon the audience to which he was talking. He could claim to be everything a United States senator with higher ambitions needed to be.

The one thing Baker could not claim was that he was a good soldier.

Baker started maneuvering for public office in 1832 at age twenty-one when he volunteered for the Black Hawk War, a nice, safe little conflict involving the forced relocation of Indians where participants had little chance to suffer injuries. He may have met a young man named Abraham Lincoln, who also used the war to build a war record to decorate his political résumé.

When the Mexican War came in 1846, Baker went to war again, leading an Illinois regiment. That service was enough to get him elected to the Illinois legislature, in which he served at the same time as his old Black Hawk War comrade Abraham Lincoln. The two became such fast friends that Lincoln named his second son Edward Baker Lincoln.

The gold rush of California called Baker westward, where he again became prominent in political circles. In 1859, he moved to Oregon to organize that newly accepted state's Republican Party. Baker's oratory against slavery so inspired the people that they appointed him a United States senator, saving him the trouble of running for the post.

Lincoln put much trust in his senator friend. On Inauguration Day in 1861, Baker rode in Lincoln's carriage. He introduced the president-elect at the inaugural address, in which Lincoln made the famous challenge to the South that war lay in its hands, not his.

Baker was fiery in his speeches about the South. After the Confederates shelled Fort Sumter, he demanded on the Senate floor that he wanted "sudden, bold, forward, determined war!" And as he made clear to the president, he wouldn't mind leading a few charges himself. Nothing real fancy, just a few victories that he could point to in some future election.

Still, Baker was careful enough in his politics to know that one does not give up everything for the sake of a military career. Lincoln offered to make him a major general, skipping even the rank of brigadier general, but Baker refused. While some observers praised Baker's modesty in accepting a colonelcy, others pointed out that law required he give up his Senate seat to serve as a general. As a regimental colonel, he could keep both his field command and his seat in Congress. Baker was no fool. He was not about to give up one seat of power for another. He wanted both at the same time.

Baker knew how to make an appearance before a crowd. Several times, he rode right from the field to the Capitol, slapping the dust from his uniform onto the floor of the Senate as he unbuckled his sword and pistol in full view of his stay-in-Washington-away-from-the-fighting colleagues. The man had style, but it was difficult to keep up appearances when there was no fighting going on that would allow him to really be heroic.

After the Federal defeats at Big Bethel and Manassas in June and July 1861, the war was virtually at a standstill as fall started. In October, Union major general George McClellan, the Federal army commander, learned through intelligence that the Confederates might be evacuating Leesburg, a small Virginia town on the west bank of the Potomac

River not far from Washington. He ordered Brigadier General Charles P. Stone to check out the reports.

Stone had graduated from West Point in 1845, just in time to go to Mexico as a young lieutenant and win two brevets (honorary promotions). When he returned to the army at the outbreak of the Civil War, one of his first duties was providing security for Lincoln's inauguration. He handled that assignment well enough to get a promotion to brigadier general, an honor that brought with it trouble—the assignment of Baker as one of his colonels.

Remembering his training as a professional soldier, Stone was cautious in making plans to investigate Leesburg. After all, he was on the Maryland shore of the Potomac. Just getting across the river to reconnoiter in force would be a major task, as there were few boats in the region large enough to carry his men.

There was also another, more dangerous problem. The Potomac at that point did not have many wide beaches on which to land. The best ford appeared to be heavily defended by Confederates. The second, much poorer choice was a narrow strip of land above which was a bluff, Ball's Bluff, which rose nearly a hundred feet above the river. A narrow, one-man path led from the beach to the top of the bluff, beyond which lay Leesburg. If the Union men were to get caught on the wrong side of the river by Confederates who were not supposed to be there, it would be difficult getting them back down to the boats.

Stone was nervous about the proposed action. The night before, a scouting party on the west side of the river had seen what it described as a Confederate camp without sentries. In fact, the Federals had seen several rows of haystacks sticking up through the fog. Later, a Massachusetts regiment had crossed the river for further investigation and still had not encountered any resistance. It was quiet—too quiet.

Stone was suspicious that the Confederates were still in the area, mainly because there was no reason for them to leave Leesburg, since there were no Federal forces pushing them. He ordered Baker across the river with instructions to evaluate the situation personally and to either reenforce the men already on the other side or withdraw if he deemed it advisable.

Baker may have acknowledged Stone's orders, but he didn't follow them. Perhaps the dream of battlefield glory crowded out the sensible thoughts in his head when he heard firing coming from above the bluff, indicating the unseen Massachusetts regiment had found some Confederates. Whatever the reason, Baker started pushing his entire seventeen-hundred-man brigade across the river. He held up the first companies at the base of the bluff until he had a crowd ready to march up the little path. With scarcely a patrol in front of him, Baker started marching blindly up the bluff.

Baker, full of himself, did not have a care in the world. He told subordinates to look for the white plume of his hat if they wanted to find the war. When he reached the fearful Massachusetts colonel, he grabbed the surprised man's hand and shook it, congratulating him for finding a battle they could fight.

Instead of sending out skirmishers to determine the strength of the Confederates, Baker gave the signal to land still more Union soldiers on the narrow beachhead. Soon, there were four regiments on the western shore. As the colonel of the last regiment, a professional soldier trained at West Point, crested the bluff trail, he was shocked to discover what Baker, the professional politician, had not recognized.

The Confederates were safely ensconced in heavy woods with all their guns trained down into the open area where the Federals were pinned. In front of the Federals was a perfect ring of Confederate fire. Behind them was the worst fall-back position imaginable—a hundred feet of air above a narrow beach. The battle had hardly started and already the Union brigade was trapped. Worse still, the brigade commander, Baker, didn't even know it.

Soon, the Confederates began to press the Federals backward, something that even Baker couldn't miss. The political colonel who had been happily quoting inspirational messages from classic poems a few moments before was now urging his men to hold their position. That was easier said than done. There were no earthworks, no breastworks, no log forts, no streams, no underbrush on which to anchor the line. All the Federals had were their bodies, their muskets, and their cannons.

Within a few moments, they did not even have two of the latter. One cannon's crew was cut down. Another fired a round and was astonished to see the recoil send the cannon careening off the cliff to the beach below.

Too late, Baker realized he had led his men into a trap. The Confederates had allowed the Federals to land virtually unopposed so they would suspect nothing. Now that the Union forces were crowded into an open battlefield of less than ten acres, it was time to shoot fish in a barrel.

The Confederates charged. Baker, in the open trying to rally his men, went down with a bullet in the brain, killed instantly. His was the merciful death. His panicked men were not so lucky. Pushed to the cliff, some jumped, sometimes landing on the bayonets of their fellow soldiers running on the narrow path below. Some landed on rocks, bashing their heads or smashing their legs and breaking their backs.

As the blue wave disappeared over the cliff, the gray wave reached it. The Confederates fired down on the helpless Federals as fast as they could. Some threw rocks, finding great sport in being able to bean Federals faster than they could load muskets and shoot them. As the Confederates watched, even they were horrified when they saw healthy men swimming into the river in pursuit of two boats loaded with wounded Union soldiers. When the swimmers caught up to the two boats, they tried to board them. Both boats were swamped, the wounded men tossed into the Potomac. A third boat was quickly loaded, and it, too, was swamped by wild-eyed Union soldiers. After a while, the stunned Confederates simply watched the Federals killing each other in their quest to survive in the water.

Ball's Bluff, designed to be nothing more than a "demonstration" to see if Leesburg was still occupied by the Confederates, turned out to be a Union military disaster thanks to the poetry-quoting Oregon senator. More than 200 Federal soldiers were confirmed killed or wounded. Another 700 were listed as missing, which meant they were either captured on the beach or drowned in the Potomac. Out of the force of 1,700 that crossed the river and climbed Ball's Bluff, fewer than 700 made it back in one piece. Baker managed to kill just 36 Confederates and wound 114.

When Lincoln heard that Baker was dead, he was devastated. Only five months earlier, he had lost another friend, Colonel Ephraim Elmer Ellsworth, a twenty-four-year-old who had read law in Lincoln's Illinois law office. On May 24, 1861, Ellsworth had become the first Federal officer to die when he ripped a Confederate flag from a hotel in Alexandria, Virginia. The owner shot him dead. Now, the war was only six months old and the president had already lost two close friends.

After watching his shattered brigade slip back across the river, General Stone likely muttered that this was what happened when Washington politicians appointed other Washington politicians to be officers. Stone was shocked several months later when he was arrested and charged with treason for the Ball's Bluff debacle by the Committee on the Conduct of the War. Though Baker had clearly disobeyed orders, Stone was accused of intentionally sending his men across the river to be butchered. Stone was from Massachusetts and had no ties to the South, but he was accused of secretly being in favor of slavery because he had once ordered his men not to encourage insubordination among slaves. This was enough to make the members of the committee suspicious that Stone was some kind of double agent who knew he was sending their good friend Baker to his death. Stone spent nearly six months in Federal prisons without formally being charged with anything criminal. Finally released, his career ruined, Stone resigned from the army.

Baker, the do-everything, be-everywhere political military officer, was quickly forgotten by everyone, with the probable exception of Lincoln and Stone. The headline-grabbing disaster at Ball's Bluff was easily overshadowed by other battles that grew ever larger in their carnage.

Had Baker followed orders to just cross the river for a look-see and extricated the men already on the wrong side of the Potomac, he and a thousand new Federal soldiers would have lived. Who knows? By 1864, he might have joined his friend Lincoln as vice president.

If only he had listened to orders.

THE STONE FLEET

On occasion, what seems like a good idea to the top brass is executed by line men who know they are completing a fool's mission.

That was the story of "the Stone Fleet," a nonlethal military weapon thought up by Secretary of the Navy Gideon Welles and the politicians who made up the Union's Blockade Strategy Board. Early in the war, these men sat down to think of something to help them blockade the ports of Savannah and Charleston. Knowing that there were only a few channels to each city and that the harbors were otherwise subject to sandbars, they hit on the idea of sinking old wooden ships in the channels. Any blockade runner that tried to run past the ships would either get tangled in them or run aground.

The idea was beautiful in its simplicity. The Union went to every little whaling town in New England and bought twenty-five old, weather-beaten, barely floating whalers. The old ships were then loaded with seventy-five hundred tons of rocks, which would hold them in place once they were sunk in the channels.

New Englanders loved the idea of the Stone Fleet. They were paid good money for rotting ships that were no longer of use to them. And the government even paid for the rocks cluttering their fields! In some cases, enterprising citizens broke into warehouses and sold Washington municipal-government paving stones.

On their way south, the civilian sea captains set off like they were racing, ignoring the military commander's suggestion that they hug the coast in case any of the ships came apart under the strain of such a long voyage.

Originally, the Stone Fleet was to be split between Savannah and Charleston, but the target became Charleston when it was learned that the Confederates themselves had sunk some old hulks to try to keep Federals from running up the Savannah River.

On December 19, 1861, several old whalers were sunk in the two main shipping channels to Charleston. Engineers laid out an elaborate grid and tried to place the hulks so no Confederate ship could slip out to sea. On January 20, 1862, more ships were sunk in a secondary channel.

The politicians in Washington chortled at their success in closing down Charleston Harbor. They never wondered why the old salts who had obediently sunk the fleet did not seem so enthusiastic.

The old whaling ships had been coming apart at the seams as they sailed south. The boards were worm-eaten, and the caulking no longer kept out water. Most of the ships would have sunk at their moorings within months had the Federal government not bought them. Within weeks of the time the hulks were sunk, most of them were broken up by the action of the waves entering Charleston Harbor. The planks washed up on shore and were used as firewood. As for the seventy-five hundred tons of stone in their holds, their effect on the tides and the currents of the Ashley and Cooper Rivers entering the Atlantic helped mother nature dig an even deeper channel than had existed before the Yankees came to help.

Welles was embarrassed by the failure of his idea. But the North did buy some time by sinking the old ships. The disruption of the harbor gave the Union several precious weeks to complete dozens of brand-new warships that made an effective blockade of Charleston.

DOUBLE-BARRELED CANNONS AND GREEK FIRE: THE BAD-WEAPONS FOLLIES

Every army wants to enter war armed with the best weapons available. Well, that's not quite true. The Union army was the exception.

For decades before the war, the Ordnance Department was run as a fiefdom by line officers too old to ride horses across the plains. They may not have been able to swing a saber anymore, but they learned they could wield even more power with their pens. Colonel Henry Knox Craig was sixty and a veteran of the War of 1812 when he was named head of the Ordnance Department in 1851. Resistant to modernization of arms, Craig was pushed into a change from smoothbore .69-caliber muskets to .58-caliber rifles by an aggressive secretary of war. That secretary was Jefferson Davis.

Craig was forced into relinquishing the Ordnance Department in April 1861, but control was handed over to a man just three years younger, Colonel James W. Ripley, age sixty-seven, an army veteran with forty-seven years of service.

Ripley was an honest man who succeeded in organizing a stagnant bureaucracy. His problem was that he was resistant to changes in the standard infantry arm. He believed each soldier should load one round at a time, take steady aim, and fire, which was the way Napoleon had fought his wars. Ripley was against breechloading weapons and those equipped with magazines that held multiple rounds of jacketed bullets. He felt that if soldiers could load and fire faster, they would take less time to aim and would waste ammunition. Not even President Lincoln, who liked to shoot proposed new weapons over the Potomac River, could change Ripley's mind. The man responsible for purchasing more than seven hundred thousand long arms for the Union bought only eight thousand breechloaders, the arm of the future.

The resistance to change exemplified by Craig and Ripley hampered the Union army for more than half the war. In fact, the effect of such recalcitrance was demonstrated as early as 1859. That was the year John Brown raided Harpers Ferry, Virginia, with the intention of starting a slave rebellion. Brown and his followers were armed with more than a hundred Sharps carbines, a single-shot breechloader rifle patented in 1848. Their privately purchased weapons were much more advanced than the army-issue muskets used to capture them.

Ripley finally became such a roadblock that he was replaced halfway through the war. The new man, Brigadier General George Douglas Ramsay, was extremely open to new ideas. In one year, he more than doubled the purchase of breechloading rifles and paved the way for other inventors to bring their weapons in for inspection and evaluation. Ramsay was the man the Union had been looking for, though he served in the position just a year, finally resigning in a political dispute with Secretary of War Stanton.

While Craig and Ripley can be criticized for not recognizing the future, they are to be congratulated for not giving in to every professor, politician, doctor, and handyman who approached them with an idea for a weapon that would end the war. Both sides saw their share of weapons that turned out to be not quite as good as their inventors claimed.

Ambrose Burnside, the future major general, invented the Burnside carbine, which he patented in 1856 when he was a civilian. Burnside had resigned his lieutenant's rank in the regular army in 1853 to become an arms manufacturer. He might have checked with General Craig first. Craig hated the idea of anything as efficient as a breechloader, so Burnside did not get the government contract he needed to stay in business. Forced into bankruptcy, he sold his patents to his creditors. When the war came along, they were ready to manufacture Burnside's invention. More than fifty-five thousand of the carbines were manufactured and sold to the Union.

Though later versions of the arm were popular with soldiers, early versions proved that Burnside was a better lieutenant than an arms designer. His major mistakes were using a Maynard priming tape (a balky system of caps on a roll, much like today's children's cap pistols) and not designing the carbine with a forestock (a grooved wooden sleeve in which the barrel rests). Within a few shots, the Maynard tape was prone to jamming. If the carbine did fire several times, the barrel became too hot for the shooter to hold, even if he was wearing gloves.

Even the best manufacturers faltered on occasion, producing weapons as dangerous to their users as they were to the enemy. That was the case with the Colt repeating rifle. This weapon looked like a cross between a rifle and the Colt revolver, which was popular with both sides during the war. Only about five thousand Colt repeating rifles were purchased for the United States Army. The reason was the rifle's nasty habit of blowing the fingers off the person who shot it.

All percussion-cap revolvers of the 1860s suffered from the potential problem of "chain firing." The hammer of the pistol normally fell on the selected cylinder's percussion cap, firing the bullet down the barrel. However, if the shooter had not properly plugged the other chambers with grease, it was possible for black-powder flames from the fired cylinder to leak into the unfired cylinders. The other chambers would then explode, and the bullets would go downrange without benefit of being fired through the barrel. This was more an annoyance than a major problem, as the pistol was held with one hand away from the body. Since the fingers were curled around the grip, no appendages were in the way.

The Colt repeating rifle was different. It was designed with a forestock, with the result that the shooter's left hand was in front of the cylinder when the weapon fired. If chain fire occurred on the left side of the cylinder, it was possible for the shooter to blow his fingers off. Soldiers, being generally in favor of keeping their digits, told their superiors they would not use the Colt repeating rifle. They preferred breechloaders, which kept the bullets away from their hands.

Perhaps the best arm that never got a fair chance on the Civil War battlefield was the Henry rifle. Had reluctant Federal ordnance officials bought large numbers when it was invented in 1860, the war would have been over sooner.

In a war when the word *cartridge* generally referred to a paper cylinder that had to be torn open by a soldier's front teeth, the Henry used a brass cartridge with the bullet firmly seated so the powder would not get wet, as it frequently did with paper. While most Civil War arms required the placement of a musket cap on a nipple over the breech, the Henry featured a firing pin that struck the brass cartridge on two different points, thereby reducing the chance of a misfire, a frequent occurrence with "nippled" muskets.

An experienced rifleman could fire a musket no more than three times a minute. For each shot, he had to reach around his side to his cartridge box, grab a cartridge, tear it open, drop the powder and bullet down the barrel, ram the bullet home, put on a musket cap, cock the musket, and fire. The Henry had a fifteen-round magazine that allowed a soldier to fire as fast as he could pull the trigger and work the two-motion lever that ejected the cartridge and cocked the hammer.

Colonel Ripley of the Ordnance Department rejected the Henry on the dubious grounds that it was too fragile for the field. He was afraid that its ejection and cocking mechanism would jam with sand. Only seventeen hundred Henrys were purchased by the United States government, but as many as ten thousand were purchased by states and wealthy regimental commanders who recognized what superior firepower could do to an enemy. In several battles late in the war, regiments armed with the Henry rolled right over Confederates armed with single-shot muskets.

As to the charge that the Henry rifle was delicate, it evolved into the Winchester, the rifle used to settle the West. But even as the Henry was being improved, the army wouldn't buy it. When George Armstrong Custer and his Seventh Cavalry were surrounded at the Little Bighorn in 1876, they were armed with single-shot breechloading carbines, while the Sioux and Cheyenne had repeating Winchesters. The Indians' purchasing was not controlled by the Ordnance Department of the United States Army.

Sometimes, resistance to modern arms reached ridiculous proportions. No man was more stupid in this regard than Georgia governor Joe Brown. A forty-year-old radical secessionist when the war started, Brown had absolutely no military training, which may account for why he proposed that Georgia troops be armed with pikes, long knives mounted on the ends of wooden poles. These were the same sort of arms used by the Romans in their conquest of Europe. Brown, a teacher and lawyer, must have assumed that if the pike was good enough for Julius Caesar, it was good enough for his Georgians. He said pikes "never fail to fire and never waste a single load." Only thirteen hundred pikes were issued before Georgia's military men were able to convince Brown that he was sending potential voters to certain death. That got his attention.

Likewise, there were men on the Union side who failed to understand that they were living in the nineteenth century. One such officer was Colonel Richard H. Rush, who recruited the Sixth Pennsylvania Cavalry from among his wealthy friends in Philadelphia. These men may have been the elite of the city, but they were not the smartest fellows ever to climb on horses. "Rush's Lancers" were armed with nine-foot-long lances topped by an eleven-inch blade. Each lance was decorated with a red ribbon. These men carried pig stickers as their main weapon! Early in the war, they performed well, running down inexperienced foot soldiers afraid of horses carrying men with sharp poles. But as the Confederates gained battlefield experience, they learned they could shoot the lancers long before they faced danger from their sharp sticks. Finally equipped with real arms in April 1863, Rush's men developed into a first-class cavalry brigade.

Some silly-sounding weapons may have been based on defensible ideas. That applies to the double-barreled cannon. Only one cannon of this description is known to have been manufactured. A Georgia weapons designer got the idea that waiting to fire canister until the enemy was only a few hundred yards away was not safe. Canister was a tin can full of minie balls. When the cannon was fired, the tin can would fling the balls in a wide arc, cutting down enemy infantry rushing a position. It was a deadly—but close-range—option for artillery. By the time the cannon could be reloaded, surviving infantry might be overrunning the gun's position.

The Georgian got the idea that if one cannon barrel was good, two would be great. He envisioned a cannon with two barrels firing simultaneously. Attached to both cannonballs—and hanging outside the barrels—would be a chain. The designer envisioned that when the barrels were fired, the chain between them would act like a giant sickle, cutting down enemy soldiers hundreds of yards away. Such a weapon would also reduce the danger cannon crews faced in firing canister when enemy soldiers got close.

The Georgian cast his cannon, loaded it with the chained balls, and fired a test round. His weapon didn't work quite like he hoped it would. The twin cannon barrels didn't fire at precisely the same instant, which resulted in the early ball's pulling the late ball in an entirely different direction from where the cannon was aimed. Whether Confederate observers were killed or injured in the experiment is not known. But it is known that the cannon was only fired once.

All good ideas do not work as expected. Take "Greek fire," an incendiary substance made by mixing phosphorous with bisulfide of carbon, an extremely unstable combination. During the siege of Charleston, South Carolina, in the summer of 1863, the Federals tried filling artillery shells containing Greek fire. They hoped the shells would explode once they struck a house, church, or store. The cannon they first experimented with was "the Swamp Angel," a giant Parrott rifle with an eight-inch bore that fired two-hundred-pound shells.

The Federals set up the cannon in a swamp on James Island several miles from downtown Charleston, an engineering feat in itself considering the swamp's mud. The Swamp Angel blew up on the thirty-sixth round when the Greek fire inside the shell exploded as the powder charge for the shell ignited. A very expensive cannon that had taken weeks to place was ruined thanks to experimentation with an unstable substance.

The Confederates did not have much better luck with Greek fire. On November 24, 1864, eight Confederate spies journeyed to New York City with a supply of the stuff. Their plan was to set fire to the entire city by igniting the Greek fire at their hotels and selected other sites such as P. T. Barnum's museum.

The Greek fire ignited just fine, but the eight men had apparently never taken a chemistry course. They did not know that fires need oxygen to burn and spread. Concerned with the chilly temperatures in New York that November, they did not open their hotel-room windows on the night of the plot. Their fires burned so slowly that other guests were able to put them out before the hotels caught. Only the Barnum museum burned, and no one was harmed in the fire.

Had the Confederates studied how to use their weapon, they might have created the worst fire in American history.

1862

"That I must *have made*

mistakes, I cannot deny. I

do not see any great blun-

ders; but no one can judge

of himself."

–GEORGE B. McCLELLAN

"A NAME IN SONG AND STORY": THE DEATH OF FELIX ZOLLICOFFER

Confederate brigadier general Felix Kirk Zollicoffer was, to put it mildly, blind as a bat. His severe nearsightedness and his political ambition killed him.

Zollicoffer started life humbly enough—as humbly as the son of a Tennessee plantation owner could. He worked on the plantation until an interest in writing took him into the newspaper business, then worked his way up from a journeyman printer all the way to associate editor of the *Nashville Republican Banner* before entering politics. In the 1840s, he served as state comptroller and later as a state senator. Zollicoffer gained a little military experience while serving as a lieutenant in the Second Seminole War in Florida. In 1852, he worked for the election campaign of Mexican War hero Winfield Scott. At the same time, Zollicoffer ran for and won a seat in the United States House of Representatives.

He served four terms in the House, where he watched with alarm the signs that the nation was moving toward war. In the 1860 presidential election, he pushed John Bell as a compromise candidate, hoping Bell could keep Lincoln out of the White House. Like most Southerners,

Zollicoffer believed Lincoln's election would send the Southern states spiraling out of the Union.

When Tennessee left the Union, so did Zollicoffer. Governor Isham Harris, under apparent pressure to bow to politicians, made Zollicoffer a brigadier general of volunteers. Put in command of eastern Tennessee, with orders to repel invasion, Zollicoffer was in way over his head.

After securing the famous Cumberland Gap, Zollicoffer and his men were ordered to move to Mill Springs, Kentucky, about seventy miles to the northwest, to meet an approaching force led by Brigadier General George Thomas, a Virginia-born professional soldier who had remained loyal to the Union.

When Major General George Crittenden, Zollicoffer's superior back at headquarters in Knoxville, asked about troop dispositions, he was stunned to discover that the inexperienced Zollicoffer had set up camp on the north side of the Cumberland River. Military common sense should have told Zollicoffer to remain on the south bank, so he could use the river as a defense against surprise attack by Thomas. When asked why he was on the north side, Zollicoffer told Crittenden the campsite there looked better. Zollicoffer was facing a professional general leading more and better-trained soldiers, and his main concern was flat ground on which to pitch his tent.

Crittenden, a West Pointer who had resigned his commission in 1832 to go adventuring in Texas, dropped what he was doing and rushed to Mill Springs to take over command of the four thousand Confederates under Zollicoffer. He decided against trying to recross the rain-swollen river, knowing that if Thomas discovered that move, he would attack even faster. Through intelligence, Crittenden learned that Thomas had set up camp barely nine miles—a half-day's march—away. He also learned that the Federals had split their forces on either side of Fishing Creek. If it continued to rain all night, Fishing Creek would be unfordable. Crittenden figured that, with luck, he could smash one part of Thomas's force while the other was forced to watch from the far side of the creek.

His back to the Cumberland River, Crittenden decided to go on the offensive. Before midnight on January 18, 1862, he and Zollicoffer, now second in command, started marching north toward Thomas on the same muddy roads that they hoped had worn out the Federals on their march south. The Confederates tired and fell behind schedule. They also lost the element of surprise when they bumped into Thomas's cavalrymen, who were out scouting the roads leading to the Confederate camp. While the Confederates expended time and ammunition shooting at the cavalry and then Federal pickets, the men in the Union camp were boiling out of their tents, arming themselves, and forming battle lines. Worse, the Union soldiers on the north side of Fishing Creek were wading across to join their fellows. The creek Crittenden had counted on was not yet deep enough.

Still, there was a chance, and Zollicoffer bravely took it. He launched an attack that broke the Federal lines. They fell back, then stabilized near a fence. Some of the more poorly equipped Confederates had to fall back to the rear because the old flintlocks they were using started misfiring in the heavy rain.

Then Zollicoffer made his fatal mistake—as if he needed to make a blunder beyond the one when he had gotten dressed at midnight. When he left camp, Zollicoffer had put on the perfect thing to make himself a target on a dark, rainy day—a brilliant white raincoat.

While wheeling his horse in circles between the two battle lines, Zollicoffer lost his sense of direction. Without realizing what he was doing, the nearsighted general spurred his horse and rode full-tilt toward the Federal lines.

He must have been able to make out shapes, because he rode up to a Federal colonel and started shouting orders to stop firing on his own men. The startled Yankee colonel, a man with the unlikely name of Speed Fry, was turning to give the order to stop firing when someone from the Confederate lines fired at him, hitting his horse. With this proof that he was shooting at the men he was supposed to be shooting at, Fry must have taken another look at the visitor in the white raincoat. Without waiting for another order from the general, Fry pulled a pistol and shot Zollicoffer point-blank in the chest.

Zollicoffer's Tennesseans crumbled when they saw their general fall. In running to the rear, they caused Crittenden's whole force to fall apart. The Confederates began a wholesale retreat toward the river. Thomas did not pursue right away. He needed to issue dry ammunition.

When Thomas did cautiously approach Zollicoffer's cozy little camp the next day, he discovered that Crittenden had abandoned twelve cannons and more than 150 wagons in his rush to get his men across the Cumberland River.

The Battle of Mill Springs (sometimes called the Battle of Fishing Creek or the Battle of Logan's Crossroads, where Thomas's men were actually camped) was a Confederate disaster, though small in number of deaths. The Confederates lost 125 killed and more than 300 wounded, compared to 40 killed and 200 wounded for the Federals. Crittenden's army virtually dissolved after the battle, as the men deserted into the hills of eastern Tennessee. They had gotten their taste of fighting, and they did not like it.

Thomas was unable to follow up his victory and advance farther into eastern Tennessee, though no Confederates were in his front. His men were tired, wet, hungry, and far in advance of any hope of reenforcement. He pulled back, leaving the region to be invaded another time.

Nearsighted Felix Zollicoffer, the general who didn't know the first thing about using the natural features of the land to protect his men, lived on in poetry. For some reason, the public ignored the fact that this poor excuse for a battlefield tactician had essentially killed himself. Verse was written to praise him. One started, "A name in song and story—he died on the field of glory."

Actually, he died because he didn't wear his glasses.

THE SELFRIDGE JINX

If Captain Thomas Oliver Selfridge, Jr., hadn't had bad luck, he would have had no luck at all. The man survived numerous shellings, sinkings, and ill-conceived assaults throughout the Civil War.

Selfridge was the son of a seaman who had joined the navy in 1818 when he was just fourteen. By the time the junior Selfridge was old enough, there was a United States Naval Academy. Thomas Selfridge, Jr., won an appointment at age fifteen and graduated in 1854. By 1861, he was a twenty-five-year-old lieutenant.

Assigned to the *Cumberland*, a fighting sloop that was one of the last United States Navy ships powered just by sail, Selfridge participated in the first Union victory of the war, the capture of Forts Clark and Hatteras at Hatteras Inlet, North Carolina, on August 29, 1861. Coming little more than a month after the defeat at Manassas, the capture of the two Confederate forts was welcome news in the North, though it was not something the Union claimed as a great tactical victory, since it had advance information on the forts' meager defenses.

Selfridge's most famous fight came on March 8, 1862, when the *Cumberland* became the second target and the second victim of the second ironclad of the war, the CSS *Virginia*. Selfridge, in command of the forward ten-inch pivot gun, watched the ironclad approach from a distance. He was confidant at first. After all, there were several Federal ships, all armed with heavy cannons firing shells and cannonballs weighing more than sixty pounds. He was sure they could crack the iron plating on any rebel ship.

What Selfridge did not count on—not that it really mattered—was the angle of attack. The *Virginia* came at his ship head-on. He could not even fire his cannon because forward rigging was in the way. Before anyone aboard the sailing ship could do anything, the ironclad rammed at full speed, burying her iron-tipped prow deep inside the *Cumberland*. As the *Virginia* backed away, water rushed into the gaping hole. The *Cumberland* was doomed, but her men stood by their guns. The ship's nine-inch Dahlgrens fired point-blank range at the ironclad, knocking some guns out of commission.

As the cannonballs hit the *Virginia*, Union sailors heard a sizzling sound, then smelled a terrible odor. One young sailor asked what that odor was. "It is the smell of hell, my boy," came the reply. Actually, it was the smell of pig fat being hit by a Yankee shell. The captain of the

Virginia had coated his ship with the gunk in the belief that it would help shells slide off, and that it would make the vessel slippery if the enemy tried to board. The captain had not counted on the nauseating stink drifting onto the already hot, smelly gun deck. Some of the ironclad's own sailors became sick.

Though the *Cumberland* hurt the *Virginia*, she did not sink her. The ironclad pulled away just far enough to rake the wooden ship. Selfridge and all of the gun crews stood to their guns, firing at the ironclad though they knew their shells would bounce off. Selfridge watched one gun captain hobble on the stumps of his blown-away legs to pull the lanyard of a cannon. Selfridge himself walked from gun to gun firing them, since the crews were so decimated by cannon fire from the ironclad that they had no gun captains to pull the lanyards. The *Cumberland* was sinking, but the men stayed and fired even as the water lapped over the gunwales and into the barrels of the cannons. When a shout came from the ironclad offering to back off if the *Cumberland* surrendered, the acting captain cried, "Never! I'll sink first!"

The *Cumberland* went down with 121 men, a third of her crew, killed. Most of the victims had been horribly mangled by shot, shell, and splinters sent flying when the shells exploded against the ship's wooden sides. The vessel settled on the bottom of Hampton Roads in water shallow enough for her masts to stand out of the water. From one of them, the colors still flew.

For the first time—but not the last—Selfridge swam safely from a sinking ship. He would have left by the hatch, but a fat drummer boy was struggling up with his drum and blocked the way. Selfridge went out a gunport. He later saw the boy using his drum as a raft.

Selfridge was later promoted to lieutenant commander and transferred west, where the navy was supposed to play a vital role in taking the Mississippi River. He was given command of a type of ironclad called a "Pook turtle," after its designer. The lightly armored vessels looked roughly similar to the *Virginia*, though they were sternwheelers rather than screw-powered ships. Selfridge commanded the USS *Cairo*, a fourteen-gun ironclad with a draft of only six feet, making her a valuable vessel in patrolling the tributaries of the Mississippi.

For several months, everything went fine. Then, on December 12, 1862, Selfridge's bad luck showed up again. Ordered to lead an expedition of three ironclads up the Yazoo River in Mississippi to clear the river of mines, he was cautioned, "Be careful not to run the vessels among the torpedoes."

As the ships arrived, sailors observed five-gallon glass jugs floating on the water. Selfridge did not react quickly enough to avoid them. One critic suggested that Selfridge "found two torpedoes and removed them by placing his vessel over them." The *Cairo* went down within minutes, but no lives were lost. The *Cairo's* smokestacks stayed above the water, just as had the *Cumberland's* masts. Selfridge again swam away unharmed.

He expected to be court-martialed for losing his ship to a torpedo. Instead, Admiral David Porter gave him another one, the USS *Conestoga*. This ship was quite a comedown from the *Cairo* and the *Cumberland*. She was little more than a small riverboat with built-up sides of lumber to keep small-arms fire from sweeping the deck. One inspector called the work done on the boat to convert her from a riverboat into a gunboat "disgraceful."

Selfridge did well on the *Conestoga*, at least until he sank her after colliding with the USS *General Price* on March 8, 1864. He was lucky he didn't blow himself up. On board was a load of ammunition. Like the *Cairo*, the *Conestoga* went down in a few minutes. Again, Selfridge swam away.

Almost before Selfridge's uniform was dry from sinking the *Conestoga*, Porter gave him the USS *Osage*, a step back up the ladder. The *Osage* was a river monitor, an ironclad that looked something like the original USS *Monitor*. Selfridge now headed up the Red River on Major General Nathaniel Banks's campaign to capture Shreveport, Louisiana.

The Union fleet of ironclads and "tinclads" (more lightly armored vessels without turrets) got to within forty miles of Shreveport on the twisting, shallow Red River before its infantry element was defeated on land. Without infantry support, the Union ships were at the mercy of

Confederate attackers shooting both cannons and rifles from shore. They turned around and started downriver, moving as fast as they could because the depth was falling thanks to slack spring rains.

The *Osage* was assigned the task of bringing up the rear of the column of ships. She grounded at a place called Blair's Landing, Louisiana. While struggling to free his ship, Selfridge saw several hundred Confederates moving in to attack. He loaded canister in both his eleven-inch guns and waited. Using a new device called a periscope, Selfridge watched the Confederates approach his ship. He waited until the Confederates, under the command of Brigadier General Thomas Green, were within point-blank range, then fired. Reports say as many as three hundred Confederates, including General Green, were cut down by the blast. One report said Green lost his head—literally.

Selfridge got his ship freed, then caught up with the rest of the fleet at Alexandria, Louisiana, where dams had to be built to make the river rise enough for the vessels to negotiate the falls they had barely passed on the way up. The Red River Campaign was a disaster shared by the navy and the army, but for once, nothing that happened was Selfridge's fault.

Selfridge did not sink anything the rest of his navy career. Admiral Porter gave him command of the USS *Huron* for the assault on Fort Fisher, North Carolina, in December 1864 and January 1865. Selfridge emerged unscathed from that epic naval bombardment—as well as from Porter's disastrous land assault on the fort.

After the war, Selfridge made a career of the United States Navy, commanding explorations into South America. After Selfridge was promoted from commander to captain, one of his superiors with a sense of whimsy assigned him to the command of the Naval Torpedo Station at Newport, Rhode Island. That must have reminded Selfridge daily of his sunken ship *Cairo*, which sat on the bottom of the Yazoo River until it was raised in 1956. Selfridge was promoted to rear admiral in 1896. He retired in 1898 and died in 1924 at the ripe old age of eighty-eight. The victim of three sinkings—two of which he was responsible for—and a survivor of some of the most intense musket and cannon fire of the Civil War, he emerged from the conflict with little more than scratches and died an old man, on land, in a nice, warm, dry bed.

THE BAPTISM OF COLONEL ZEBULON VANCE

Colonel Zebulon Vance was not a trained soldier but a natural politician given to smooth talk, storytelling, and promising anything to everybody if they would just vote for him or follow him. At the Battle of New Bern, North Carolina, he tried to set an example for his men and almost died in the process.

Born the son of a farmer in the mountains north of Asheville, North Carolina, Vance was forced to work to support his family after his father died. His formal education was interrupted from ages fourteen to twenty-one, when he studied law at the University of North Carolina. After just a year of legal training, Vance hung out his shingle, then launched a lifelong career as a politician when he ran for solicitor of the county court. When his opponent questioned his youth, Vance replied that he could not help being born when he was, that his parents were to blame for that, but that he would do better next time. Such homespun, self-deprecating humor went over well with his constituents. Five years earlier, a certain Illinois politician had used the same tactics to win a seat in the United States Congress.

Within two years, Vance ran for and won a seat in the North Carolina General Assembly. In 1858, he was elected to the United States House of Representatives. Over the next three years, Vance pushed hard for North Carolina to remain in the Union. He campaigned against secession based on assurances from his Northern friends that President Lincoln would not try to reenforce Federal forts. He later felt betrayed. As Vance put it, "I literally had my arm extended upward, pleading for peace and the Union of our fathers when the telegraphic news was announced of the firing on Fort Sumter and the President's call for seventy-five thousand volunteers. When my hand came down from that impassioned gesticulation, it fell slowly and sadly, by the side of a Secessionist."

Vance left Washington and returned to the mountains, where he organized his own company, the Rough and Ready Guards. Before going into combat, the company was absorbed into the Fourteenth North Carolina, and Vance was elected colonel of the Twenty-sixth North Carolina.

Organizing and training a regiment did not come naturally to Vance. He left most of the drilling to Lieutenant Colonel Henry K. Burgwyn, a twenty-year-old. Burgwyn was not impressed with Vance. "Colonel Vance is a man without any system or regularity whatever. His abilities appear to me to be more overrated than those of any other person I know of," he wrote.

The regiment's baptism of fire came at the Battle of New Bern on March 14, 1862. Union major general Ambrose Burnside had more than eleven thousand men, compared to around four thousand under the overall command of Confederate brigadier general Lawrence O'Bryan Branch, a former United States congressman with no military training. Branch built earthworks in anticipation of attack, but they were not placed to defend in the direction from which the Federals would come. One whole line of very fine earthworks was abandoned without a shot fired because Branch figured he had about half the men necessary to use it.

Most dangerous of all, Branch built his defensive line with breaks in it at a railroad line running from New Bern to Morehead City and at a brick kiln near the railroad line. At the center of the line, he placed his least-skilled troops, a militia unit formed just days earlier from the shopkeepers and businessmen of New Bern. Most of them were armed with shotguns and hunting rifles.

The Federals, fresh off capturing Roanoke Island the previous month, came barreling right at the untested Confederates. One wing hit at Fort Thompson, a dirt fort partially facing the river. Another rushed down the railroad bed toward the frightened militia. Hundreds of the Twenty-first Massachusetts found themselves suddenly inside the Confederate lines facing a frightened bunch of civilians clutching shotguns. One or two volleys and the Confederate civilians were on their way back to New Bern.

The Federals, now caught behind Confederate lines, poured a volley of fire into the Thirty-fifth North Carolina. The Twenty-sixth started edging forward, trying to protect the Confederate center so the reserves of the Thirty-third North Carolina could come up from the rear. While the Twenty-sixth and the Thirty-third were shoring up the center, the Federals were renewing their attack on Fort Thompson.

Branch, seeing his whole line fiercely engaged, and already having committed his reserves, panicked. He ordered a general retreat to New Bern. There was one problem. He either forgot to issue the retreat order to both the Twenty-sixth and the Thirty-third or the courier was cut down without reaching them. Before Vance's men and those of the Thirty-third knew what was happening, both regiments were alone. To his left, where four Confederate regiments should have been, Vance saw only bluecoats. To his rear, where a road led to New Bern, he saw the same.

For the better part of two hours, the two Confederate regiments held off sniping Federals, but the men realized that the plans to retreat to New Bern were off. The only way open to them was to head west through the swamps fed by Bryce's Creek.

With Vance leading the way, the Twenty-sixth and the Thirty-third ran toward the creek as their rear guard kept the Yankees at bay. The same rains that had slowed the Federal advance now worked against the Confederates. Bryce's Creek was out of its banks and moving swiftly. Still, it was the only choice the Confederates had.

Vance surveyed the situation and decided he would set the example. Plunging his horse into the creek, he promptly fell off and sank to the bottom. Several men dove in after him. After a number of tries, they found him and dragged him sputtering and coughing to the surface.

Vance's swim proved one thing: the creek was too deep to wade. While Vance recovered from his near-death experience, Burgwyn sent out scouts to find a ford. A black body servant located a boat, which was used to ferry the men across eighteen at a time. Burgwyn was the last man across, a point of honor that won him the men's respect and loyalty.

The Battle of New Bern was over. New Bern itself was captured without resistance. The Twenty-sixth would go on to write its place in Civil War history by being the Confederate regiment that suffered the most casualties at Gettysburg. Burgwyn, the boy colonel, fell dead on the first day in a vicious fight with the Twenty-fourth Michigan of the "Iron Brigade." His men buried him in a gun case where he fell. Two days later, what was left of the Twenty-sixth advanced beyond the stone wall on Cemetery Ridge, helping create North Carolina's battlefield motto of going "farthest at Gettysburg."

Vance would lead the regiment through the Seven Days' Battles on the peninsula of Virginia the following year. He left the regiment in August upon his election as governor of North Carolina. He did not make a single speech on his own behalf, his entire campaign being waged by a North Carolina newspaper editor. Vance's term in office was marked by his commitment to "fight with the Yankees and fuss with the Confederacy." He and Confederate president Jefferson Davis traded bitter letters and telegraph messages as Vance fought to keep control of North Carolina's troops and supplies.

After the war, Vance returned to Washington, where he spent the next fifteen years as a United States senator. The humor that had entertained Southern and Northern legislators alike was heard in the halls of Congress once more. Vance never again made the mistake of diving into a raging creek wearing a heavy wool uniform, boots, sword, and pistol. He died in 1894.

A Scraped Shin Fells a Great General

Union major general Charles Ferguson Smith might have been venerated one day as one of the army's most capable generals. His background was impeccable. An 1825 graduate of West Point at age eighteen, Smith was named commandant of cadets just four years later. During the Mexican War, he was praised for bravery by two different American generals leading two different armies. Over the next decade, he worked his way through the ranks until he reached lieutenant colonel, an outstanding achievement in the small peacetime army in the days when most officers struggled to move from lieutenant to captain.

When the Civil War started, Smith was named a brigadier general. Within a year, he was promoted to major general. Though he was a bit long in the tooth at age fifty-four, his on-field performance was impressive. It looked like Smith was destined for great things, perhaps one day commanding all Union forces in the Western theater.

Then he skinned his shin.

Smith was an army brat, born in 1807 to an army surgeon. During his tenure as commandant of cadets at West Point, he was in a prime position to observe and instruct many future Civil War officers on both sides. His charges from 1829 through 1845 included scores of generals, among them George Meade, John Sedgwick, Henry Halleck, and John Reynolds for the Union and Braxton Bragg, Jubal Early, P. G. T. Beauregard, and Richard Ewell for the Confederacy. Two of Smith's favorites were William T. Sherman (class of 1840) and Ulysses S. Grant (class of 1843).

Smith left West Point during the Mexican War to test his theories alongside his students. Generals Zachary Taylor and Winfield Scott praised his courage and recommended him three times for brevet promotions. After the war, he returned to the regular army and continued his good service. During the expedition to put down the Mormons in Utah in 1857, Smith found himself under the command of West Pointer Albert Sidney Johnston, who had graduated a year behind him.

When war came in 1861, Smith was one of the country's most experienced soldiers, with more than twenty-five years of active service. At first, his combat record was ignored by Washington war planners, who believed in giving commands to younger men. Smith was shuttled around to various staff commands before finally being named a brigadier general of volunteers in August 1861. Smith looked like a general. One army regular described him by saying he was the only officer on the

Western front who "could ride along a line of volunteers in the regulation uniform of a brigadier general, plume, chapeau, epaulets and all, without exciting laughter."

By January 1862, Smith, a stern-eyed, white-haired warrior with a drooping white mustache that reached past his chin, found himself under the command of one of his former students, Brigadier General Ulysses S. Grant. Grant needed his old commandant to help attack Forts Henry and Donelson, two Confederate installations in western Tennessee.

Fort Henry fell almost immediately with little fighting by the Union army. In fact, naval gunboats shelled the Confederate fort until its garrison asked for terms.

Fort Donelson did not go so easily. Grant wanted time to encircle the fort before moving in, so he told his division commanders to do nothing more than "demonstrate" to keep the Confederates occupied.

General Smith must not have attended that staff meeting. After eating breakfast on February 13, he ordered his own attack with two brigades and lost more than a hundred men before he could pull back. Smith made himself scarce so he would not have to face Grant, then realized that the general was not on the battlefield. Grant, believing the Confederates were too timid to try anything, had left to confer with the Union naval commander.

On February 15, while Grant was still at his meeting, the Confederates made a surprise attack, pushing the Federals back and opening an escape route. General Grant returned to the battlefield and discovered that the victory he had been planning was about to slip through his fingers. He felt there was only one man on whom he could count, his old commandant, Smith.

Grant found Smith sitting under a tree. He described how Confederates had been captured with several days' rations in their haversacks, an indication that they must not believe Fort Donelson was defensible. They were trying to break out, not defend the fort. If Smith were to recapture the ground lost that day, the Federals still might be able to win a victory.

Smith readily agreed to the counterattack. He mounted a horse and rode at the head of his division. The Federals charged through shot and shell, one man claiming he focused on following "the Old Man's white mustache." By night, Smith's division pushed the Confederates back to their outer trenches. The ground that the Union army had lost was retaken.

That night, two Confederate generals passed responsibility for the fort to a third, Simon Bolivar Buckner, an old friend of Grant's. When Buckner sent word to Grant asking for his terms of surrender, Grant asked Smith what he should offer. "No terms to the damned rebels" was Smith's reply. Grant agreed, and more than twelve thousand Confederates made an unconditional surrender. After the battle, Northern newspapers stuck him with the nickname "Unconditional Surrender" (or "U. S.") Grant. Privately, Grant thanked Smith for his prominent role in capturing the forts. Smith humbly accepted Grant's thanks, probably breathing a sigh of relief that Grant did not bring him up on charges for attacking in direct disregard of orders.

The aftermath of the capture of Forts Henry and Donelson demonstrated how even victories could harm a general's career. Grant was hailed as a hero by nearly everyone in the Union command structure. Once written off for his well-known problems with the bottle, Grant was promoted to major general. Smith was similarly rewarded, though he would remain a subordinate of Grant's, since his promotion came after Grant's.

But one man was not happy with Grant's newfound prominence. That was Major General Henry Halleck, Grant's boss. Halleck reveled in his nickname, "Old Brains," believing it accurately described him. He wired Washington asking to be put in overall command of the armies in the West. While waiting for an answer, he looked for a chink in Grant's armor. It did not take long to find it.

After Grant had taken the forts, he had disappeared for a week—at least in the view of Halleck, who expected daily reports from his subordinate general. On March 4, barely three weeks after the taking of the forts, Halleck wired Major General George McClellan in Washington, "It is hard to censure a successful general immediately after a victory, but I think he richly deserves it. I can get no returns, no reports, no information of any kind from him. Satisfied with his victory, he sits down and enjoys it without any regard to the future."

McClellan, always a stickler for military etiquette, gave Halleck permission to arrest Grant on charges of dereliction of duty. Halleck then telegraphed Grant, "You will place General C. F. Smith in command of expedition and remain at Fort Henry. Why do you not obey my orders to report strength and positions of your command?"

In an attempt to seal Grant's fate, Halleck started spreading the rumor that Grant was drinking again, wiring McClellan that Grant had "resumed his former bad habits. I do not deem it advisable to arrest him at present, but have placed General Smith in command of the expedition up the Tennessee. I think Smith will restore order and discipline."

The history books do not charge anyone with bringing Halleck the rumors that Grant was drinking, but Smith was the general who benefited. He was handed command of Grant's army.

Grant was livid at the charge of dereliction. During the period he was out of touch with Halleck, he had been in Nashville conferring with other generals on how best to move their armies up the Tennessee River. He demanded that Halleck formally relieve him of command, not just replace him for the current expedition. If Halleck did not support him, then he would go home.

The debate continued for two weeks as Smith transported the army upriver to a place called Pittsburg Landing near a little church called Shiloh. What Smith did not know was that the Confederates were secretly concentrating their forces at Corinth, Mississippi, less than a day's march from the spot Smith had picked as a campsite.

Meanwhile, Grant was still demanding to be relieved of command. Almost without warning, the opposite happened. Halleck reinstated Grant to command the Army of the Tennessee (named after the river, not the state, unlike the similarly named Confederate army). Halleck's only explanation was that he needed his best general in the field. What Halleck did not say was that he had received a stern warning from the army's inspector general in Washington demanding proof that Grant was neglecting his duty. Halleck had nothing but rumors, so he withdrew the charges.

Smith, the old warrior, must have been disappointed when Grant reappeared with orders giving him back his army. Smith retook his old position as commander of the Second Division. He plunged back into his duties as vigorously as always.

On April 2, Smith was climbing into a rowboat on the Tennessee River to go inspect troops when he skinned his shin on the sharp wooden edge of the seat. Like almost everyone who suffers such an abrasion, he ignored it. He probably did not bother pouring alcohol on it, a simple first-aid measure that most mothers would take today if their children suffered the same injury. He could have borrowed some from Grant but didn't. It was just a slight annoyance during a routine day.

Within days, the scrape turned worse. Smith developed a blood infection so severe he was forced into bed. Even that did not dampen his fighting spirit. Talk swirled among low-ranking Federal officers that if the Confederates found them and attacked, the Union army was in a precarious, poorly defended position, its back to the Tennessee River. Smith, who had selected the ground on which the army was camped, scoffed at the idea: "I ask nothing better than to have the rebels come out and attack us! We can whip them to hell! Our men suppose we have come here to fight, and if we begin to spade [dig earthworks] it will make them think that we fear the enemy!"

The rebels did come, much sooner than Smith or Grant expected. Smith was in bed on April 6 when he heard the crash of gunfire from the west. Nervous officers of his division came in to report that the Confederates were attacking in force. Smith laughed at them, chiding them for misinterpreting the fire of a few skirmishers as the start of a great battle.

He was wrong. Coming through the woods at a dead run toward the Federals camped around Shiloh Church were forty thousand Confederates under General Albert Sidney Johnston, Smith's old West Point mate. Smith, who had served in the army more than thirty-seven years, missed the largest two-day battle ever staged on the North American continent. All he could do was listen from his sickbed. His subordinates in the field were too busy fighting for their lives to even keep him informed.

The men of Smith's Second Division, commanded in his absence by

Brigadier General W. H. L. Wallace, were heavily engaged from the start. They initially rushed to the front to hold back the charging Confederates. Forced into a sunken road that history would call "the Hornets' Nest" because of the sound of bullets whizzing into and out of it, the division held out for six hours until Wallace was shot in the head. Seeing their new commander fall, many men of the Second Division broke and ran, leaving the Sixth Division to its fate.

The Second Division recorded more than thirteen hundred missing. Some were among the unidentified dead or captured on the field, but many were absent without leave. The men who had earlier said they would follow "the Old Man's white mustache" anywhere were probably on their way back to Iowa and Illinois.

Smith never got the chance to be proud of his division's initial performance—or embarrassed at how many of his men ran. He never even got to see the battlefield, having been moved to a hospital miles away so doctors could concentrate on stopping the infection. They failed.

On April 25, 1862, Major General Charles Ferguson Smith passed away in bed. The man who had taught and inspired more than a hundred Union and Confederate generals died of a scraped shin that would not even slow today's seven-year-olds.

A Well-Concealed Wound

Civil War generals were front-line fighters. Some were wounded several times. Some claimed to have been wounded more times than they really were.

Some wounds were dramatic. Some came simply from being in the wrong place at the wrong time.

One general may have even been shot by one of his own excitable soldiers in broad daylight. The blunder, though, lay just as heavily on the general's own shoulders, as he had sent away the one man who might have saved him.

Albert Sidney Johnston, fifty-eight, was a veteran of the revolution in Texas, the Black Hawk War, the Mexican War, and the Mormon Expedition by the time the Civil War flared. He was also considered one of the best officers in the service. It was a blow for the United States Army when he resigned his brevet brigadier general's commission to join his adopted state of Texas in leaving the Union.

Johnston had become close friends with Jefferson Davis at West Point. The Confederate president awarded him a commission to full general and command of the region stretching from Tennessee to Texas. But hardly had Johnston settled into his duties than the Union army threatened. In January 1862, the Confederates lost at Mill Springs, Kentucky. The following month, Forts Henry and Donelson fell in western Tennessee, leaving that part of the state and eastern Kentucky open to Federal control. Johnston, touted to the citizens of the new Confederacy as the best general on either side, was watching his command rapidly fold in on him. He had to move.

That move came in early April 1862 when Johnston marched his forty-four-thousand-man army out of Corinth, Mississippi, in what he hoped would be a surprise assault against Grant's thirty-nine-thousand-man army camped at Pittsburg Landing near Shiloh Church. Rain and inexperience hampered the Confederate movement. It took three exhausting days to get near Grant, time enough that watchful Union soldiers should have spotted the massive movement. Johnston was confident they wouldn't. The night before the assault, he boasted to his subordinates, "Tomorrow we will water our horses in the Tennessee River."

Not only did Grant neglect to fortify his position along the river's bluffs, he told his officers that the Confederates were nowhere near. His subordinates also took up the theme. When one skeptical regimental colonel who had been doing his own scouting warned Major General William T. Sherman that Confederates were moving in front of his position, Sherman replied, "Take your damned regiment back to Ohio," insisting that the man was seeing rebels where none existed.

Sherman and Grant were forced to change their minds on the morning of April 6, 1862, when tens of thousands of Confederates came pouring out of the woods into the Union camps. Sherman still had a hard time believing the attack and at first thought his Union regiments were firing into the woods needlessly. It wasn't until the Confederates started coming directly at him that he realized the colonel had been right all along. That same colonel was later blamed for not being strong enough in his suspicions, but charges were never brought against him, since he was killed in the heavy fighting.

Johnston's biggest problem during the attack was that his men stopped to loot the Federal camps they were overrunning. Some men stacked arms and sat down to eat the breakfasts still steaming over the Yankee campfires. Johnston at first admonished them, then realized they were proud of their attack and felt they deserved some reward. He grabbed a tin cup as a symbolic souvenir and waved it—instead of his sword—the rest of the battle. When he reached a group of men hesitating to move forward into a peach orchard filled with Yankees, he rode down their line touching their bayonets with the tin cup and telling them, "These must do the work."

The men surged forward and pushed the Yankees out of the orchard. Johnston turned back and rode toward his aides, pleased that he had been able to inspire one little victory on the big battlefield. An aide noticed that the heel of Johnston's left boot had been shot away and that the sole was split all the way to the toe. Johnston laughed and shook his leg as one might do to awaken a limb that has fallen asleep. Another aide noticed that Johnston's horse had suffered two minor wounds. Then Johnston reeled from his horse. One of his aides, Tennessee governor Isham Harris, grabbed the general before he fell, held him in the saddle, and guided his horse to a safe area. Harris then eased the general to the ground and searched for a wound. Though Johnston's coat was torn in several places by spent bullets, there was no blood on his upper body.

Then Harris noticed the blood dripping from Johnston's right boot. There, in the upper leather, Harris found a small hole just in back of the knee. A bullet had severed an artery, and Johnston's blood was flowing from him. Normally, the general would have had his personal surgeon at his side, but he had sent the man away to attend wounded Federals. The doctor had protested, only to have Johnston insist, "These men were our enemies a moment ago. They are our prisoners now. Take care of them."

Johnston's last words came in answer to Harris's inquiry as to whether the general was hurt. "Yes, and I fear badly," he said.

General Albert Sidney Johnston thus became the highest-ranking Confederate officer to die in the war and one of the first to perish on the battlefield.

There are unanswered questions about his death. Did he hide his wound in fear that his men would waver if they saw their leader removed from the field? Was he so excited by the battle that he didn't even feel the bullet pass through his leg? Most important, who fired the fatal shot? The entry wound was in back of the general's knee, which opens the possibility that one of his inexperienced soldiers might have shot his own commander. The minie ball was identified as coming from an Enfield, which was the type of weapon issued to one Tennessee regiment behind Johnston. On the other hand, had Johnston been hit by a musket ball fired at close range, his leg should have been shattered. Perhaps the bullet was fired by an Enfield-equipped Yankee and had just enough power to penetrate the general's leg without smashing it.

There is speculation that had Harris put a tourniquet on Johnston's leg, he could have slowed the blood loss and kept the general alive until the doctor arrived. Johnston died from loss of blood, which suggests he was wounded at least forty-five minutes to an hour before he expired. Had he alerted his staff, an amputation of his leg might have allowed him to survive. In the end, it was his concern for his wounded enemies that killed him.

Two Governors Find Death at Shiloh

At first glance, Governors Louis Powell Harvey and George W. Johnson wouldn't seem to have much in common. One represented a Northern state, while the other drew support from secessionists in a border state. One was legally elected, the other not.

The one thing they shared was a noble instinct to aid their constituents on the battlefield—an instinct that got them both killed.

Louis Powell Harvey's private and political careers were remarkably like those of Abraham Lincoln. Harvey was born in Connecticut in 1820. His family later moved to the Ohio frontier, where he had little opportunity for formal schooling. What he learned, he taught himself. But it was good enough to get him into college, where he stayed two years before dropping out due to illness. Through the 1830s and 1840s, he held a succession of jobs in Wisconsin—schoolteacher, shopkeeper, and editor of a newspaper, where he first drew attention from Whig politicians.

In a period when frontier politics was rough and tumble, Harvey kept his image squeaky-clean. By 1853, he was a Whig state senator. He easily made the transition to the new Republican Party in 1855. By 1859, he had moved higher up in state government, to secretary of state. In 1861, he was elected Wisconsin's governor by a large margin over the Democratic candidate.

In early 1862, the North was not fully united in the war effort. Many citizens, believing the early hype that the war would be over in less than ninety days, were now becoming disillusioned. One of Harvey's first problems was convincing his legislature to vote funds to support its soldiers in the field and their dependents at home.

The Battle of Shiloh shocked Northern sensibilities when it was revealed that more than seventeen hundred Union men had been killed and another eighty-five hundred had been wounded. Many were from Wisconsin—so many that Harvey decided to personally lead a relief mission carrying food and medicine. He traveled down the Mississippi, visited hospital ships making their way home, and reached the scene of the battle on the Tennessee River on April 19.

While trying to cross from one boat to another, Governor Harvey slipped and fell into the river. Apparently, the Tennessee was running too swiftly for anyone to save him by throwing a line or diving in after him. He disappeared, and his body was not discovered until several weeks later, sixty-five miles downstream.

Harvey had been in high office barely more than three months, so he is little remembered by Civil War historians. Though he never heard the crash of cannons and may have never even seen the battlefield where so many of his citizens died, the compassionate governor might be considered the last victim of Shiloh.

George W. Johnson was not the legal governor of Kentucky, but in the eyes of the secessionists of the state, he was their leader right up to his death on the bloody plains of Shiloh.

Johnson was a lawyer, planter, and state legislator from one of the oldest families in Kentucky when his state began to talk of secession. Though Kentucky never officially left the Union, a large number its men joined the Confederate army, particularly after the Union army invaded the state to enforce Federal control. In November 1861, a number of delegates from Union-occupied counties met to secede from the state and declare a provisional Confederate government. Johnson was elected governor, though the office was mostly symbolic, since the state capitol remained in Federal hands.

Realizing he was a governor on the run, Johnson attached himself to the command of John C. Breckinridge, a man he had supported for president in the 1860 election. He followed the general to Shiloh and served as a civilian aide on the first day. Feeling he was more in the way than helping, he decided to do something worthwhile. That night, he found the First Kentucky Regiment, asked for a musket, and was sworn in as a private. Johnson hadn't a clue how to be a soldier. The same night, his fellow soldiers drilled him on how to load and fire his musket and take care of himself on the battlefield.

The lessons didn't do much good. Johnson was wounded the next day. He lingered for two days before dying in a Union hospital.

Like Powell, who died just ten days later, Johnson was a politician who couldn't stand by while his citizens were fighting and dying on a battlefield. He had to be there with them. Though Johnson chose to pick up a musket and Powell to bring medicine, both perished while doing what they thought was right.

"SAM" BLALOCK AND THE "SHE DRAGOON": FEMALE SOLDIERS WHO POSED AS MALES

Waging war is man's work. Rolling bandages, loading cartridges, and nursing the wounded is woman's work.

Blundering Civil War recruiters remained comfortable in that logic even when faced with soft-talking, feminine-looking "boys" who wanted to join the army. Some women cut their hair, bound their breasts tightly against their bodies, wore loose-fitting clothes, and talked as deep as they could in an effort to gain a place alongside the men in the front lines. Needless to say, recruiters who neglected to do even cursory physical exams were not doing their jobs. While the number of women who successfully posed as men will never be known, researchers believe it happened hundreds of times on both sides.

Often, the women weren't discovered until they were wounded or killed. At least one North Carolina woman soldier marched all the way to the stone wall on the third day of Gettysburg in the Pettigrew-Pickett-Trimble Assault, becoming one of the few members of the fifteen-thousand-man (and -woman) contingent to make it all the way across that mile-wide field filled with bursting cannon shells and whining musket balls. She did not make it back. Her body was discovered after the battle was over.

In Vicksburg, the bones of several Federal soldiers were found on the battlefield in the 1930s. A routine pathology study was done, and the shape of the hipbones of one soldier proved conclusively that "he" was a woman.

When Confederate brigadier general John Hunt Morgan crossed into Indiana in July 1863 to begin his month-long raid, he ran into a stubborn defense from a Union regiment. Some of the wounded soldiers were captured. As Morgan's surgeon pulled the coat off one boy, he discovered a female. The nineteen-year-old woman was a Canadian named Lizzie who had crossed the border and joined a Michigan regiment by pretending to be a man.

Union major general Phil Sheridan wrote in his memoirs about two people in his ranks—a teamster and a soldier—who were discovered to be women only after they got drunk, fell in a river, and nearly drowned in January 1863. When Sheridan went looking for them, he found the teamster smoking a corncob pipe. According to Sheridan, "Her features were very large and so coarse and masculine was her general appearance that she would readily have passed as a man and in her case the deception was no doubt easily practiced."

The other was prettier than her companion. As Sheridan put it, "The 'she dragoon' proved to be a rather prepossessing young woman and though necessarily bronzed and hardened by exposure, I doubt if, even with these marks of campaigning, she could have deceived as readily as did her companion. How the two got acquainted I never learned, and though they had joined the army independently of each other, an intimacy had sprung up between them long before the mishaps of the foraging expedition."

Sheridan didn't ask and didn't tell. He put the two into dresses and shipped them to Louisville, Kentucky.

At least two female Union soldiers participated in the Red River Campaign in Louisiana in 1864. One made it back. One did not. The one who died on the field was Private Lyons Wakeman of the 153rd Regiment, New York State Volunteers. The private was really Sarah Rosetta Wakeman, a nineteen-year-old farm girl who had left home, lied about her age, and enlisted. She stood just five feet tall, six inches shorter than the average man. She took part in two battles and apparently acquitted herself well. She died from diarrhea and was buried under her adopted name. Her adventure was kept a secret for more than a century before her family released her letters. At first, she had signed them under her real name. Then, coming to realize they might fall into the wrong hands, she had started signing them with her male name.

Private Albert Cashier of the Ninety-fifth Illinois was a man from 1862, when he enlisted, until 1911, when he was hit by a car. In taking off his clothes to set his leg, doctors discovered that Albert was really a woman—Jennie Hodgers, an Irish immigrant who had lived as a man for nearly sixty years. During the Civil War, she had fought at Vicksburg, on the Red River, at Brice's Crossroads, in Mississippi, and in Nashville before ending the war at Fort Blakely, Alabama. She had carried a musket for three years in tough, wide-ranging campaigns. Her secret was never discovered. Her photo shows a slight, five-foot-three-inch figure with short hair who easily passed for a man.

In her later years, Hodgers lost her mind and was put into an asylum. She died in 1915 and was buried in her uniform. Her regimental mates fondly remembered a soldier who never shirked duty and never ran from the Confederates.

The best-known female Confederate soldier was better known as a Unionist bushwhacker.

Private Sam Blalock, from near Grandfather Mountain, North Carolina, joined the Twenty-sixth North Carolina Regiment with his brother Keith. Regimental mates remembered Sam as a slight boy who never went skinny-dipping with them but liked to watch them swimming in the creek near camp.

That was because Sam was really Malinda, Keith's wife. Both Blalocks joined the Confederate army early in the war—not to fight Yankees but to get close enough to them to desert. When it occurred to Keith that he could die before he figured out where the Yankee lines were, he threw himself into a patch of poison sumac in order to give himself a rash, which he hoped would look like some kind of disease worthy of getting him discharged. It worked. He was mustered out of Confederate service on April 10, 1862. Sam then turned himself in and proved he was a she.

The Blalocks' military careers were over, but their Civil War careers were just beginning. The two became bushwhackers near Grandfather Mountain. They would wait in the woods beside roads at night to rob late-night travelers, be they Confederates or Unionists. They also raided known Confederate farms, including the house of the only man besides Keith who had initially known Sam was Malinda. He was the recruiting officer for that district of the state. That did not buy him any slack from the two robbers. They raided his farm twice, which turned out to be a mistake for Keith. His eye was shot out in the second raid.

The two survived the war, though they went on numerous raids and are rumored to have killed some of their victims. Malinda was wounded at least once. She died first, of natural causes. Keith stayed the same irascible man he always was. He died when he lost control of a railroad handcar on a steep mountain grade. The handcar ran off the rails and landed on top of him. He was seventy-seven.

One of the most puzzling cases of a woman posing as a man was that of Florena Budwin. She disguised her sex and joined a Pennsylvania regiment with her husband. Both were captured in 1864 and sent to Andersonville Prison, a crowded stockade in southern Georgia. Even in prison, Florena did not reveal her sex. Had she simply walked up to a guard, she would have been immediately removed from the crowded camp that eventually saw the deaths of thirteen thousand Federal prisoners. At some point, her husband died. Still, Florena did not show herself.

She was transferred to a prison camp in Florence, South Carolina, early in 1865. When she was subjected to a routine medical exam, her sex was finally discovered. The prison doctor took her out of the camp's population and made her his nurse. It was too late. She died in February 1865, just a few months before the war was over and she would have been sent home. Her tombstone is the only one marked among the Union soldiers who died at Florence. She may have been the first person buried in a national cemetery who was known to be a woman.

"PLUCKY AFRICANS" STEAL
A CONFEDERATE SHIP

Robert Smalls, a twenty-two-year-old slave, did much more than embarrass his owner and his employer when they inadvertently gave him the opportunity to escape in May 1862. Not only did he humiliate the whole Confederate military structure in Charleston, South Carolina, he also proved to skeptical Northerners and nervous Southerners that skin color had nothing to do with ingenuity. He also proved that if people look only at what they expect to see, they may miss what they are really seeing.

Born in 1840 in Beaufort, South Carolina, into a family owned by the white McKees, Smalls had it better than most slaves. His peers worked on plantations on the small islands off the coast, cultivating high-quality sea-island cotton, which was so delicate that its seeds were picked out by hand rather than by being run through a gin. Tending sea-island cotton was unusually hard because the owners used the nutrient-rich tidal muck from the area's creeks for fertilizer. Slaves spent hours at a time in water digging up the muck, which was then spread on the dry fields.

His owner recognized that Smalls's intelligence could prove profitable if he were trained to perform skilled labor. At that time, it was common for slaves to be taught trades such as barrel making and blacksmithing. They performed these trades for their masters. In addition, the products of their work or their time was sold to other whites. The master usually collected most of the profits, while the slave was given some of the money as an incentive to do good work.

McKee trained Smalls to be a ship's pilot. It was the pilot's job to determine where currents had deposited sandbars in bays and remember where underwater snags were in rivers. It was a highly skilled job that required a long memory, a quick mind, and good judgment, so orders could be instantly given to the ship's helmsman to make corrections in course.

In early 1862, Smalls's skills were sold to C. J. Relyea, the captain of the *Planter*, a 147-foot-long twin-engine supply ship based in Charleston. Though armed with two cannons, the *Planter* was not really a warship. Her job was to run supplies from Charleston to the various forts protecting the harbor. Her draft of less than 4 feet enabled her to negotiate the shallowest harbors, rivers, and creeks. Since she was also the fastest ship in the harbor, the *Planter* also acted as a dispatch boat for Confederate brigadier general Roswell S. Ripley, the commander of the city's harbor defenses. Ripley stationed the ship close to his headquarters.

Little is known about Captain Relyea other than that he was a man of habit. When his ship got under way, he would put on a wide-brimmed white straw hat he kept in the wheelhouse. He would then walk the deck, frequently standing at the bow with his arms folded. Regular observers who may not have known the captain's name knew his ship when they saw the straw hat moving about.

One day, the slave crew of the *Planter* was lounging aboard while Relyea was on shore tending to business. Smalls playfully put the white hat on his head and struck the familiar pose of the captain. Everyone laughed at the imitation. One of the slaves remarked that Smalls looked just like Relyea.

Everyone laughed again, but the casual remark gave Smalls an idea. If his imitation looked that much like the captain to the rest of the crew, could he also fool the harbor sentries? Could he play the captain convincingly enough to cast off with just his fellow slaves on board? More important, could he fool the Confederates manning the deadly cannons at Fort Sumter? If the ship could get past those cannons, the Union blockading squadron was just a few miles away.

Smalls explained his dangerous plan to the other slaves. If they were caught, they would be whipped at the very least and possibly executed for staging a slave rebellion. But if they could reach those Yankee ships, the men on the *Planter* would be free. The crew voted for freedom.

On the night of May 12, 1862, they walked down to the harbor one by one so as not to attract attention. At about three-thirty in the morning, the crew, who had been building steam pressure in the *Planter's* boilers, cast off. Though the ship was leaving her moorings at least an hour earlier than on a normal day, the sentries apparently did not give it much thought. They were used to the ship's coming and going every day.

The *Planter* moved slowly up the Cooper River before putting in next to another steamer. As the helmsman shifted into reverse, the wives and children of the crew jumped on board the *Planter*, and she started back downriver. Smalls donned the captain's straw hat and started walking around the ship as he had seen Relyea do many times. Whenever he saw a sentry on shore, he waved, then turned away "so the sentinel could not see my color," as he wrote years later.

As the *Planter* passed the guns on the point of shore called "the Battery," she turned east toward the cannons of Fort Sumter, held for the past year by the Confederacy. Smalls slowed the ship, checking his pocket watch to be sure he passed the fort when its sentries were expecting him. As he neared, Smalls blew the correct recognition signal on the ship's whistle, then stood on the bow so the sentry could easily distinguish the familiar white straw hat. The sentry waved, and the ship passed without incident. When the *Planter* reached the point where she normally turned south toward the first Confederate fort on her regular route, Smalls ordered the helmsman to go full throttle toward the Union ships.

Surprised Confederate sentries wondered what was happening, but no one ordered the cannons to fire. The Federals were just as puzzled by a Confederate ship barreling toward them in the predawn darkness. They assumed she was attacking, so they went to general quarters and were preparing to fire when they noticed that the ship was flying a white sheet as a surrender flag.

The Federals were delighted at the resourceful Smalls's theft of a Confederate ship and her cargo, which consisted of the two mounted cannons, a quantity of black powder, and four unmounted cannons which had been destined for installation on a Charleston-area fort. The Federals awarded the crew about five thousand dollars for the captured ship, of which Smalls kept fifteen hundred dollars, since he acted as captain.

The Northern press spread Smalls's fame nationwide as evidence that blacks could think just as clearly as whites. *Harper's Weekly* gushed about the "plucky Africans" and published a picture of Smalls. The *New York Commercial Advertiser* commented,

> We suppose few events that have taken place during the war have produced a heartier chuckle of satisfaction than the capture of the rebel armed steamer *Planter*. It is a remarkable instance, even in these times, of riches taking themselves to wing and flying away. Here were eight contrabands, made out of the commonest clay imaginable, and they actually emancipated not only themselves, but as many others, bringing a highly valuable present to Uncle Sam. The fellow who managed this affair proves that, in spite of his name, he is no Small man.

The Southern press was not at all impressed. Besides noting that the *Planter* had little military value, Southern newspapers speculated that Smalls must have had help from white people in getting away with the theft. After all, he was just a slave.

The Smalls story does not end there. The *Planter* was pressed into service as a Union raider because of her shallow draft. Smalls stayed with her as a pilot on at least seventeen raids the Yankees conducted up creeks and rivers he knew. Once, the ship came under artillery fire, and her white captain abandoned his post in the wheelhouse to seek cover. Smalls took over the ship and brought her out of danger. His courage was recognized, and he was given command of the ship.

Smalls used his fifteen hundred dollars in prize money to return to Beaufort and buy his former master's house at a tax sale of confiscated Confederate property conducted by the United States government. Smalls, born in the slave quarters behind the big house, now owned the big house.

During Reconstruction, many blacks were appointed congressmen from the former Confederate states. Smalls, certainly the most famous former slave in South Carolina, was appointed for his district. He quickly got the hang of congressional wheeling and dealing, successfully pushed through a bill appropriating money for a small naval coaling station on an island just south of Beaufort. He reasoned that its expansion would help both his white and black constituents.

That little naval installation is now the United States Marine Corps training depot on Parris Island. Every marine recruited east of the Mississippi River receives his or her basic training there. They can thank— or curse—Robert Smalls, whose accomplishments thus continue to have a major impact on South Carolina more than 135 years after he became famous.

Smalls staked his life on fooling hundreds of Confederate soldiers into believing he was a white man. Used to seeing the same thing day after day, they failed to pay attention to the man beneath the hat.

LITTLE MAC AND THE PRIVATE EYE

The Confederates never had a propaganda minister better than Allan Pinkerton. To hear Pinkerton tell it, the Confederate army in 1862 was the largest, most efficient, fastest-moving, best-equipped, most dangerous war machine on the planet. That description was exactly what the Confederates wanted the North to believe, and they had Pinkerton to thank.

The interesting thing is that Pinkerton was not some Confederate psychological-warfare genius who planted false information in the heads of the Federals. He was the head of the Secret Service—the United States Secret Service.

Who knows why the United States government, particularly Major General George McClellan, trusted Pinkerton? Nothing in his background indicated an inherent ability to root out spies. He had no training in police work or espionage. Most important, the man did not show any ability to analyze the information that came his way. He could not even fill that most basic military-intelligence need, accurately counting the number of opposing troops in the field.

Born in Scotland, Pinkerton immigrated to the United States in 1842. He settled in Chicago, where he was employed as a cooper. While working in the city, he learned of the activities of a Chicago counterfeiting gang. He helped the police bust the racket, which was just the break he needed to get out of barrels and into law enforcement. By 1850, he was a deputy sheriff of Cook County, Illinois.

Pinkerton did not stay a sheriff long. That same year, he organized what is usually regarded as the first detective agency in the world, the Pinkerton National Detective Agency. He adopted a line drawing of a large eye as his company's logo to suggest that his agency was always watching, thus creating the euphemism for detective, "private eye."

While trying to find thieves preying on the Illinois Central Railroad, Pinkerton met a young lawyer who also had the railroad as a client. That man was Abraham Lincoln. The two became good friends over the next decade. When Lincoln was elected president, it was a Pinkerton bodyguard who escorted him to Washington early in 1861. The escort was more than an honor guard. In most places Lincoln visited on his twelve-day train trip from Springfield to Washington, he was greeted warmly by curious crowds. Most people had never even seen a picture of the man they had elected president and knew little about him. Once they got a good look, some had second thoughts. Lincoln had not even left some Eastern cities before newspapers in those towns were calling him a country bumpkin. Some even insulted his ungainly physical appearance by calling him a gorilla or a baboon. More darkly, some Southern sympathizers began to question whether he would live to take office.

While Lincoln was preparing to pass into Maryland, a slave state, his old friend Pinkerton told the president-elect that he had seen his last friendly crowd. Pinkerton claimed that his operatives, working undercover as secessionist sympathizers, had infiltrated a number of violent secret societies that intended to kidnap or kill Lincoln when he passed through Baltimore. One organization that had sworn to harm the new president was called "the Bloody Tubs."

Pinkerton's plan to protect Lincoln was radical at best and dangerous at worst. Instead of bypassing Baltimore's railroad station and sending Lincoln to Washington by carriage with a military escort, Pinkerton suggested sending Lincoln's railroad car through Baltimore as planned, but in the dead of night and without notifying local politicians who were organizing public rallies. And instead of surrounding Lincoln with bodyguards, Pinkerton assigned only one—a nervous operative armed with four pistols and two knives. Pinkerton even asked Lincoln to pack away his signature stovepipe hat in favor of a soft, nondescript type. It would be impossible to disguise Lincoln's lanky six-foot-four-inch frame when most people stood less than five-foot-seven, but ditching the stovepipe couldn't hurt.

It was three-thirty in the morning when Lincoln's railroad car passed through the quiet streets of Baltimore. No one seemed to pay it any attention. No attempt on his life was made, though he did hear a drunk singing "Dixie" at the top of his lungs.

Historians are still divided as to whether the Bloody Tubs really existed and whether they really intended to harm the president-elect. If they were real, Pinkerton took a major chance by sending Lincoln into their lair. If Pinkerton made them up in order to enhance his reputation, he did a masterful job of selling the administration on his unorthodox protection scheme.

Though Pinkerton's plan got Lincoln to Washington in one unbloody piece, it did terrible damage to the president-elect's reputation. When the hostile Eastern press got wind of how Lincoln had been spirited through Baltimore in the dead of night, it ran editorial cartoons showing him cowering in a boxcar wearing a Scotsman's disguise (based on his wearing the soft hat instead of his stovepipe).

This would not be the last time Lincoln questioned his old friend's judgment.

By the late summer of 1861, Pinkerton hooked up with another old Illinois Central friend, Union major general George McClellan. McClellan had accepted the detective's reports when he held a job as vice president of the railroad. Now, he used Pinkerton to help him estimate the number of Confederate soldiers facing his army at Centreville, Virginia, not far from the site of the great Federal defeat at Manassas in July.

According to Pinkerton, it was by the grace of God that the Confederate army had not rolled right over the Union army. Judging by Pinkerton's estimates, every tree hid a dozen Confederates. It was enough to scare the pants off McClellan. "I am here in a terrible place. The enemy have from three to four times my force," wrote McClellan in a report to Washington.

McClellan found himself held back by a bristling array of artillery at Centreville. When the line was finally occupied, Union soldiers discovered that the Confederates had withdrawn in the night, leaving only an impressive collection of black oak trunks masquerading as cannons. The calls for McClellan's removal started then.

Pinkerton's reports of troop strength kept growing. McClellan believed that the Confederates were getting stronger by the day. At one point, McClellan, quoting Pinkerton's intelligence, estimated the Confederate army at "150,000 strong, well drilled and equipped, ably commanded." None of it was true, although Southerners might have agreed with the "ably commanded" part. Since no one but the Confederate commanding general could dispute Pinkerton's claims about troop strength, Pinkerton's reputation steadily increased over the summer.

One real success he had as head of the newly formed United States Secret Service was arresting Washington socialite Rose O'Neal Greenhow as a Confederate spy. In early July 1861, Greenhow had successfully sent messages to the Confederates that Union forces would move on Manassas Junction, Virginia. Though modern historians suspect that the Confederates already possessed this knowledge, the Federals believed her messages had helped the Confederates win the first major battle of the war.

Greenhow's system of spying was rather simple. She threw great parties attended by all the right people in Washington. Historians have never been bold enough to confirm that the forty-five-year-old widow was trading sex for information, but a surprising number of congressmen, senators, and military officers vied for invitations to her parties. One regular, Henry Wilson, later became vice president of the United States under President Ulysses S. Grant. Greenhow was good at collecting information but terrible about concealing the fact that she was doing it. Pinkerton put her under surveillance and easily caught her passing information to contacts. Pinkerton was all for hanging her, but cooler (and more embarrassed) heads in Washington deported her south.

The war started anew in March 1862 when McClellan launched a bold plan to capture Richmond by marching his army up Virginia's peninsula, the landmass between the James and York Rivers. McClellan faced a formidable opponent. According to Pinkerton, anywhere from 50,000 to 150,000 Confederates could be quickly dispatched to the area. That would have been welcome news to the Confederates, who counted about 39,000 effectives in all of northern Virginia.

Trusting Pinkerton, McClellan spent a month laying siege to Yorktown, Virginia, the Confederates' first line of resistance. Looking through his binoculars, McClellan could see that the Confederate entrenchments, some of them left over from the American Revolution, bristled with cannons. Watching all day and listening all night, he could see and hear tens of thousands of Confederates moving in their giant fortress.

That was not quite true. Facing McClellan's 105,000-man army were fewer than 15,000 Confederates under Major General John Bankhead Magruder. Called "Prince John" for his fancy uniforms and huge parties, Magruder had been the hero of lower Virginia since he was in overall command at Big Bethel in June 1861. Now, Magruder correctly recognized that the only way he could hope to hold out against McClellan was to make the cautious Federal general believe he was at a disadvantage. To do that, Magruder had scores of trees cut down, stripped of their branches, and painted with several coats of black paint. Dubbed "Quaker guns" after the religion that teaches pacifism, the fake cannons were interspersed among real ones. From a distance, the Quaker guns looked real and dangerous. To complete the effect, Magruder had his regiments march back and forth in full view of the Federals. Sometimes, he marched them quietly to the rear, then marched them noisily back to the front to make it look like reenforcements were arriving.

The ruse worked better than Magruder could even know. McClellan, with almost a ten-to-one advantage, was fooled a second time by the same trick. He halted his advance and wired President Lincoln for reenforcements. When Lincoln refused, McClellan declined to move forward, convinced that he would be sending his men to their deaths in front of those fearsome black cannons.

After a month, the Confederates realized they had played the game as far as they could. They quietly evacuated Yorktown and pulled back to set up another defense on better ground. McClellan, who was then planning to unleash a hundred-cannon bombardment, was chagrined to discover that Quaker guns had fooled him for so long. By contrast, the Union soldiers were relieved. They amused themselves by staging photos showing soldiers holding lighted sticks to the tree trunks where a torch hole would normally be on a cannon.

The Confederates used their easily bought time putting together a real army to face the Federals. As spring wore into summer, McClellan slowly pushed toward Richmond. At one point, he could see the church spires of the city. All the while, Pinkerton was gathering and evaluating reports from his spy network, in addition to reports by earnest but excitable captured slaves, who were likely as not to misidentify which generals were in the city. Nearly every day, Pinkerton issued warnings of gathering Confederate forces.

On May 31, 1862, the Confederate army commander, General Joseph Johnston, suffered a debilitating wound. Robert E. Lee was given field command of Johnston's army. Instead of slowly retreating as Johnston had been doing, Lee struck back in the Seven Days' Battles. With this sudden counterattack, McClellan now viewed Pinkerton's inflated Confederate figures with even more alarm. Thinking his army had been lured into a trap by superior forces, he went into a full-scale retreat down the James River.

Oddly enough, the Peninsula Campaign, five months of slogging through Virginia's swamps, ended rather abruptly with a major Union victory when Lee rashly sent several brigades charging into the mouths of Federal cannons dug in on Malvern Hill, losing more than five thousand men. This was little more than a year before he would repeat the same mistake at Gettysburg. Though he actually won Malvern Hill, McClellan refused to fight Lee again. He embarked on his ships and headed back north, convinced by Pinkerton that he was outnumbered by the Confederates.

At most, Lee had 70,000 troops during the final days of the Peninsula Campaign. But Pinkerton, sometimes combining and double-counting reports from his spies, convinced McClellan that the Confederates numbered as many as 200,000. In truth, if the two largest armies of the Confederacy—the Army of Northern Virginia and the Army of Tennessee—had ever combined at their prime, the total would have been fewer than 120,000 men. The entire Confederate enlistment, counting every militiaman who never left his home county and every sailor who never set foot on a battlefield, was around 1,000,000 men. In effect, Pinkerton convinced McClellan that he was facing a fifth of all the men who served the Confederacy over the four years of the war.

Even the debacle on the peninsula did not convince McClellan that Pinkerton's service was unreliable. Three months later, in September 1862, McClellan was still listening to Pinkerton when the detective placed the strength of Lee's Maryland invasion army above 120,000. As usual, McClellan was frightened. The Union army had just 75,000 men.

The faulty intelligence worked to Lee's advantage, because he had just 40,000 men. When a Union cavalryman found a copy of Lee's battle orders lying in the grass, the orders were sent directly to McClellan, who claimed he now had what he needed to defeat Lee. Lee's orders detailed how he would split his forces to capture Harpers Ferry before concentrating at the town of Sharpsburg near Antietam Creek. McClellan believed Lee's splitting of forces meant both armies were now equal in size, when the split actually gave McClellan far superior numbers. Throughout the battle, McClellan kept reserves out of action as he waited for the rest of Lee's vast army to appear. It never did. McClellan allowed Lee to leave Antietam though the Southerners were trapped on the north side of the Potomac. McClellan, still believing Pinkerton's reports, never made an effort to pursue the Confederates down to the water's edge. Had he done so, Lee probably would not have been able to mount much of a defense, and his army would have been crushed.

The lost opportunity at Antietam was the last straw for Lincoln, who had been pushing McClellan to use his well-equipped army. When McClellan refused a direct order to pursue Lee, Lincoln fired him.

When McClellan was replaced by Major General Ambrose Burnside, Pinkerton lost his sponsor. Burnside did not like the scruffy little Scot, and Pinkerton had no confidence in Burnside—as if he would know a competent general if he met one. Pinkerton later claimed that he was offered the job of top detective in the War Department, but he might have been fibbing about that. For the rest of the war, he did little more than investigate civil crimes committed against the government.

Allan Pinkerton and George McClellan were the best friends the Confederates had in the Union army. For the first eighteen months of the war, McClellan implicitly trusted Pinkerton's outrageous estimates of Confederate strength. By believing those figures, McClellan developed a fear of fighting rebels he could not see but who he knew were out there.

After the fighting ended, Pinkerton ruined whatever good reputation he had in the South before and during the war. In Missouri during the 1870s, his detective agency aggressively pursued the train-robbing gang led by Jesse James. Most members of the gang were former Confederate guerrillas. In their zeal to make a capture, Pinkerton men threw a bomb into a house where they thought James was hiding. He was not there, but his mother and eight-year-old brother were. The boy was killed, and Mrs. James's arm was blown off in the explosion.

From that moment, the name Pinkerton was spat out in revulsion throughout the South and the border states.

How Stovepipe Johnson Got His Name

Fooling the enemy is one of the joys of warfare. If one side can defeat the other without dismembering anyone, the winning side is happy and the losing side is embarrassed, but both sides are all in one piece. In one incident during the war, a small force of Confederates fooled a Yankee garrison into believing it would be blown to bits unless it gave up. At most, the Yankees would have gotten a little soot on them.

Major Adam Rankin Johnson was more than a rough-hewn, frontier-educated Indian fighter when he started his own band of partisan rangers in Kentucky. He was a protégé of Brigadier General Nathan Bedford Forrest, which meant he was not educated in the traditional means of combat. Forrest did not have much regular schooling, much less a West Point degree. Neither did Johnson. What both men had was an innate sense of what worked on the battlefield. In February 1862, when the commanders at Fort Donelson, Tennessee, feared that the Federals had them surrounded, it was Johnson who crawled through freezing mud and water to scout a way out. Forrest followed his trusted scout and took out his entire cavalry command, rather than letting them be captured.

Johnson left Forrest's command to form his own band of "partisan rangers," a controversial attempt by Confederates to employ men who would remain outside regular military control so they could raid behind Federal lines. In the daytime, they appeared to be farmers. At night, they became soldiers. Forrest was sorry to lose his scout. He was also convinced Johnson had become involved in something unsavory. Forrest wrote, "The authorities given to would-be colonels, and by them delegated to would-be captains and lieutenants, have created squads of men who are dodging from pillar to post, preying upon the people, robbing them of their horses and other property, to the manifest injury of the country and our cause."

That may have been the case, but unsavory methods hardly came into play in the old-fashioned ruse Johnson pulled on July 18, 1862. He and twelve men crossed the Ohio River and moved on Newburgh, Indiana, a small town with a Union garrison. Johnson surprised the Federals by demanding their surrender. The Union commander asked Johnson what made him think they would surrender to a scraggly little ranger.

Johnson turned and pointed to a nearby hill. There, looking down on the town, were two large cannons manned by the rest of Johnson's men. He told the Union officer that he was prepared to shell the town if the Federals did not surrender immediately. The Federals were only a small infantry detachment. They had no heavy guns to shell the Confederate position. The officer decided to comply.

Johnson took all the Federals' arms and ammunition and departed Newburgh as quickly as he could. He left behind the two cannons that had intimidated the Federals into surrendering. They were really two lengths of stovepipe mounted on wagon wheels.

In July 1863, Johnson joined Brigadier General John Hunt Morgan and seventeen hundred cavalrymen on a month-long raid into Ohio and Indiana that was supposed to draw off Federal soldiers from Kentucky. The raiders fought a skirmish a day, as militia tried to stop the fast-riding Confederates. Finally, a force did catch them. At Buffington Island, Ohio, Johnson and about two hundred of Morgan's men crossed the Ohio River into West Virginia. Morgan and the rest of his command were caught on the Ohio side and later sent to prison, but Johnson escaped.

Promoted to brigadier general, Johnson continued his partisan activities until August 21, 1864, when he was leading a raid in Kentucky. In a hot, confusing firefight, one of his own men shot him in the head. Johnson survived but was blinded. Even then, he refused to resign from the Confederate army.

After the war, Johnson, by then known as "Stovepipe," lived a full life in Texas, even dictating a popular book about his activities with the partisan rangers. Blinded at age thirty, Johnson lived to be eighty-eight, a pillar of his community.

The name of the Federal commander who surrendered his garrison and the town of Newburgh, Indiana, to a single Confederate officer with soot on his hands has been lost to history.

ERICSSON'S RIVER MONITORS
SUFFER A REDESIGN

If there is one thing that upsets brilliant inventors, it's when upstarts come along behind them to "improve" the original designs.

———————

John Ericsson always had problems convincing the powers that be that he knew what he was doing. Part of his problem was that sixteen years before the Civil War, one of Ericsson's business partners accidentally blew the United States secretary of state and secretary of the navy to bits when an experimental cannon exploded. Ericsson had the misfortune of being blamed for killing his primary customer.

In late 1861, Ericsson and the navy agreed to work together to design an ironclad ship to counter the Confederate ironclad *Virginia*, then under construction. The government gave Ericsson less than a hundred days to build his ironclad.

Though Ericsson's design was accepted, the navy made at least two changes in his plans. Ericsson suggested mounting two fifteen-inch cannons, the largest guns that could be forged. Worried that the gun crew would not be able to stand the noise and concussion of such guns, the navy instead gave Ericsson two eleven-inch Dahlgrens, still formidable guns that fired shells weighing 184 pounds. The navy also did something else that Ericsson didn't like—it instructed him that his cannons would fire shells using only 15 pounds of powder. The cannons were designed to be fired with 30 pounds per shell, but the navy men insisted that the recoil from larger charges could injure the crew and Ericsson's turret.

As "Ericsson's battery" started to take shape in New York Harbor, word of her innovations spread throughout the North. She would have only two feet of freeboard (deck above normal water level), meaning that waves would likely wash over her. Her engines would be below deck. Two steam engines would suck surface air into the engine room to feed the two boilers and provide fresh air to the crew. There was even a toilet that flushed using compressed air. In all, Ericsson had more than forty patentable innovations on board his battery.

Ericsson settled on a name for his "impregnable battery" in January 1862 when he wrote, "This structure will admonish the leaders of the Southern Rebellion that the batteries on the banks of their rivers will no longer present barriers to the entrance of the Union forces. The iron-clad steamer will thus prove a severe Monitor on those leaders."

Even on the day the *Monitor* was launched, bookies were taking bets that she would sink. To prove them and his ever-present navy critics wrong, Ericsson stationed himself on board the vessel near the stern and ordered the wooden chocks removed. If the vessel sank, he would go down with her.

The *Monitor* floated just fine. A newspaper reporter wrote that the ship "had no intention of sinking."

Within weeks, the *Monitor* set out to meet the *Virginia* at Hampton Roads. On March 9, 1862, the world saw the first battle between ironclads. It was a draw, as neither vessel sank the other, although the *Virginia*'s iron plating was cracked and she technically left the battle site to her opponent. Ironically, the battle was a draw primarily because the navy had limited the *Monitor*'s firepower. Some balls and shells fired by the *Monitor* cracked the *Virginia*'s iron plating. Had thirty pounds of powder been used, they might have penetrated the Confederate iron-clad, and the battle might have been over within minutes. The *Monitor*'s captain had the opportunity to try using thirty pounds, but being an old, by-the-book navy man, he refused to disobey orders under battle conditions.

In August 1862, Ericsson was asked to design a class of shallow-draft "monitors" (the name had by then become generic) for use on shallow Western rivers. Within two days, he returned plans for a vessel with a six-foot draft.

Weeks later, he discovered that his plans had been altered. Upon investigation, Ericsson learned that the government had gone behind his back and had the navy's chief engineer, Alban C. Stimers, redesign the plans to include such modifications as water tanks that could be flooded to lower the level of the ironclad. Ericsson looked at Stimers's plans and confidently said the redesign was unstable at best and capable of sinking at worst. Ericsson offered to correct the plans for the ironclad, officially called the "Casco" class of monitors, but he was refused. With Stimers in charge, construction got under way on the first of twenty planned vessels. The construction budget was fourteen million dollars, a tremendous sum.

When the first Casco-class monitor, the USS *Chimo*, was launched, she had a draft of less than six feet, as expected. But she also had a freeboard of just three inches, instead of the fifteen Stimers expected. Worse, this was before the boat was loaded with coal, supplies, and crew. Waves would constantly sweep the deck and cause leaks that would swamp the ship. Ericsson was right. The design was unsound. When asked to redesign the monitors now that they were under construction, he refused lest he get the blame for wasting millions of dollars on a design that was no longer his.

Construction on the Cascos continued once modifications were made. Five were easily converted into gunboats without turrets. Their only use was as floating gun platforms for a single cannon. The rest of the vessels underwent extensive and expensive modifications. The best of them had a draft of eight feet, two feet more than Ericsson's design.

One historian told a story of how Stimers was transferred in disgrace from his high-level Washington-based design job and assigned to one of the gunboats he had ruined with his modifications. He was chagrined to find that someone had erected a brass plate on the ship giving him credit for its design. When last seen, Stimers was going at the plate with a coal chisel, trying to remove his name from the million-dollar blunder.

BRIGADIER GENERAL THOMAS WILLIAMS EXPERIENCES PAYBACK

While official military records say Union brigadier general Thomas Williams was shot to death by a Confederate bullet while defending Baton Rouge, Louisiana, some of Williams's own men started a rumor that they killed him by holding his head in front of one of his own cannons.

It appears Williams's blunder was in carrying strict discipline too far.

***

Williams was born a military man, the son of a militia general who convinced his young son to join up to fight Indians in the Black Hawk War in Illinois in the 1830s. Williams graduated from West Point in 1837 and spent the next twenty-four years fighting Indians and Mexicans.

Appointed a major of artillery at the start of the Civil War, Williams took part in the early Union victories in North Carolina. It was also in North Carolina that regular soldiers learned to hate him. Williams participated in the capture of Forts Clark and Hatteras at Hatteras Inlet in the summer of 1861. Once the forts were captured, Williams put his soldiers to work in the hot sun building the sand walls of Fort Clark higher. The soldiers thought the work a punishment, since it was unlikely that the forts would be of military use to Union forces now that all Confederate threats had ended along that part of the coast. One Union soldier wrote in his diary, "It is only the infernal foolishness of the thing that makes it irksome."

The soldiers disliked their commander so much that they dug pitfalls for him outside the fort, covering the holes with brush. Followed by an aide who mimicked the general's walk to the amusement of watching soldiers, Williams fell into one trap. Pulled out of that one, he promptly fell into another. Within a few days, a soldier took a potshot at him. Things got so bad that even Williams's subordinate officers avoided him.

The Union army knew how to deal with a bad egg like Williams—it transferred him to another command. He was given a brigade under Major General Ben Butler, who was making plans to attack New Orleans.

Williams's next assignment was to help figure out a way to capture Vicksburg. One of his responsibilities was evaluating the chances of digging a canal that would divert the Mississippi River away from the cannons protecting the city. Just as he had been fascinated with digging on North Carolina's Outer Banks, Williams now pushed an even bigger digging project. His soldiers were again none too happy with their commander. They were supposed to be fighting Confederates, not digging ditches.

By the summer of 1862, the canal scheme had been abandoned and Williams was stationed at Baton Rouge. The Union position there was exposed, and the Confederates took advantage of it on August 5, 1862. Confederate major general John C. Breckinridge attacked the city as a diversion so the Confederates could have time to build a formidable position at Port Hudson, between Vicksburg and Baton Rouge.

It was a confusing battle fought in the fog. Confederates fired on Confederates and Federals fired on Federals when the two sides were not shooting at each other. Both sides were forced to employ the walking sick. Large numbers of men were ill because of the extreme heat, the poor food and water, and the fevers associated with living along a river surrounded by swamps that bred millions of mosquitos.

The Federals were forced back through the outskirts of Baton Rouge, where Williams demanded that his men make a stand. It was here also that Williams met his death. The official report said that Williams died with a bullet in the heart while rallying his men to counterattack. Unofficially, the rumor mill said that his men finally got even with their bullying commander by grabbing him by both arms and holding him in front of a cannon, which was then touched off. One rumor said he was decapitated. Whatever happened, Williams was the second Union general killed in combat to that date.

The truth of Williams's death was never determined and never will be. The Union army had a vested interest in hiding any story of a general's being murdered by his own soldiers—it did not want to give other regiments ideas. In another odd twist on the final fate of Williams, the ship carrying his body down to New Orleans sank, and his coffin had to be rescued from the river.

Few people in the Union army mourned the death of General Williams, least of all the men who served under him. The general had not absorbed the first lesson every officer in every army should learn: officers should do everything in their power to get the men under their command to respect them. After all, they wield just as many muskets—and cannons—as the enemy.

"POOR KEARNY": THE EMBARRASSING DEATH OF A GLORIOUS FIGHTER

Union major general Phil Kearny gave up a fortune to follow his dream of being a soldier. He wanted to die a glorious death on the battlefield. As it turned out, his death was more embarrassing than glorious.

Kearny's mother died when he was nine, so he went to live with his maternal grandfather, a wealthy New Yorker who demanded only one thing of his grandson—that he not join the army. That was a difficult thing to promise for the impressionable Kearny. His uncle was a United States Army dragoon, a saber-toting, fancy-dressing cavalryman. Still, Kearny did what his grandfather wanted. He graduated from Princeton University and opened a law practice.

When Kearny's grandfather died, he left Phil more than a million dollars, an immense sum in the 1830s. With no one left to object, Kearny put his money in the bank and did what he had always wanted to do. He joined the dragoons as a lieutenant. He must have showed promise, because the United States sent him to cavalry school in France. While there, he volunteered for service in France's war in Algiers. His bravery won him the French Legion of Honor.

When Kearny returned to the United States, he became an aide to General Winfield Scott and followed his mentor to Mexico for that war. There, he exhibited two traits common to many Mexican War veterans who later fought in the Civil War: bravery and foolishness. He was wounded so severely at Churubusco that his left arm was amputated.

Even that did not slow Kearny. After a short retirement from the army, he rejoined in 1859 and traveled to Europe, where he fought for France in a war with Italy.

When the Civil War started, Kearny must have thought it the answer to his prayers. At last, a war he could fight without leaving the country! He accepted a brigadier generalship leading New Jersey troops. He did so well during the Peninsula Campaign in Virginia that he was promoted to major general.

Kearny's men loved him. He was fearless. He would put his horse's reins in his teeth, grip his sword in his right hand, and ride along his lines encouraging his men, his left sleeve flapping in the wind.

His last battle came two days after the humiliating Union defeat at Second Manassas on August 30, 1862. On September 1, Lee sent Stonewall Jackson and A. P. Hill around the Federals' flank, hoping to catch the Union army before it retreated to Washington. Kearny and Brigadier General Isaac Stevens were waiting in the woods at Chantilly, a few miles outside Fairfax Court House. Though the main part of the army was in retreat, they were not.

It was a dark, rainy day with lightning crashing when the unsuspecting Confederates entered the woods where Stevens, Kearny, and their men were waiting. Charges from both sides followed. During one, Stevens fell dead with a bullet in the head.

Riding ahead of his men, Kearny lost his sense of direction in the gathering darkness and rode directly into Confederate lines. Surrounded by hundreds of Confederates, he could have—should have—surrendered. He would have been given special treatment, then been exchanged for a high-ranking Confederate officer. He would have been a prisoner no longer than a few months, most likely less, and his stay would probably have been easy. After all, he was the most famous cavalryman in America. The Confederates would have enjoyed hosting him awhile.

But Kearny did not do what everyone expected. Instead, he wheeled his horse and ignored the shouts of "Surrender!" and the hands reaching out to grab his reins. He stood in his stirrups and leaned forward to urge his horse back to his lines. Before he had ridden more than a few yards, a volley of muskets fired. Bullets crashed into his back and buttocks. At least one entered his anus and passed through his head. Kearny fell to the muddy, bloody ground.

The men who had reluctantly killed Kearny knew who he was. They tenderly took his body to the rear, where General Hill said, "Poor Kearny. He deserved a better death than that." The next day, Robert E. Lee ordered a truce under a white flag so Kearny's body and his effects could be sent through the lines.

Kearny lived the life he wanted to live, though his death probably would have embarrassed him. The details were not widely reported in the North. Even today, few biographies of Kearny describe the severity and location of his wounds.

"IF I CAN'T WHIP BOBBIE LEE WITH THIS . . ."

Union major general George McClellan unwittingly sealed his fate as commander of the Army of the Potomac in September 1862 when he grasped a piece of paper in his hands and exclaimed to his staff, "If I can't whip Bobbie Lee with this, I will be willing to go home!"

He didn't and he did.

What McClellan had was a piece of paper that could have ended the war within a week. What he did with it resulted in the war's dragging on for another two and a half years. No general on either side had as many chances to end the war as did McClellan. No general on either side had as many supporters as McClellan. And no general on either side had as inflated an opinion of himself as McClellan.

George Brinton McClellan seemed destined for great things. Born in 1826 in Philadelphia to an old-line Yankee family, he left the University of Pennsylvania in 1842 at age sixteen to accept an appointment at West Point. He graduated in the illustrious class of 1846, just before the Mexican War. That class of fifty-nine second lieutenants eventually yielded twenty Union and Confederate generals, the most of any class. McClellan finished second in his class.

Sent to Mexico, McClellan earned the plaudits of General Winfield Scott for his skill in transporting an army invading a foreign country. It was in the Mexican War that McClellan developed his slow, methodical system of operation. This application of his classroom training as a civil engineer served him well in building bridges but came back to haunt him fifteen years later in commanding his own army.

After the Mexican War, McClellan was hand-picked by his superiors to be the army's golden boy. Indeed, he made his mark. During an assignment back at West Point, he instructed cadets on the French bayonet drill, which he conveniently renamed the McClellan bayonet drill. Before accepting an extended assignment in Europe to study the Crimean War, he helped survey some potential transcontinental railroad routes, the key to truly uniting the nation. While in Europe, he amused himself by redesigning the standard Hungarian horse saddle, which he naturally dubbed the McClellan saddle. The concave, hornless saddle with wood underlying the leather for increased stability would be standard army issue during the Civil War and remain unchanged until the 1920s, when the United States Army finally abandoned horses in favor of mechanized cavalry—tanks.

Though it was clear by 1857 that the nation was edging toward war, McClellan apparently grew tired of the slow process of promotion in a peacetime army that still found him ranked captain more than a decade after his graduation from West Point. He resigned his commission in the cavalry and accepted a lucrative position as chief civil engineer of the Illinois Central Railroad. While in this position, he met an Illinois congressman who was also attorney for the Illinois Central. He would cross paths and egos with Abraham Lincoln on many future occasions.

When war broke out, McClellan was living in Cincinnati and making a handsome living as president of the Ohio & Mississippi Railroad. But the chance to command men in battle again proved too difficult a temptation to resist. He accepted a position as major general of Ohio volunteers.

McClellan immediately began to apply all the skills he had developed as a civil engineer and railroad president into organizing his men. He quickly gained notice for these talents. Through a bit of political maneuvering by some politician friends beholden to the railroad, he was appointed major general in the regular army. This sudden promotion put him ahead of many Union officers who had seniority in graduation from West Point and had not resigned from the army to accept private riches. McClellan's self-promoting habits, which would win him as many enemies as his organizational talents won him friends, had begun.

When Virginia seceded in April 1861, the mountaineers in its western counties objected. They were small farmers scratching out a living on the sides of mountains. They saw no reason to leave the Union just so the wealthy cotton-plantation owners in eastern Virginia could keep their slaves. Less than two months after Virginia seceded, the western counties of the state seceded from Virginia and declared that they were staying in the Union.

To help this mini-rebellion against the larger rebellion, McClellan invaded western Virginia with twenty thousand men in mid-June, the largest movement of Federal soldiers to date. Resisting him were around forty-five hundred Confederates under Brigadier General Robert S. Garnett, a 1841 West Point graduate who was acquainted with McClellan from the Mexican War. On July 11, ten days before the big battle at Manassas Junction, McClellan attacked Garnett at Rich Mountain. Garnett had dispersed his men, so McClellan was able to easily overrun the Confederate positions. Two days later, McClellan's forces caught the retreating Confederates at Corrick's Ford. Garnett was killed as he foolishly exposed himself with the rear guard in an attempt to make sure his men were across. He was the first general on either side to die.

Both battles were small in reality but large in the eyes of Washington politicians still reeling from the loss at Big Bethel, Virginia, in June. McClellan's victories grew even more significant after Irvin McDowell was soundly defeated by the Confederates at Manassas on July 21.

The thinking in Washington was simple. McDowell, with his thirty-five-thousand-man army, had been defeated. McClellan, with his twenty-thousand-man army, had been victorious. So the answer to all the Union's problems was to bring McClellan out of the mountains and give him command of what would soon be known as the Army of the Potomac. By August, McClellan was hankering for an even larger command—all the Union armies. Only one man stood in his way, General in Chief Winfield Scott.

McClellan launched a psychological war against Scott, acting like an energetic puppy intentionally irritating an old dog. During war councils, McClellan would disagree on parts of Scott's plan for a slow, strangling "Anaconda" campaign against the South. In public, he would bound up stairs as the fat, infirm, arthritic Scott struggled behind.

This baiting was not lost on Scott, who was planning his retirement anyway. Once, he turned to McClellan in a meeting and said, "When I proposed that you should come here to aid, not supersede me, you had my friendship and confidence. You still have my confidence."

Though he liked to harass Scott over his Anaconda Plan, McClellan was not for the all-out immediate strikes into the South that many in the War Department wanted. Keeping with his training as a civil engineer, he was cautious. His chief of espionage, Allan Pinkerton, was telling him that the Confederates had more than a hundred thousand men poised to strike at Washington. McClellan said he needed to buy time before he moved against them. He reluctantly allowed some regiments to venture toward Leesburg, Virginia, to see how many Confederates were there. That resulted in the disastrous Battle of Ball's Bluff, where scores of Union soldiers drowned in the Potomac River in a panicked retreat. The loss played heavily on McClellan's mind, particularly since some of the bodies floated all the way to Washington before they were pulled out.

Despite the Ball's Bluff setback, McClellan was appointed general in chief in November when Scott finally stepped down. Lincoln was unsure if the thirty-five-year-old major general who had been a cavalry captain just five years earlier understood all his responsibilities.

"I can do it all," McClellan replied. The answer was characteristic of his overreaching.

As the winter of 1861–62 yielded to spring, McClellan began to feel the same heat that McDowell had the previous summer. Washington politicians, Lincoln among them, demanded that he do something with the vast army he had been training for nine months. Finally, he moved more than 105,000 soldiers by navy transport from Washington to the Virginia peninsula between the James and York Rivers. It was an engineering and logistical feat McClellan was born to do.

What McClellan was not born to do was send that army toward Richmond in a crushing blow, sweeping everything before him. He marched like his feet were in molasses. It took him from March to July 1 to travel less than a hundred miles. All along the way, he sent fright-filled messages back to the War Department claiming that his army was outnumbered and about to be jumped by unseen hordes of Confederates. He demanded more men and ammunition. He actually got within sight of the church steeples of Richmond before being driven back during the Seven Days' Battles. McClellan actually won most of those battles, particularly the last and the largest, Malvern Hill, in which well-placed Federal artillery on the hill decimated an ill-conceived frontal assault ordered by the new leader of the largest Confederate army in the field, Robert E. Lee. Had McClellan discontinued his retreat and marched again toward Richmond, Lee might not have had the men to stop him. As it was, McClellan continued retreating. He blamed his defeat on the War Department. If only he had been given reenforcements, he could have crushed Lee. McClellan probably never knew—and certainly never acknowledged—that he had at least a third more men than Lee and maybe twice as many.

Lincoln had experienced enough of McClellan's slowness and belly-aching. Without formally firing him, the president simply transferred his men to Major General John Pope, who was organizing his Army of Virginia and preparing to attack Lee from the north. Pope led the Union's largest army for barely more than two months before Lee thrashed him at Second Manassas in August 1862. About the time Pope learned the names of his subordinates, he, too, lost a major battle and found himself out of a job.

Lee now headed into Maryland, hoping to find new recruits for his army from this border slave state, fresh food for his men and animals, and perhaps new allies in Europe. English and French officials were hinting that all they needed to officially recognize the Confederacy was a major victory—on Northern soil. Lee and Davis also thought that a Confederate victory in the North might demoralize citizens enough that they would demand their politicians let the South go in peace. In the view of Davis and Lee, who had been handily beating the Union army for several months, an invasion was worth a try. Pennsylvania would be the final objective.

The only man considered for the job of heading off Lee was McClellan. The smug McClellan—who had once gone to bed without meeting with President Lincoln, who was sitting in the general's parlor—had his Washington enemies exactly where he wanted them. Even his critics had to admit that he and only he could stop the Confederates. McClellan rode through his army to their great cheers and told them that their leader had returned. He headed his great force into Maryland in pursuit of Lee.

Lee was not overly worried. He said of McClellan, "He is an able general, but a cautious one. His army is in a very demoralized and chaotic condition and will not be prepared for offensive operations for three or four weeks. Before that time I hope to be on the Susquehanna [in Pennsylvania]." Lee's objective was to capture Harrisburg, destroy bridges to slow Federal reenforcements, and then turn toward Philadelphia, Baltimore, or Washington.

His strategy in invading Maryland involved splitting his forces into four parts. Three of them would converge on Harpers Ferry, Virginia, capturing it and its Union supplies. Lee could then proceed with the invasion, secure that he did not have a large Union force too close to his rear. Splitting his forces was risky, particularly since he had just forty thousand men, but Lee felt McClellan was too cautious to even discover the size of his army.

On September 9, Lee wrote out Special Orders 191, which detailed his objectives and which forces were assigned to do what. He then broke his army into four pieces (later five). What Lee was about to do was top-secret. Major General James Longstreet, realizing the importance of the order, ate his copy after reading it.

Two copies of the orders, one copied by Stonewall Jackson himself, were inadvertently prepared for Major General Daniel Harvey Hill, who was assigned to take one of the heights overlooking Harpers Ferry. Since Hill already had Jackson's copy, one of Hill's staff officers pocketed the official document as a war souvenir. He wrapped it around three cigars and stuffed it inside his coat pocket. The officer thought nothing of it, but pocketing the order was a major security breach neither Lee nor Hill would have ever permitted. There was now a copy floating around that, if captured by the Union, could destroy Lee, his army, and any chance the South had of winning the war.

By the time Lee wrote the order, McClellan had discovered that the invasion of Maryland was in full swing. On September 13, his Army of the Potomac was marching through Frederick, Maryland, a city the Confederates had passed though just days earlier. McClellan was pleased that the citizens of the slave-holding border state greeted him warmly. That morning, some soldiers were walking across a field outside town when they were ordered to stack arms and take a rest. Three of them were lounging in the grass when one noticed an envelope. Inside were three cigars with a paper wrapped around them. While they searched for some matches to light the cigars, one of the soldiers started reading the paper, which started "Headquarters Army Of Northern Virginia."

That was all it took for the soldiers to realize they had something important. They rushed the copy of General Orders 191 to their commander, who relieved them of it and the three cigars and rushed the paper to McClellan. The ever-cautious general at first suspected the Confederates were trying to trick him, but one of his staff officers identified the handwriting of Lee's assistant adjutant general, who had actually written the orders for Lee.

McClellan now knew exactly what Lee was going to do and even where he was at that particular moment. All he had to do was march to the nearest piece of Lee's army, crush it with his superior numbers, then march to the next piece. He wired Lincoln, "I have a difficult task to perform, but with God's blessing will accomplish it."

The handful of Confederates holding Turner's Gap on South Mountain, the gap through which the Federals had to pass, were puzzled when they saw the Union forces marching toward them. It was almost as if they knew where they were going.

Within hours, a civilian who had been at Union headquarters when McClellan shouted out his glee brought Lee the sad news. McClellan did know where to go. He knew everything Lee knew.

Lee threw reenforcements under Major General Longstreet toward Turner's Gap, which was held by Major General A. P. Hill. They fought all day, slowing the Union army for vital hours while Lee called for the rest of his army to assemble near the small town of Sharpsburg on Antietam Creek for an all-out battle.

McClellan, confident for once, wired Washington that he had won a major battle at South Mountain and that the Confederates were in full retreat. He assured his superiors that he would catch Lee and dispose of his army.

He could have, too, had he moved immediately on the men Lee had on September 15. The pieces of Lee's army had not yet come back together. Lee had just eighteen thousand men in place, facing more than eighty thousand of McClellan's. Still, McClellan thought that Lee had a hundred thousand men total, and he was not sure whether they had merged after the day-long battle at South Mountain. McClellan decided to wait—and wait, and wait. He waited two days before finally attacking Lee on September 17. By that time, Lee's army had swollen back to forty thousand men, still fewer than half what McClellan had.

Sharpsburg (or Antietam), the war's bloodiest single day, opened at dawn when Union forces under Major General Joseph Hooker swarmed through a cornfield toward the Confederates dug in along the West Woods. All morning long, that pretty green cornfield changed hands every few minutes. By midmorning, all of the corn had been shot down or knocked down by falling bodies.

The battle shifted to the center, where Confederates under Major General D. H. Hill held a road that had sunk below ground level through years of service. These tough soldiers were the same men who had held Turner's Gap three days earlier.

Some of the Yankees advancing on the Sunken Road broke line before even getting to the action, but not because of Confederate fire. One regiment was told not to break ranks as it marched through a farmhouse yard. The soldiers, new replacements raised in the city, were to keep shoulder to shoulder. When they encountered some odd-looking round objects resting on wooden tables, they pushed them over rather than marching around them. The bees inside their hives were not amused. The regiment, which had vowed not to run from Confederates, beat a hasty retreat from several thousand angry insects.

Some military tacticians have questioned Hill's initial placement of troops in the Sunken Road. He likely should have put them on the hill in front of the road, then fought back to the Sunken Road if necessary. By starting the defense in the road behind a rail fence, Hill gave his men no safe haven. If the Federals took the high ground in front of the road, they would be able to shoot down into it. Eventually, a mistaken order took one Confederate regiment out of the road. The Federals poured into the hole, where they started firing down the line of Confederates. The Sunken Road would forever become known as "Bloody Lane" once the Federals gained its flank.

As the Federals gained control of Bloody Lane, the fighting shifted to the southern part of the battlefield, near a stone bridge over Antietam Creek. McClellan had ordered that the bridge be taken early that morning, but by midafternoon, Major General Ambrose Burnside and his fourteen thousand soldiers were still on the wrong side. All day long, Burnside had been firing on several hundred Georgians dug in on the heights above the opposite bank, directly above the bridge. Though Burnside had forty times as many men, he had not been able to dislodge them. Finally, after more than eight hours of trying, Burnside ordered two regiments into the narrow path to hell that lay across the bridge. The regiments asked if they would get the ration of whiskey that had been withheld from them if they took the bridge. Burnside assured them they would. His men then took that bridge.

While some men were drinking their whiskey, others were placing orders for coffee with the commissary. The waiter was a young Ohio sergeant named William McKinley. McKinley, later the nation's twenty-fourth president, would have a battlefield monument erected to his hero-ism for literally serving on the field. It may be the only monument to the heroic delivery of caffeine ever placed on any battlefield.

It was later, after the battle, that curious Union soldiers discovered something that made them boil with anger. Burnside had been ordered to take the bridge, and those were the orders on which he focused. He never bothered checking the creek running under the bridge. It was barely thigh deep in most places. Had his divisions swarmed across en masse, they would have easily overwhelmed the Georgia sharpshooters who controlled the bridge all day.

His line now breached, Lee planned for the final attack, which he knew would crush him. He reluctantly urged a shattered Confederate artillery battery back into action. One of the cannoneers looked at him, waiting for recognition. When Lee didn't say anything, Robert Jr., his son, his features hidden by caked black powder and sweat, finally spoke up and told his father they were ready to continue fighting.

As Lee waited on the approaching Union army, he saw a column approaching from the southwest. Although the men appeared to be wear-ing Union uniforms, they were flying the Confederate flag. It was A. P. Hill, who had marched all day after capturing Harpers Ferry. Hill's men fooled the first Union regiment they met. The Yankees never suspected the blue-clad soldiers approaching them were Confederates until a single musket volley cut down nearly half the real bluecoats. Confused Federals still milled around wondering who these other bluecoats were until more Confederate muskets tore into them. Hill's Confederates now charged, giving the rebel yell. At last, McClellan's men realized who they were facing. The whole lot crumbled and ran.

McClellan thought for a full day about attacking Lee again. Lee waited, expecting such an attack. For reasons still unclear today, McClellan continued to believe—without a shred of evidence—that Lee's army numbered more than a hundred thousand men. McClellan had decimated Lee's forty-thousand-man force, killing or wounding more than eleven thousand, yet he still believed Lee's true force had been kept in reserve. Lee was able to pull back across the Potomac. His army was severely hurt, but it was intact.

Though he made only a halfhearted effort to pursue, McClellan saw a great victory. "Those in whose judgement I rely tell me that I fought the battle splendidly and that it is a masterpiece of art," he wrote his wife.

Well, not quite everyone thought that. The War Department and Abraham Lincoln, to name two critics, were furious that a beaten, bloodied Lee was allowed to return to Virginia without any effort at contesting his crossing of the wide Potomac River. Lincoln personally visited McClellan more than two weeks after the battle to urge him to move into Virginia, to go after Lee, to invade Virginia, to do something— anything! McClellan made it clear to Lincoln that his army was not moving anytime soon. Lincoln remarked to a friend that the Army of the Potomac was really "General McClellan's bodyguard!"

On November 9, McClellan received an order telling him to turn over command of his army to Major General Ambrose Burnside. This was the same Burnside who had twice turned down command of the army claiming his own incompetence, the general who had dawdled more than eight hours in front of a bridge when he could have waded across the stream.

McClellan accepted his firing as any good soldier would, but his army did not. Thousands of men threatened to mutiny, even to march on

Washington to demand his reinstatement. McClellan calmed them and asked that they give Burnside the same loyalty they had shown him.

To the end, McClellan never understood what his problem was. He said, "That I must have made mistakes, I cannot deny. I do not see any great blunders; but no one can judge of himself."

The blunder McClellan kept making was overestimating his opponent's strength. Often fooled by faulty intelligence, he never understood or believed that he was fighting an underfed, underequipped, undermanned army that never was the match of his except in fighting spirit.

To his credit, McClellan created the Army of the Potomac out of the rabble that had streamed back into Washington after the disaster at Bull Run. He taught it discipline, tactics, and even how to shoot straight. He alone built the Federal army.

In the end, McClellan was forced to keep the promise he made when handed Special Orders 191. He was not able to beat Bobbie Lee, so he had to go home.

THE SOUTHERN-TALKING COLONEL OF THE EIGHTH NEW YORK CAVALRY

What is a subordinate officer to do when his frightened superior wants to surrender his command to an enemy who has him surrounded and outnumbered? In the case of one officer, the answer was to break out of the trap and even bring home a bonus to the Union cause, thanks mostly to his Southern accent.

Colonel Benjamin Franklin "Grimes" Davis was one of those rare Southern-born regular-army officers who stayed loyal to the Union. An Alabaman and an 1854 graduate of West Point, the thirty-year-old Davis had spent his entire army career fighting Indians in New Mexico. When the Civil War broke out, he was named a colonel of the Eighth New York Cavalry.

Davis was assigned to Harpers Ferry, Virginia, in September 1862, just in time to find himself in the way of Robert E. Lee's grand invasion of Maryland and eventually Pennsylvania. Lee had to capture Harpers Ferry and its twelve-thousand-man Union garrison so as not to leave a large Federal force in his rear.

Like his fellow officers, Davis was stunned to discover Confederates holding the heights around the town on the evening of September 13. He was also discouraged with the command capabilities of Colonel Dixon S. Miles, an 1824 West Point graduate. Miles, though roaring drunk at the Battle of Manassas in 1861, had not been drummed out of the army. Instead, his old friends and his superiors had shifted him to the command of the vitally important Harpers Ferry. What disheartened Davis was Miles's talk of surrender. Davis did not want to hear of it and would not do it.

On the night of September 14, Davis made his move. He called his thirteen hundred cavalrymen together and told them that the infantry was going to stay in the trap, but that the cavalry would be leaving that night. He had recruited a Unionist resident of the city to show him a little-used trail for escape. Oddly enough, it was the same mountain trail John Brown had used to invade Harpers Ferry back in 1859. It had been unguarded then and was luckily unguarded now. Davis had his men tie down their equipment and cross the Potomac River on a pontoon bridge. They were on their own, with no chance of calling reenforcements if they bumped into Confederates.

It was a tough climb up Maryland Heights. The Federals passed within yards of an enemy camp. The Confederates, confident that no one would use such a steep trail, blundered in not even bothering to guard it. Somehow, thirteen hundred horses were able to pass without even attracting a warning shot.

Later that night, the Union cavalry passed around Sharpsburg, heading north on the Hagerstown Pike, the same ground where there would be deadly fighting in less than a week in a battle called Antietam. Davis heard wagons moving ahead of him. He rode up and discovered a Confederate train escorted by cavalry. He informed the Confederates he was a colonel (he was) from Alabama (he was) with an Alabama regiment (he wasn't). Thanks to the darkness, his practiced command voice, and his Southern accent, Davis was able to convince the Confederate cavalrymen to fall in at the rear of the column of wagons. He moved some of his Yankee cavalrymen in their places and left others to capture the soon-to-be-surprised rebels.

For the rest of the night, the Confederate wagon train rumbled north toward Pennsylvania. It wasn't until dawn that the teamsters noticed their escorts' uniform color. One finally asked what regiment they were. "Eight New York Cavalry," came the honest, calm reply. A few teamsters tried to break away, but drawn pistols moved the wagons back into line.

Nervous because he didn't know if there were any more Confederates around, Davis didn't stop the wagon train until he got to Greencastle, Pennsylvania. There, he counted more than 40 wagons, more than 240 mules, and 200 angry cavalrymen and teamsters—an ammunition train belonging to Confederate major general James Longstreet—as his captives. Longstreet would dearly miss that wagon train in the coming Battle of Antietam.

As for Colonel Miles back at Harpers Ferry, he and his men came under fire from Confederate cannons before Davis even reached Greencastle. Waving a tiny white handkerchief, Miles was killed in the initial barrage.

Though Davis was a hero to the Union cavalry, he did not win a promotion to general for his courageous and profitable scam on the Confederates. The following year, he was killed leading a brigade in the largest cavalry battle in history, Brandy Station.

COLONEL JOHN T. WILDER
CALLS IN A CONSULTANT

Union colonel John T. Wilder of the Seventeenth Indiana Volunteers was commander of the forty-three-hundred-man garrison at Munfordville, Kentucky, in the fall of 1862. In mid-September, he suddenly found himself cut off from Union contact as Confederate general Braxton Bragg began his invasion of Kentucky.

Wilder was unsure what to do. He was a professional man who knew more about building and running railroads and coal mines than about commanding men. He was now surrounded, or so it seemed. What should he do? Surrender his entire command? Fight to the death?

He settled on a solution with which any business executive can identify. The Union colonel called in a consultant to help him make his decision. That consultant was wearing the gray uniform of a Confederate major general.

The situation had not been so bad just a few days earlier. Confederate brigadier general James Chalmers first attacked Wilder's little fort on September 14. He sent a note congratulating the Federals on their defense, then offered them the chance to surrender. Wilder refused.

When Bragg discovered the irritating little fort in his way, he sent his whole army toward it. He also sent Wilder a note saying that he was surrounded by an entire army and that he should surrender before all his men were killed. Wilder, used to dealing with facts and figures he could read on paper, asked for proof of Bragg's claim of an overwhelming force.

The exasperated Bragg, showing more restraint toward an enemy than he normally showed his own subordinates, replied, "The only evidence I can give you of my ability to make good my assertion of the presence of a sufficient force to compel your surrender, beyond the statement that it now exceeds 20,000, will be the use of it. You are allowed one hour in which to make your decision."

Wilder had a problem. If Bragg was telling the truth, Wilder might as well surrender so he and his men could fight another day. If Bragg was lying, Wilder could face the wrath of his commanders for abandoning the fort instead of fighting for it.

The Indiana colonel reached a solution that must have puzzled even his most loyal lieutenants. He knew that Major General Simon Bolivar Buckner—the Confederate who had surrendered Fort Donelson, Tennessee, in February—was in command of a division in front of the fort. Walking out under a flag of truce, Wilder asked Buckner for his opinion. He asked if he should surrender the fort.

The highly amused Buckner, a professional soldier, said he could not make that decision for Wilder. But if Wilder wished, Buckner could show him around the Confederate positions. After counting forty-six cannons, Wilder said, "I believe I will surrender." He turned over more than forty-two hundred prisoners.

Wilder could have been court-martialed for consorting with the enemy, but no charges were filed. He went on to a distinguished career with the Union army. A brigade under his command was one of the first developed as "mounted infantry." During much of the Civil War, the cavalry was used for scouting. It was seen as the eyes and ears of the generals commanding the infantry. Wilder, taking a cue from the successful tactics of Confederate major general Nathan Bedford Forrest, helped develop the idea that horses could be used as a means of transporting large numbers of infantry to a battlefield. His unit moved so quickly and was so successful in the Western campaigns that it was called "Wilder's Lightning Brigade."

Then, at the top of his military career in 1864, Wilder resigned from the army to return to his civilian career of railroading and mining. He rarely talked about the time that he called in that consultant with the Southern accent.

THE DAY TWENTY-FIVE HUNDRED CONFEDERATES COULD HAVE CAPTURED TEN THOUSAND FEDERALS

The Battle of Goldsboro, North Carolina, on December 17, 1862, was a pretty fair fight on both sides. The Confederates under Brigadier Generals Nathan Evans and Thomas Clingman fought a good defensive battle, clearing the ground in front of their lines, rigging booby traps to catch the Yankees, and protecting their meager resources. The Federals under Major General John Foster fought an equally good battle, charging bravely and setting fire to the bridge over the Neuse River, which was the objective of the ten-day raid. Technically, the battle can be considered a draw, since the Federals withdrew from the battlefield, but only after accomplishing their mission.

What the Confederates did not know, however, was that they made a major mistake in not chasing the Federals back to their base in New Bern. Had they pressed forward with a counterattack, they would have captured the bulk of Union forces on the North Carolina coast.

General Foster's raid into the interior of North Carolina from New Bern started on December 11, 1862, partly to destroy Confederate forces and partly as a diversion to keep Confederate reenforcements from being sent to Fredericksburg, Virginia, which was under attack by Union Major General Ambrose Burnside. Foster left with 10,000 infantry, 650 cavalry, and 40 cannons. This was not going to be an ordinary out-and-back raid.

Along the way, Foster burned the town of Kinston, driving its defenders away in a hail of gunfire. He shelled the Confederate ironclad *Neuse*, under construction at Whitehall. Now, on December 17, he finally saw his main target, the Goldsboro railroad bridge over the Neuse River, one of the major links in the Wilmington & Weldon Railroad, which kept supplies moving north from blockade runners on the coast.

Foster sent his men in close. Some of them were able to set the bridge on fire, despite the efforts of an armored railway car the Confederates brought up to throw shells into the Yankees. The Federal artillery found the range of the engine that had brought the armored car. Within a few minutes, they burst its boiler.

Though the Confederates brought up reenforcements, the Federals still had a vast numerical advantage. Then Foster did something very strange. Poised to attack, he about-faced most of his men and marched them from the field. A Union artillery battery stayed behind to spray a lethal dose of canister into a regiment of South Carolinians who charged the guns. The Confederates got revenge for that as some Federals were crossing a dry millstream bed. Hidden Confederates opened a dam gate, and the rushing water knocked several Federals off their feet and drowned them.

Foster rapidly marched his men back the way they had come, arriving in New Bern on December 21. He counted his losses at around a hundred killed and nearly five hundred wounded. Most of the fighting had been on the way to Goldsboro. The Federals suffered little opposition on the way back, as the Confederates were content to let a superior force leave in peace.

It was in the 1880s when an old Federal rode the train into Goldsboro. He walked around town asking if there were any former Confederate soldiers around who would take him to see the scene of the battle. One old man who had worn gray that day agreed, and the two rode to the battlefield in a buggy. They spent the afternoon together, forgetting old differences and making new friends.

Finally, the curiosity of the old Confederate got the best of him. He asked a question that had been bugging him for more than twenty years. He wanted to know why Foster had turned around and left the field when he had more men and the railroad bridge was burning. Why had the Federals broken off the attack?

The old Yankee replied, "We were entirely out of ammunition. We did not have a round to a man and all of us expected capture. If twenty-five hundred Confederates had been thrown against us at Kinston [on the march back], they would have captured the whole fifteen thousand [actually a little over ten thousand]."

Though the Confederates had not known that Foster's men were out of ammunition, they would have discovered that fact if they had harassed his column on its way back to New Bern, since the Federals would not have been able to fire back when attacked. The Confederates thus lost a golden opportunity to rid the state of Yankees. As the war dragged on, New Bern remained a major Union base. Robert E. Lee coveted its supplies and even sent an expedition to try to capture the town. It failed.

There never was a better chance to capture New Bern than in December 1862, but it took two decades to realize that.

1863

"Do not *bring on a*

general engagement."

–A. P. HILL TO
HENRY HETH BEFORE HETH'S DIVI-
SION STARTS THE BATTLE AT
GETTYSBURG

THE MUD MARCH

Bad weather and unusual environmental conditions seemed to be factors in almost every battle of the Civil War. Gettysburg was blazing hot. Fort Donelson was freezing cold. There was an earthquake at Corinth. When Grant tried to take Vicksburg, he was faced with a falling Mississippi even though upriver rains were supposed to make it rise. Banks and Porter moved up the Red River confident that a rising river would bring them back down, but ended up almost leaving a half-dozen gunboats stranded on sandbars. Tremendous thunderstorms competed with the crash of artillery in the Battles of New Market and Chantilly.

Still, none of these has its own weather-related nickname. None can compete with Ambrose Burnside's "Mud March." What Burnside proposed made sense on paper, but mother nature and lady luck hated the thirty-seven-year-old major general almost as much as the woman who jilted him at the altar.

Virtually everyone wearing blue liked the 1847 West Point graduate who compensated for his bald-as-a-cue-ball head by connecting his facial hair to what was left on top. He had proven his bravery fighting Indians, proven he could control his emotions when his fiancée literally left him standing in church, proven his ingenuity by designing a serviceable carbine, and proven he would take chances when he left the army to try his hand at manufacturing the weapon.

When the war started, Burnside rejoined the army as colonel with the First Rhode Island Volunteers. He handled himself so well at Manassas that by August he was a brigadier general—not bad for a man who had only risen to lieutenant in the prewar army and who had spent most of his time on garrison duty.

Following Ben Butler's capture of the forts on North Carolina's Outer Banks in August 1861, Burnside launched an amphibious assault on Roanoke Island in February 1862. His landings went so well that his soldiers barely got their ankles wet. Army casualties in taking the island were very light. The next month, Burnside's men took New Bern, a port city on the Neuse River. Again, they suffered few casualties. In April, he laid siege to Fort Macon on Bogue Banks. Burnside himself took an offer of surrender to the Confederate colonel commanding the fort. The colonel thanked Burnside but politely declined for several weeks, until one day's bombardment satisfied his sense of duty to resist.

Burnside's three victories in three months sat well with war planners in Washington. He won promotion to major general and command of a corps with the real fighting army, the Army of the Potomac, under an old West Point friend, George McClellan.

It was at the Battle of Antietam in September 1862 that Burnside was first criticized for his careful style of fighting. He tried for hours to take a stone bridge over Antietam Creek on the left side of the Federal line, never discovering that thousands of his men could have swarmed across in water barely thigh-deep.

Burnside himself wondered about his ability to command an army. He recognized that he was methodical in planning, plodding in style, and single-minded once he started something. That was not the way battles were won. Knowing his own nature, Burnside twice turned down President Lincoln's offer to take command of the army from McClellan. He finally took command only after Lincoln ordered him to in November 1862, and then only after McClellan told his men to offer their devotion to the new commander of the army.

Lincoln thought he had found his leader when Burnside did what

McClellan had refused to do—pursue Lee. The Confederate general had taken up winter quarters on the south side of the Rappahannock River at Fredericksburg, Virginia. Burnside initially moved his army so fast that he outran the supply of pontoon boats needed to bridge the river. While his men sat on the north side of the river waiting for the pontoons, Lee's troops were digging trenches and placing cannons on a long ridge that looked down on the river. When they were finished, Confederate lieutenant general James Longstreet told his commander that "a chicken couldn't live on that ground when we open on it."

Burnside, a professional soldier, looked at the same ground and may have thought the same thing. He hoped crossing the Rappahannock in downtown Fredericksburg would give his men cover to take those heights. He also hoped Lee would be stunned at a Federal army coming right at his center, rather than both flanks.

Actually, Lee hoped Burnside would try his center. He even issued orders to resist the crossing—but not so much that the Federals would get discouraged and try elsewhere. Lee wanted them to cross the river and move into town. He wanted them on that field where a chicken couldn't live.

On December 11, 1862, the pontoons were laid. The following day, most of Burnside's army crossed. On December 13, his men started charging up that open plain toward a stone wall behind which ran a sunken road. All day long, the Federals ran at that wall, as they did farther southeast across a flatter plain. All day long, they failed. By nightfall, more than 12,600 Federals lay dead and wounded. Confederate losses were less than 5,600.

Burnside was convinced that his army could take that wall. He ordered more charges for dawn on December 14. When he woke to make final preparations, he was met by his division commanders, who told him that the battle was over and the Federals had lost. Forcing their men forward again would be slaughter. Reluctantly, Burnside called a truce to bury his dead. By the morning of December 16, all of his men—the live ones—pulled back across the Rappahannock.

Brooding about the loss of men, Burnside offered his resignation to

President Lincoln, who rejected it. To make amends, Burnside planned another crossing attempt in January. In his mind, the situation was simple. The Union army was still there. The Confederate army was still there. He had to try again. Knowing Lee's tremendous strength on Marye's Heights, and knowing that Jackson still remained to the south, Burnside looked north to Banks' Ford, about six miles from downtown Fredericksburg. Perhaps he could cross there. Once across, he could attack Lee's flank.

On the morning of January 20, 1863, nineteen days after President Lincoln had declared that the war's purpose was now to free the slaves, Burnside's hundred-thousand-man army started marching north along the Rappahannock. Just before leaving, Burnside issued an order stating that "the auspicious moment seems to have arrived to strike a great and mortal blow to the rebellion and to gain that decisive victory which is due to the country."

He was confident his plan would work. December had been cold, but the January weather was mild. The roads were in good shape. He saw no reason why his entire army couldn't be across the river in one or two days and why he wouldn't be celebrating a great victory in less than a week.

Mother nature wore gray the day the march started. As the men grimly moved out of camp, it began to drizzle. Then it began to rain steadily. Then the rain turned to torrents. For two days, it came down. The roads, which Burnside had personally inspected and pronounced ready for his army, disappeared. In their place were miles of muddy strips. Mules sank up to their chests. The cannons they were hauling sank up to their barrels. Almost as soon as the men pulled the mules free, the frightened animals mired themselves again, sometimes breaking legs, sometimes dying from sheer exhaustion at trying to pull the weight behind them.

The frustration sometimes caused men to boil over. On one occasion, two of Burnside's corps found themselves at a crossroads. Instead of halting one corps to let the other pass, both commanders ordered their men to continue marching. It looked like a giant demolition derby, with men crashing into each other as they slogged through the mud.

Burnside sought to raise the spirits of his men with the aid of alcohol, as was commonly done. At Antietam four months earlier, he had promised his soldiers a ration of whiskey if they took the bridge. They had done just that. Burnside figured the same thing would work in getting his men to march. The whiskey flowed, at least until a fight started between a Massachusetts regiment and a Pennsylvania regiment. When a Maine regiment tried to make peace, the Massachusetts and Pennsylvania men turned on the third regiment. Soon, more than twenty-five hundred Yankees were having a fistfight in the Virginia mud as watching Confederates and other Yankee regiments roared with laughter.

Desperate to get his men moving and keep them from killing each other, Burnside ordered them off the roads and into the adjacent fields, as if this ground would somehow be drier. It wasn't. Men sank just as deep in the fields as they had on the roads. When detailed to pull out the cannons and wagons, they could do nothing. One soldier wrote of a wagon loaded with a pontoon boat that had sixteen mules and dozens of men pulling it, yet remained stuck fast. It was perhaps an exaggeration, but one man claimed that when the mules were too exhausted to move, they were simply cut out of their harnesses, shot, and walked over until their bodies disappeared in the mud. Sometimes, whole regiments of a thousand men were hooked to cannons to pull them forward. If the men stopped moving, the cannons sank out of sight.

When Burnside himself came riding through the disaster, a soldier called to him that the auspicious moment had arrived. Burnside didn't answer. To add insult to injury, the whole fiasco took place in view of the Confederate army. The Confederates knew what the Federals had been planning and stood ready to repel any attack. But now that the rain had come, they had nothing to do but stay high and dry under their tents. As the Union soldiers struggled to extricate one muddy leg after another just to keep from drowning, Confederates called across the Rappahannock. They shouted encouragement, telling the soldiers how many more miles they had to walk. They offered to take the pontoons and have them in place when the Union army arrived, just as they had allowed the pontoons to be placed in December. They even offered to let the Yankees borrow boards from the plank road on their side of the river if it would help them get to Banks' Ford any faster. Signs proclaiming "This is the way to Richmond!" showed up along the march. The Federals were too tired to shoot at their tormentors.

Officers began to beg Burnside to call off the march before all the horses and mules fell over dead, leaving no way to remove their cannons should the Confederates attack. Finally, he gave the order to return to camp. By January 24, the Mud March was over. A march that should have taken no more than four hours at two miles an hour had become a four-day, out-and-back disaster. Hundreds of men—perhaps more—died of exhaustion by the side of the road. Hundreds more deserted and started the long walk north. Many of these deserters made it, as the roads were too muddy to mount an effective roundup campaign.

For weeks, men who decided to stick with the army struggled back to their camps around Falmouth, just north of Fredericksburg. Exhausted officers did not even bother going out to find their stragglers, secure that the men had either deserted, were dead, or were on their way back to camp. The most common notation in the daily roster kept on the soldiers was "died at Falmouth," an indication of just how exhausting the march had been.

The Confederates did not fire a shot at the Army of the Potomac during January 1863. Even General Lee could not resist taking a straight-faced poke at the muddy, cold, exhausted Yankees. On January 29, five days after the Mud March, he filed a report with Confederate secretary of war Seddon stating, "Whether the storm or other causes frustrated the designs of the enemy I do not know; but no attempt has been made to cross the Rappahannock, and some of the enemy's forces have resumed their former positions. The ground is covered with six inches of snow and the probabilities are that the roads will be impractical for some time."

As for Burnside, he returned to his tent and continued muttering about "those men over there," referring to the 12,600 soldiers he had sent to destruction on the south side of the Rappahannock. One of his generals wrote that he thought Burnside had lost his mind.

Burnside had not lost his mind, but he would soon lose his army.

Burnside's Whistle-Blowers Tempt Their Fate

After Major General Ambrose Burnside suffered more than 12,600 casualties on the slopes of Marye's Heights at Fredericksburg, Virginia, in December 1862, his fellow Union generals began to doubt his ability to lead an army. One watched a distraught Burnside wave his arm across the river and wail about "those men over there," meaning the thousands of dead Federals in front of the stone wall protecting Lee's army. The subordinate general thought Burnside was having a nervous breakdown.

It was not only generals who thought Burnside and his army were coming apart at the seams. The soldiers in the ranks had no confidence in him. They started comparing Fredericksburg unfavorably to Valley Forge. Men started writing home pondering whether it would be better to just let the South go, since the Union army had no generals who could beat the Confederates.

At the end of December, two weeks after the disastrous crossing of the Rappahannock, two brigadier generals left their divisions and took a train to Washington. They departed without Burnside's knowledge in hopes of alerting their senator that Burnside was planning a second try at Lee's army. In the view of the generals, such a move so soon after the previous slaughter could result in the mutiny of the entire army. Instead of scores of men deserting and heading home, there would be thousands.

The two brigadiers did not find their senator, who had gone home for the holidays. They did find the secretary of war, who took them to see the president of the United States. The president listened to the generals' worries about morale and dashed off a telegram to Burnside, asking him not to make any movement across the Rappahannock without consulting Washington.

The two generals thought they were doing the right thing by alerting higher authorities to the morale problems within the army. They thought they were saving the lives of their men. But they gave no thought at all to their own careers. Had they done so, they would have realized that criticizing Burnside was a blunder, a one-way ticket to oblivion.

President Lincoln thanked the two generals. He probably didn't tell them about a letter mailed to Washington after the battle by two other generals who also questioned Burnside's competence. The president then relegated both his visitors and the letter-writing generals to the trash heap of history. Lincoln did not like whistle-blowers any more than did Burnside. Saving thousands of lives was one thing. Staying loyal to your boss was more important.

What Lincoln did was inform Burnside that two brigadiers had told him of the unhappiness of the army with Burnside's performance. While Lincoln coyly refused to name the generals, an incensed Burnside simply checked regimental records to see which two brigadiers had left camp on unspecified leaves. He easily determined that the two disloyal generals were in the Sixth Corps. They were Brigadier General John Newton, a Virginian who had stayed loyal to the Union, and Brigadier General John Cochrane, a former New York congressman.

Burnside seethed for the next several weeks, during which he undertook the Mud March against the advice of his generals. Upon returning to camp after the march, he wrote out some secret orders, then took off for Washington. He wanted President Lincoln to read the orders in person.

He handed the president General Orders Number 8, which charged Major General Joseph Hooker with being "guilty of unjust and unnecessary criticisms of the actions of his superior officers"; Brigadier General W. T. H. Brooks with "complaining of the policy of the government"; and Brigadier General John Newton and Brigadier General John Cochrane with "going directly to the President of the United States with criticisms upon the plans of their commanding officer." Pending Lincoln's approval, all four were to be dismissed from the service of the

United States. Burnside went on to request that Major General W. B. Franklin, Major General W. F. Smith, Brigadier General Samuel Sturgis, Brigadier General John Cochrane, and Brigadier General Edward Ferrero all be reassigned from the Army of the Potomac. The order demonstrated just how furious Burnside was when he wrote it, as he mistakenly mentioned Cochrane twice—once when he demanded Cochrane be banned from the service of the United States and again when he requested Cochrane be transferred to another army.

Burnside gave Lincoln a take-it-or-leave-it choice. Either the president fire all the men mentioned in the order or he, Burnside, would resign.

It took the president less than a day to react to Burnside's demands. He accepted Burnside's resignation and put Joseph Hooker in command of the Army of the Potomac. Of all the generals Burnside demanded be fired, only Franklin got the ax. Though Hooker would be in command of the Army of the Potomac barely five months, he was the only winner in the confrontation. The rest of the generals learned their lesson about bucking authority.

Franklin, who had graduated number one in the West Point class of 1843—twenty spots ahead of Ulysses S. Grant—had a spotless record in the army until the Civil War. He got plum engineering jobs, including the chance to put the new dome on the Capitol in Washington. Appointed a brigadier just a month after the war started, Franklin steadily rose up the command chain under McClellan. When McClellan was replaced, Burnside showed his faith in Franklin by giving him command of two corps, creating a "grand division." This grand division was assigned to the left flank at Fredericksburg. Operating under Burnside's vague orders, Franklin sent his men against Stonewall Jackson's position but never committed all his resources, a mistake that set Burnside boiling with anger. Burnside blamed Franklin for not carrying the left, which did not have stone-wall defenses and expansive field of cannon fire that the right did. Franklin blamed Burnside's vague orders on his not understanding exactly what was expected of his men.

It was after the battle that Franklin made his biggest mistake. He and another general, William Farrar "Baldy" Smith, sent a letter to Washington commenting on Burnside's inability to tell his subordinates what was expected of them and suggesting that other generals had better ideas. The contents of that letter got back to Burnside after the battle.

Based on Burnside's recommendation, Franklin was relieved of command for the first half of 1863 until he was finally transferred to Louisiana in June to take over the Nineteenth Corps. There, he served under bumbling politically appointed generals like Butler and Banks, and his talents wasted away. Wounded in the Red River Campaign, he was sent home to convalesce. When he recovered, he requested more combat duty. Ulysses S. Grant petitioned to have him assigned, but the specter of Burnside's blacklist lingered. It finally dawned on Franklin that his military career was over.

While Franklin was the only general officially relieved by the president, the others all suffered from unofficial ostracism.

Brigadier General William Thomas Harbaugh Brooks, an 1841 graduate of West Point, was a professional soldier for more than twenty years before the war. He initially served as an aide to Brigadier General David E. Twiggs, a Confederate sympathizer who turned over United States government supplies to the Texas Confederates without a fight. Brooks was commanding a division in the Sixth Corps and had been wounded twice on the battlefield when he ran afoul of Burnside. Brooks was under Franklin, which was good enough to get him fired in Burnside's book.

At first, crossing Burnside didn't seem to matter. Then the hints started. Brooks's promotion to major general was revoked within weeks after it had been granted, a sign that the system still supported Burnside. As a brigadier, Brooks fought in Grant's army until poor health and old wounds forced his retirement. After the war, he moved to Huntsville, Alabama, where he acted like a simple farmer instead of a former Yankee general, developing friendships that ignored past allegiances. When Brooks died just five years after the war, his neighbors paid him the ultimate compliment. They decorated this grave of a Yankee general with a Confederate emblem.

Brigadier General John Newton at first seemed to escape Burnside's wrath. Two months after Burnside was replaced, Newton was promoted to major general. Then the military bureaucracy caught up with him. His major generalship was revoked. Crushed, Newton accepted a transfer west and another division command. Even that was taken from him when he was transferred to the Department of Key West and the Dry Tortugas, the outer limits of the Civil War. After the war, Newton sought to be repromoted to major general, but the Burnside curse continued. Though he was breveted a major general, his regular army rank remained brigadier.

Brigadier General John Cochrane, a political general, resigned his commission rather than fight Burnside and his unseen supporters in Washington. He returned to politics and enjoyed a brief fling as a vice presidential candidate in John C. Fremont's abortive run for the presidency in 1864. In the end, he threw his support back to Lincoln. In the general election, Cochrane at least got some satisfaction when Lincoln easily defeated Burnside's old West Point friend, McClellan.

Of all the whistle-blowers, only Major General William Farrar "Baldy" Smith recovered during the war. Smith had spent his prewar years in a variety of engineering roles, as was expected of top graduates of West Point. A colonel at First Manassas, he climbed the ladder quickly, reaching major general and command of the Sixth Corps at Fredericksburg. After the battle, he and Franklin wrote the letter to Lincoln independent of Cochrane and Newton's personal visit. After Lincoln shared the letter with the secretary of war, Smith watched his commission to major general disappear. He was transferred to several unimportant, behind-the-lines commands.

After a transfer to Grant's army in Tennessee, Smith's star began to rise again. Grant pushed through his reappointment to major general, and this time Congress reluctantly granted it. Assigned command of the Eighteenth Corps under Ben Butler, Smith must have chafed under the old political hack from Massachusetts. He held his tongue as long as he could but ultimately clashed with Butler. He even criticized Major General George Meade, the commander of the Army of the Potomac and Grant's right-hand man. Grant was finally forced to remove Smith, the engineering genius he had credited with helping him win the war in the West.

And Hooker, the man who won control of the Army of the Potomac from Burnside? Lincoln warned him in a letter that he had better live up to his high opinion of himself:

> I think it best for you to know that there are some things in regard to which I am not quite satisfied with you. . . . I think that during General Burnside's command of the army you have taken counsel of your ambition and thwarted him as much as you could, in which you did a great wrong to the country and to a most meritorious and honorable brother officer. I have heard, in such way as to believe it, of your recently saying that both the army and the government needed a dictator. Of course it was not for this, but in spite of it, that I have given you the command. Only those generals who gain successes can set up dictators. . . . And now, beware of rashness. Beware of rashness, but with energy and sleepless vigilance go forward and give us victories.

Hooker's big chance to destroy Lee and give Lincoln that victory came in May 1863, five months after he sent Burnside packing. Lee's handling of his forces at Chancellorsville proved him to be a great commander. Hooker's handling of Federal forces proved him to be as bad as—or worse than—Burnside. Burnside might have allowed himself a few chuckles after the Union defeat, but the men whose careers he destroyed assuredly did not.

"I Fear It Will Do Infinite Mischief": A Lincoln Appointee Gives His Opinion of the Emancipation Proclamation

For most of the first two years of the war, President Abraham Lincoln insisted that all the fighting boiled down to one thing: the North believed in a strong union of all the states and the South wrongly believed it could leave that union.

Lincoln then changed tactics to rally a war-weary Northern populace that was beginning to think it would not be so bad if the Southern states went their own way. In the fall of 1862, he started shifting the focus onto the abolition of slavery. If Northerners did not think the Union was worth fighting for, maybe they would buy the idea that all men should be free—at least all men in the Southern states.

Someone forgot to tell the man Lincoln had appointed war governor of North Carolina. Had he been asked, he would have said he was all in favor of slavery.

While portions of Virginia and Florida had never left United States control, it was a major Union accomplishment to recapture much of coastal North Carolina in the nine months from August 1861 to April 1862. Northern forces under Major Generals Ben Butler and Ambrose Burnside captured key installations like the forts on the Outer Banks and Roanoke Island; those at New Bern, Morehead City, and Beaufort; and Fort Macon. These were the first victories for the Federals, and they gave the Northern public hope that the war would not last long.

Almost before the smoke cleared, Unionists started popping up in North Carolina claiming that they could bring the state back into the Federal fold. Little came of their activities, although a regiment of Unionist men was raised in the coastal counties. Also active along the coast were bands of Unionist irregulars called "Buffaloes," apparently after their roaming style of never having headquarters. These men helped keep alive the idea that the state would come back into the Union.

In May 1862, the Union had such a hold on eastern North Carolina that Lincoln was willing to try putting a provisional governor in charge of all the counties under Federal control. The governor's duty would be to reestablish a civilian government loyal to the Union, which would free the military for more pressing duties.

The man chosen for this task, for reasons even he was unsure of, was

Edward Stanly, a native of New Bern who had long ago left the South and settled in California. Lured back to North Carolina by Secretary of War Edwin Stanton's appeal to his sense of duty, Stanly set up his "capital" in his old hometown of New Bern, which had been captured in March 1862.

He went right to work soothing the fears of North Carolina civilians—which might have raised the eyebrows of abolitionists in Washington. One of his first measures was to tell slave owners that they would get their runaway slaves back if they pledged support to the Union. He also called for the shutdown of a newly organized school for slave children in the belief that it would anger citizens of the region. Before Stanly was in office two weeks, Northern members of Congress were peppering Lincoln with questions about this man's sympathy toward the South.

Lincoln, too, must have begun having misgivings, since he was looking for an opportunity to declare slaves in the rebelling states free. When the victory at Antietam in September 1862 gave the president his opening to free the slaves, Stanly was appalled. But he decided to wait and see if Lincoln would really go through with such a drastic measure.

While Stanly was waiting, the Union army at New Bern, under Major General John Foster, was leading raids into the interior of North Carolina. Along the way, the men destroyed private property while they were supposed to be attacking military targets. Stanly found it difficult to make speeches that the Union administration in Washington felt the pain of the citizens while the Union army in North Carolina was burning barns, stealing pocket watches, and killing livestock.

Stanly resigned as provisional governor within two weeks of the time the Emancipation Proclamation was issued on January 1, 1863. He wrote of the document that freed slaves in the states in rebellion, "I fear it will do infinite mischief. It will fill the hearts of Union men with despair and strengthen the hands of the detestable traitors whose mad ambition has spread desolation and sorrow over our country."

Stanly returned to California, and Lincoln decided to wait until North Carolina was totally defeated before he tried to install another provisional governor.

THE "BLACK TERROR,"
SCOURGE OF VICKSBURG

Fooling the enemy is a time-honored tradition in warfare. It is embarrassing, however, when one side fools the other by displaying weapons that exist only in the minds of frightened opponents.

The prize on the Mississippi River was Vicksburg. The Confederacy controlled only about a hundred miles of the river, from Vicksburg south to Port Hudson, Louisiana. But that hundred miles was enough to help bring in supplies from Texas that could be shipped either to the Army of Tennessee or the Trans-Mississippi Department. If the South lost Vicksburg, it would mean the loss of the western half of the Confederacy. If the North won Vicksburg, it would be able to start a march eastward to strangle the South.

From mid-1862 to early 1863, the Federal navy went on a spree building river gunboats, deemed necessary to take Vicksburg. Just about anything that floated was pressed into service. "River rams," usually flat-bottomed and narrow, were designed to operate in the shallow tributaries along the big river. The theory was that if the Union could control the small waters, it would eventually control the big river. The Union figured that once it had enough gunboats, it would be able to shell the guns of Vicksburg into submission.

That should not suggest the river rams were well designed. Some were leaky and were equipped with engines that could barely keep them in place going upriver. The boats' armor plates—when they had them—might not fit well and might not be thick enough to stop a projectile much larger than a minie ball. Some boats even resorted to "armoring" themselves with cotton bales in hopes that the padding would absorb musket balls and at least slow down cannon rounds. If the cotton bales caught fire, they could be shoved overboard. That was assuming, of course, that sailors could be persuaded to go on deck in a hailstorm of lead to shove them.

In mid-February 1863, the USS *Queen of the West* successfully ran past Vicksburg, headed south for the Red River. Her nineteen-year-old "captain" was really an army colonel, Charles Ellet, son of the man who had designed many of the Union's river rams. He caught and burned several Confederate ships on the river, which inspired the Union to send another ship downriver to help him on his wrecking mission. That ship was the USS *Indianola*. Like the *Queen*, she was an ugly thing, just 175 feet long, little more than a rectangular box with sidewheels and smokestacks. She was, however, armed with two eleven-inch and two nine-inch Dahlgren cannons, plus some smaller cannons that could be wheeled around the deck to where they were needed.

When the *Indianola* made it downriver on February 23, her captain learned that Ellet had gone up one river too many and lost the *Queen* to capture. Ellet himself had escaped on one of the smaller Confederate vessels he had captured. Knowing his luck had run out, Ellet was headed back home when he ran into the *Indianola*.

Four ships launched by the Confederates, including the rapidly repaired *Queen*, caught the Federals on the Mississippi. One of the Confederate ships was a fast, hardheaded ram, the *William H. Webb*. The *Webb* and the *Queen* repeatedly rammed the *Indianola* until the Federal ship started to sink. Her captain beached her but was unable to destroy her. He apparently never hit his attackers with return cannon fire.

The Confederates towed the *Indianola* to the east bank of the Mississippi and immediately set about trying to repair her so they could add her to their own fleet, just as they had done with the *Queen*.

Upriver above Vicksburg, Union admiral David Porter hit the roof. Not only had he lost two gunboats because their captains failed to destroy them, but now both would be turned against him by the Confederates, who were apparently experts at quick repairs. Porter aimed to do what he could to stop the repairs.

As he put it in his postwar writings, Porter "hit upon a cheap expedient." Instead of sending a real ironclad gunboat downriver—a boat he did not have at his immediate disposal anyway—Porter set his men to building a fake one. They appropriated an old coal barge and attached logs to it so that it was more than three hundred feet long. They then built a superstructure and fake sidewheel covers on each side. In the center, they mounted empty salt-pork barrels on top of each other to make them look like smokestacks. At the bottom of each stack was a pot filled with slow-burning pine pitch and oakum. Once lit, the pots would produce black smoke, making the gunboat look real. Since the sidewheel covers extended all the way to the water, even casual observers—at night—would think the fake ironclad was under power. To complete the ruse, Porter had lifeboats mounted and logs poked through the sides of the vessel to make it look like the "ironclad" was well armed.

Porter was trying to make the Confederates think they were facing the USS *Lafayette*, a three-hundred-foot ironclad that had not yet made it that far downriver. He assumed Confederate intelligence had spread the word that the *Lafayette* was almost finished and would show up near Vicksburg soon.

When the fake ironclad was finished—supposedly within twelve hours of the time the idea was hatched—it was dubbed the "Black Terror." Some wag painted a message on the sidewheel covers: "Deluded Rebels—Cave In." Another sailor added two flagpoles, from which flew a skull and crossbones and the United States flag.

On February 24, one night after the *Indianola*'s capture, towboats cast the "Black Terror" off above Vicksburg with a fervent prayer that it would not run aground. It was entirely unmanned and at the mercy of the river's current.

Mother nature, who had not often smiled on Union efforts to control her river, cooperated that night. The fake ironclad was seen by Confederate pickets, and the heavy cannons protecting the city roared to life. Incredibly, almost all the shells missed it. The few that hit the "Black Terror" did nothing more than shatter the lifeboats on deck. The Confederate gunners whom the Federals feared couldn't hit a wooden raft floating at the predictable rate of the river's current.

The raft grounded below Vicksburg, but Union soldiers waded out and pushed it back into the main channel. Once again, the "Black Terror" was on its way.

When the Confederate crew of the *Queen of the West* saw the ironclad headed downriver, it rushed to tell the salvage crew plugging the holes on the *Indianola*. It never occurred to the captain of the *Queen* to do battle with the "ironclad." He must have thought it too formidable, as he didn't even throw a shell to slow it down. Had he done so, he would have discovered that the wooden guns couldn't hurt him.

The *Indianola's* salvage crew didn't wait around to see what the unidentified Federal ironclad would do. The men threw the smaller cannons and the nine-inch guns into the river. They then loaded and aimed the two eleven-inch cannons mouth to mouth and primed them with slow-burning fuses. When the fuses burned down, the two valuable cannons, which had been destined to join the Confederate forts at Vicksburg, blew themselves up. That in turn started an explosion that consumed the *Indianola*. The Union ship that had been a Confederate ship for less than twenty-four hours was destroyed for both sides.

The "Black Terror" never even got close to the *Indianola*. It grounded upriver, and the secret of its phony construction was finally discovered by the Confederates in the morning. News of the fakery could not be contained. Newspapers as far away as Richmond joked about the idiocy of the Southerners who had run scared from an unmanned, unarmed, un-iron ironclad.

Though the Confederates did not get to use the *Indianola*, the Union was still out an expensive gunboat whose loss would make it that much more difficult to capture Vicksburg. Union lieutenant commander George Brown, captain of the *Indianola*, filed a report on the action, but a careful reading shows how he attempted to avoid punishment for abandoning his ship to the Confederates. Brown ended his report by noting how the *Indianola's* weapons had been "rendered useless." What he implied is that he destroyed the cannons to keep them from the Confederates. The truth was that the Confederates destroyed the cannons to keep them from being recaptured by the phantom Federals aboard that huge ironclad.

GRANT AND BUTLER TINKER
WITH MOTHER NATURE

There's an old, rollicking, folk song about the glories of working all day on the Erie Canal.

There is no such song about working all day on DeSoto Point Canal in Louisiana or Dutch Gap Canal in Virginia. These Union projects, described as both brilliant and ill-conceived, ended as total failures in helping the war effort.

DeSoto Point Canal was first thought of in the spring of 1862 as a means of bypassing the heavy Confederate cannons atop the bluffs at Vicksburg, Mississippi. The concept of the canal was simple, if ambitious. Vicksburg is located on the outside of a horseshoe bend in the river. Union war planners had only to look at a map to see that if they could somehow cut across the DeSoto Point peninsula, three-quarters of a mile wide, they could eliminate the threat Confederate cannons posed to their gunboats.

What they proposed was something nature did not yet intend. The Union army wanted to move the Mississippi River away from Vicksburg. If it could accomplish that, the Mississippi would be open to the Union all the way to the North and Vicksburg would be little more than a small town to be dealt with at the army's pleasure.

The canal concept was not new. As early as 1853, a civil engineer had suggested a canal be built across DeSoto Point as a means of straightening the river. The citizens of Vicksburg were appalled that someone would even think of cutting them off from the river. They had a law passed in 1858 that forbade any such artificial changes in the river's flow.

The Union army began digging DeSoto Point Canal in early June 1862 after surveying a route that would be about a mile and a half long. Doing the digging were slaves confiscated from surrounding plantations and white soldiers under Brigadier General Thomas Williams.

By July 1, more than a thousand slaves and many of Williams's three thousand men had almost completed the canal. The design, in theory, was ingenious. The canal would slope slightly from north to south, so once the northernmost part of the point was removed, the natural flow of the river would scour the canal's bottom, deepening it for gunboats that needed at least six to ten feet of water to float.

The Union men counted on one uncontrollable factor to help them create the canal. That was mother nature, and she was not cooperating. All the depth charts and weather forecasts predicted that the river should rise in the summer, thanks to spring rains hundreds of miles to the north. That did not happen. Instead, the water level dropped almost a foot a day. Though thousands of men dug as fast as they could from dawn to dusk, the river fell faster. The canal's bottom remained higher than the river.

By the middle of July, the river had fallen almost twenty-five feet, far faster than the men could dig. They were exhausted. Williams had only seven hundred men reporting to work out of his force of three thousand. Even fewer slaves were reporting to work. All were broken down by the constant digging and the fever. The Union army finally gave up and pulled back down the river, abandoning both the canal and the slaves. When a force of Confederates rowed across the river to see what the Yankees had been doing, they found six hundred soldiers' graves and hundreds of slaves who had been left to fend for themselves.

That August, Williams was killed at the Battle of Baton Rouge, but his canal lived on, as Major General U. S. Grant saw no other way to land his troops south of the city except by avoiding the guns of Vicksburg. He sent his engineers to look at the canal in January 1863.

By the end of January, work had resumed. At least five feet of water stood in the bottom of the canal, but the scouring effect was not materializing. Grant even had a sternwheeler posted at the head of the canal in an attempt to move rushing water down the ditch. It did not work.

Grant then listened to some riverboat captains, who told him that the entrance to the canal was at a slow spot in the river. They told him he should move the entrance farther up the river, where the water would enter with more force. For the next two months, Grant tried redigging the canal. This time, he was hampered by high water. Grant finally got some steam shovels operating, but the Confederates parried by moving guns to cover the lower entrance to the canal.

Finally, Grant gave up efforts to open the canal that now sometimes bore his name. Unable to defeat the heavy guns on the river, he finally marched his men around Vicksburg and took the town from the east. At least a thousand men died building a canal that never saw a ship pass through it.

The Union army and Grant had not learned their lesson about fighting mother nature. The following year, Grant allowed construction to begin on Dutch Gap Canal on the James River below Richmond.

Grant may have had an ulterior motive with this canal. It was the brainchild of Major General Ben Butler, a politically appointed general Grant considered a fool. Grant may have let Butler spend his time on the canal to keep him out of the more important work of attacking Lee at Petersburg.

The objective of Dutch Gap Canal was legitimate. Just south of Richmond was Drewry's Bluff, a high spot on the James from which the Confederates commanded the lower river. No Northern gunboat could attempt a run up the James without first silencing the Confederate cannons commanding every inch of the river. Farther downriver was Trent's Reach, another Confederate stronghold that held the river under control.

Butler found a place on the James below Trent's Reach. Called Dutch Gap, it was just under two hundred yards wide. If he could build a canal there, he could bypass the guns of Trent's Reach and possibly shell Drewry's Bluff from a safe distance.

From August through December, Butler had men working on the canal. Though much shorter than Grant's Mississippi River canal, Dutch Gap Canal was more dangerous to build. It was under constant, if anemic, Confederate musket and cannon attack, just enough to keep the black soldiers digging it on edge and not concentrating on throwing dirt.

Grant never told Butler that he had no intention of moving on

Richmond until he took Lee's army around Petersburg. Butler, assuming that Richmond was the object, continued digging his canal. Both men were happy, Grant because Butler was out of his hair and Butler in his belief that he was doing something worthwhile in the war effort.

On New Year's Day 1865, Butler, a lawyer with no engineering training, ordered that work on the canal be speeded up. His solution was the explosion of six tons of black powder. Mindful of the hole that Union engineers had created the previous summer in blowing up the Confederate lines at Petersburg, Butler ordered the mine placed to help excavate some of the last parts of the canal. When it exploded, tons of dirt flew high in the air—then landed where they had originated. Additional dirt was deposited in the canal when the sides caved in due to the force of the explosion.

Butler's refusal to listen to experienced engineers who counseled against the explosion put the project behind by months. When it was finally finished in April 1865, it was useless. Lee was moving out of Petersburg. The forces at Drewry's Bluff were spiking their guns, and all the stores in Richmond were being burned by the Confederates. Butler had built a canal that would allow the capture of a city that had already been abandoned.

While Grant was accepting the surrender of Lee at Appomattox Court House, Butler was on the James River staring at the muddy water in the bottom of a ditch that had consumed his imagination for more than nine months.

Mother nature heaped some final irony on the two failed canals.

In 1876, when Grant was president, the Mississippi River flooded and cut its own channel very near, but not in, the old DeSoto Point Canal. What Grant, Williams, and thousands of Union soldiers had been unable to do, nature did. Vicksburg was left high and dry. It was not until 1903 that the Corps of Engineers diverted the river back to its "natural" course and restored Vicksburg's status as a Mississippi River town.

Modern civil-engineering analysis of DeSoto Point Canal's original design has determined that if the Mississippi had not fallen so rapidly in the summer of 1862, the plan for the river to scour its way across DeSoto

Point, deepening the ditch into a true canal, would have worked. The canal would indeed have been able to carry ships out of the range of Confederate guns, and the attack on Vicksburg might have been made much sooner, possibly shortening the war by months.

And while that Mississippi River canal envisioned by Williams and Grant was ultimately a failure, Dutch Gap Canal on the James was not. Not long after the Civil War, the river diverted into the canal, which serves today as the main channel. The area where the Confederate guns were placed is now inaccessible, just as Butler intended.

THE BATTLE OF THE CLOTHESLINES

Black soldiers had to struggle the entire Civil War to prove to skeptical Union generals that they had the same right to die on battlefields as white soldiers.

Though President Lincoln eventually changed the focus of the war from preserving the Union to ending slavery, that did not mean white Union leaders actually believed black people were equal. On two occasions before the Emancipation Proclamation was issued, white generals gave slaves in Union-occupied territory their freedom. Both times, Lincoln rescinded the generals' proclamations. It took more than two years of lobbying by abolitionists before Union generals reluctantly accepted the idea that free blacks and escaped slaves could join the Union army. For many months, the generals kept black soldiers digging ditches and guarding towns far from Confederates in the belief that the blacks were inferior in intelligence and incapable of loading and firing weapons.

It wasn't until the middle of the war that black soldiers got a chance to show their courage. One such occasion came in March 1863. Union soldiers were invading Jacksonville, Florida, for the third time, having left two previous times when no Confederates seemed to be around. This time, black soldiers of the First South Carolina Volunteers, freed slaves from around the town of Beaufort, were among the Union forces.

They were led by a Massachusetts-born abolitionist colonel named Thomas Wentworth Higginson, one of the "Secret Six" supporters who had financed John Brown's 1859 Harpers Ferry raid. The First South Carolina Volunteers were among the first black men in uniform for the Union and were the first to see action, several months before the Fifty-fourth Massachusetts Regiment won fame at Battery Wagner near Charleston in July 1863.

Higginson had faith in his men. He was convinced they were as smart as, and would fight the rebels as well as, white Yankees. His opinion was not shared by his superiors, who only reluctantly allowed his black soldiers away from guard duty in South Carolina for the invasion of Jacksonville.

Higginson was itching to prove what his well-trained men could do. They were in camp one day when a breathless white scout arrived with word that his company had discovered a rebel camp of at least twenty-two tents about four miles away. His men needed help!

Eager to show their bravery, the former slaves marched toward the potential battle. An amused Higginson later described what happened: "At a certain point forces were divided, and a detachment was sent round the head of the creek, to flank the unsuspecting enemy; while we of the main body, stealing with caution nearer and nearer, through ever denser woods, swooped down at last in triumph upon a solitary farmhouse— where the family washing had been hung out to dry. This was our Rebel camp!"

He called the incident "the Battle of the Clotheslines." The white scout who had been so frightened after finding the supposed Confederate camp was accused of being "three sheets to the wind."

As for the black soldiers of the First South Carolina Volunteers, they lived to fight another day. The First South Carolina was later inducted into the United States Colored Troops as the Thirty-third Regiment. It got to fight in several minor battles. Higginson once ordered his men to stop firing on some rebels when one soldier ran up to him to complain that the government was paying him ten dollars a month to shoot his musket, and that he didn't care to stop.

By the end of the war, perhaps as many as two hundred thousand black men were in the Union army. It was this influx of manpower that helped turn the tide on many fronts. Had the North inducted blacks earlier than 1863, it might have shortened the war simply by having more men to put in more places throughout the South.

Though kept segregated from white regiments, black regiments were used with increasing frequency, as white generals grudgingly learned the bravery of freed Southern slaves and freeborn Northern blacks. They could charge as well as whites–and die as well also. At some battles—such as those at Battery Wagner, South Carolina, in July 1863 and Olustee, Florida, in February 1864—blacks were the primary troops involved and the bulk of the casualties.

DUELING OFFICERS

Confederate general Nathan Bedford Forrest once said, "War is fighting and fighting means killing." Usually—but not always—that meant killing the other side. Angry officers on the same side occasionally fought and killed each other over some perceived breach of honor. While Union officers murdered each other in the heat of the moment, Confederate officers sometimes staged formal duels, complete with chosen weapons, witnesses, and written rules of conduct.

Union brigadier general William "Bull" Nelson had already spent two decades at sea as an officer in the United States Navy when he left the ocean to become a landlubber general at the request of his old friend Abraham Lincoln. Nelson did well at the Battle of Shiloh and was rewarded with a major generalship. Later beaten at a battle in his native Kentucky, Nelson pulled in his horns to recuperate from a minor wound and to recruit more loyal Kentuckians to his command. He set up headquarters in Louisville and asked that a regular-army officer be sent to him to assist in recruiting.

The officer selected was Brigadier General Jefferson Columbus Davis (who may have been sensitive about sharing his name with the Confederate president). Davis, thirty-three, was a career army man, having joined as a private during the Mexican War. He won a battlefield commission to lieutenant during that war, a rare occurrence for an army overstaffed with West Pointers, then worked his way up in rank in the peacetime army. Davis was part of Fort Sumter's garrison at the time of the bombardment. He was appointed colonel within months and general by December 1861. Having seen hard fighting at Pea Ridge, Davis was a tough, no-nonsense regular-army man who must have chafed at being under the command of an ex-swabby who had gotten his major generalship by being friends with the president of the United States.

Davis and Nelson clashed from the moment they met. Nelson treated Davis as the underling he was, not with the respect owed a man who had worked his way up from the ranks to be a general in the United States Army. They butted heads so much that Nelson relieved Davis of command, a blot on an otherwise spotless record.

On September 29, 1862, Davis went to the hotel where Nelson made his headquarters and demanded an apology in a face-to-face meeting. Nelson refused. Davis threw a wad of paper in Nelson's face. Nelson responded by slapping Davis. He then turned around and walked away.

No one walked away from Jefferson C. Davis after slapping him. The enraged but unarmed Davis borrowed a pistol from an unthinking fellow officer, then rushed upstairs behind Nelson. He yelled Nelson's name. When Nelson turned around, Davis shot him from point-blank range.

It was a clear case of murder, but Davis was never charged or even relieved of duty. His one punishment, if it can be called that, was that he was never promoted to major general.

Davis was a fighter, which probably played the major role in keeping him in the service. He was also a cold-hearted man. While commanding the Fourteenth Corps during Sherman's March to the Sea, he found his corps last in line on the march. All around him were slaves who had fled Georgia plantations in hopes of following the Union army to freedom. When his corps came to Ebenezer Creek, east of Savannah, Davis asked the slaves to stand to one side of the road so he could get his corps across the pontoon bridge laid by earlier soldiers, after which the slaves could cross. Davis, who shared the racist views of Sherman that they were fighting to preserve the Union, not to free the slaves, had no intention of keeping his word.

Once Davis's men were across, he ordered the pontoon bridge pulled up, leaving hundreds of slaves stranded on the west side of the swollen creek. The slaves knew that Confederate cavalry was rushing to catch up to the Federals. They also knew that those same horsemen would capture them and send them back to their plantations. The lure of freedom and the fear of capture were too much. Scores of slaves dove into the swollen creek. Most of them drowned attempting to reach the other bank. Those who couldn't swim simply stared across the creek at the Yankee general who had lied to them. Davis turned around and rode away.

Sherman never relieved Davis of corps command for his actions at Ebenezer Creek. Davis stayed in the army after the war. He never made major general and never apologized for killing either Nelson or the people who just wanted to walk across his bridge.

Nathan Bedford Forrest was not above killing a fellow officer, particularly if the other guy started it.

Lieutenant Andrew Gould was in charge of two cannons captured by retreating Federals during Forrest's pursuit of Union brigadier general Abel Streight through northern Alabama in April 1863. Gould and others were surprised by an ambush and fell back, leaving the cannons.

Though Forrest got his cannons back, he ordered Gould out of his command, blaming him for the loss. He may have questioned the courage of the twenty-three-year-old. Gould was both embarrassed and determined to prove to Forrest that he belonged with him. In June, Gould caught up with Forrest at his headquarters in Columbia, Tennessee. He asked the general to reconsider his order and allow him back. The general refused out of hand and dismissed Gould.

Impulsively, Gould took out his revolver and shot Forrest in the side. The general, who was not armed since he was in his own headquarters, grabbed Gould with one hand and held him while reaching into his pocket for a penknife. He opened the tiny blade with his teeth, then jammed it into Gould's ribs. Gould broke away and ran.

The general conferred with one doctor, who predicted Forrest's wound would be fatal. Enraged that one of his own men would kill him when the Yankees could not, the general hunted Gould down and shot at him with a borrowed pistol. He missed and hit a bystander. This time, a second doctor caught up with Forrest and told him his wound was not fatal. Relieved, Forrest let Gould live and told the doctors to tend to the young lieutenant.

There was nothing they could do. While Gould's bullet had missed Forrest's vital organs, Forrest's tiny knife had found Gould's. The lieutenant died within a few days. A Forrest legend says the general visited the boy while he was in the hospital and forgave him for the assassination attempt, but historians doubt that the fiery general ever forgave anyone.

That is not to say that Forrest had no compassion. When the war started, he had offered eventual freedom to any of his male slaves who joined the army with him. At least thirty of them became teamsters for his supply wagons. After a few battles, Forrest grew concerned that he might not live out the war to keep his promise, so he amended his will to state that if he died in combat, his slaves were to be freed.

One of the oddest squabbles among officers took place in May 1863 near Suffolk, Virginia. During a raid on a Confederate camp, the Federal army made off with some precious cannons. Two officers from an Alabama brigade, Captain L. R. Terrell and Captain John Cussons, wrote a report suggesting that a neighboring regiment, the Fifty-fifth North Carolina, had run in the face of the Federals.

The Tar Heels hit the roof when they learned another regiment had questioned their courage. Colonel John Kerr Connally and Major A. H.

Belo of the Fifty-fifth challenged the Alabamans to a double duel with weapons of the Alabamans' choosing. Captain Cussons chose rifled muskets at forty paces. Captain Terrell chose double-barreled shotguns.

The staff officers of both units were stunned. Unless these men were terrible shots, someone was going to be killed. In the old days of dueling, the weapons of choice had been single-shot pistols. If the parties missed each other or even wounded each other, they sometimes went off arm in arm to have a drink, since their honor had been properly defended. That would not happen if rifles and shotguns were used.

Belo and Cussons went first with the muskets. The Tar Heel grazed the head of the Alabama officer, while the Alabaman missed his target entirely. They agreed to shoot again. This time, a hole was torn in the North Carolinian's jacket, but the Alabaman was missed entirely. After shooting at each other from forty paces with muskets rated accurate up to six hundred yards, the only marks they had to show were a grazed head and a hole in a jacket.

Next up were the colonels with the shotguns.

Since two rounds had already taken place and no one was dead, the other officers convinced Connally and Terrell that further fighting was pointless. The two sweating men quickly agreed, and the Alabamans vowed to amend their "mistaken" report on the loss of the cannons. Everyone lived to fight another day.

The Fifty-fifth North Carolina, the regiment whose courage was questioned, was one of the handful of Confederate units that made it all the way to the stone wall on Cemetery Ridge on the third day at Gettysburg. The fifteen-thousand-man Pettigrew-Pickett-Trimble Assault, made over a mile of open ground under constant fire from cannons and muskets, came just two months after the duel in Virginia.

On one occasion, a Confederate general killed another Confederate general.

Brigadier General Lucius Walker was good at reading and writing at West Point, graduating in the top third of his 1850 class. But he never amounted to much as an officer. He resigned his regular-army commission after just two years of active service to become a merchant. A nephew of former president James K. Polk, he likely used his family connections to secure a lieutenant colonelcy when the war started.

Though he rose to brigadier general, Walker was never involved in a major battle in which he proved himself. Like many other generals, he ran afoul of Braxton Bragg, who ordered Walker out of his army. Walker moved to the Trans-Mississippi Department and fought at the head of a cavalry division in the Battle of Helena, Arkansas, in July 1863.

It was in Arkansas that Walker met Brigadier General John Sappington Marmaduke, a flamboyant rolling stone who had quit both Harvard and Yale before finally winning an appointment to West Point. Marmaduke's leadership had been praised ever since Shiloh, a battle the sickly Walker missed.

At some point during the action around Little Rock and Helena, Marmaduke questioned Walker's courage. That charge called for a duel of honor. Marmaduke and Walker faced off, and Walker went face down. Marmaduke was arrested for murdering a fellow officer, but once it was established that Walker had requested the duel, all charges were dropped.

Major General John Austin Wharton, a Texas lawyer who had voted to take the state out of the Union, learned too late that he should have listened to his subordinates when they ask to be promoted.

Wharton's war experience was fraught with peril. A lawyer more used to courtrooms than battlefields, he had the measles early in the war, followed by pneumonia that damaged his lungs. He was wounded in the right leg at Shiloh, then in the arm four months later. Eight months after that, he was wounded when a bullet grazed his chest. Two months after that, his horse failed to completely clear a tree, and Wharton's leg and foot were crushed between horse and tree trunk. The man was a walking accident.

Wharton was absent so often in the Tennessee theater that he was transferred to the Trans-Mississippi Department, arriving just in time to take part in the exhausting Red River Campaign in Louisiana. He headed the cavalry after Brigadier General Tom Green was beheaded by a Federal cannon blast.

It was on April 6, 1865, just three days before Lee surrendered in Virginia, that Major General John Magruder called a meeting of all of his commanders in Houston to discuss how to conduct the rest of the war. At the meeting was Colonel George W. Baylor, a subordinate of Wharton's who had been asking for a promotion for some time. Wharton had never acted on the nomination. During an argument about the promotion, Wharton slapped Baylor. That was all it took. Baylor drew his pistol and shot the unarmed Wharton dead in the presence of the other officers.

Wharton, who had survived camp diseases, horses, and bullet wounds for four years, could not survive the anger of one of his own officers in the closing weeks of the war.

A Case of Déjà Vu

History remembers Lieutenant Generals Thomas Jonathan "Stonewall" Jackson and James Longstreet as two of Robert E. Lee's strongest tacticians, battlefield masters who knew just when to hit the Federals with devastating blows.

So how could both men neglect to inform their own regiments that they would be performing dangerous reconnoitering in front of Confederate lines?

In the case of Jackson, the answer is simple. He was a peculiar, single-minded, hardheaded orphan whose whole philosophy was built around keeping his own counsel.

Jackson was born in 1824 near what is now Clarksburg, West Virginia. His parents both died when he was a child. He and his sister were raised by an uncle. Almost by force of will, since he never had a formal early education, the backwoods boy entered and mastered West

Point. He improved his standing every year until graduating seventeenth in a class of fifty-nine in 1846. Sent to Mexico as a second lieutenant, he won two brevet honors in the artillery.

After that war, he was sent to Fort Meade, a frontier outpost in Florida named after the future Gettysburg general. Within days of his arrival, Jackson found himself in conflict with the post's commanding officer. The man appeared to be consorting with one of his female slaves, an affront to God in the eyes of Jackson, who observed strict morality. Jackson wrote the War Department about the immoral behavior, and his commander retaliated by putting him under house arrest. By the time the matter was settled, Jackson was thoroughly disgusted with the United States Army. He resigned in 1851 and took a position as professor of artillery and natural philosophy at Virginia Military Institute in Lexington.

A graceless, solitary man who was comfortable only around close family members, Jackson seemed ill-suited to be a professor dealing with prank-playing teenagers. His students delighted in playing tricks on him, such as interrupting his classes with meaningless questions. Jackson, who memorized his talks while standing for hours in a sort of self-discipline training, would be forced to start over. The students also laughed about his personal habits, which included taking frequent cold showers with the water directed at specific parts of his body in the belief that such therapy had health benefits. He would often raise one arm above his head in the belief that the blood needed to run back down into his body. He refused pepper on his bland diet, believing the spice upset his digestive system. He constantly complained of dyspepsia, or indigestion. His solution was to eat meals of raspberries, bread, and milk. If he had one indulgence, it was lemons. Cadets, and later officers and common soldiers, knew they could get on Jackson's good side if they brought him lemons.

Whether Jackson's nickname was a compliment for staying put in the face of an advancing enemy or a complaint because he would not move forward to support Confederates already fighting that enemy, it is clear that his stubbornness was both a positive and a negative trait. On the positive side, he would set a military goal and keep going after it.

On the negative side, he never told anyone anything before he thought it time. He rarely asked his subordinates for their opinions on how to handle battlefield conditions and almost never passed along details of orders he had received from General Lee.

In fact, Jackson rarely told even his highest-ranking officers where they were going when he ordered a march. As his men neared a crossroads, his brigade commanders would look around for a courier carrying Jackson's orders for what to do at the junction. If no order to turn was received, the subordinate generals continued marching straight until the next crossroads. Jackson was a stickler for military order on such marches. The book called for fifty minutes of marching with a ten-minute rest. He once ordered a general arrested for ignoring the rest period.

If any of Jackson's generals had the gall to question his reasoning or suggest something out of turn, he often reacted with rage. When one of his brigadiers, William W. Loring, went over his head to complain to Secretary of War Judah Benjamin about being posted to an exposed position during the winter of 1861–62, Jackson exploded. He offered the Confederacy his resignation, and he meant it. Amends were quickly made, and he stayed in the army.

Though Jackson was a deeply religious man who often cited "God's will" for both victories and defeats, he fully accepted that war meant killing. After the Battle of Port Republic, he heard that one of his division commanders, Major General Richard S. Ewell, had ordered his soldiers not to kill a Federal officer on a snow-white horse who was conspicuous for his bravery. Jackson called Ewell to his tent and dressed him down. "Shoot the brave officers and the cowards will run away and take the men with them," Jackson told him.

It was Jackson's hardheadedness that got him killed. As night fell on May 2, 1863, on the Chancellorsville battlefield, where his twenty-six-thousand-man corps had smashed the right flank of the Federal army, Jackson was impatient to renew the attack. The four brigades under A. P. Hill that had led the charge were trying to reorganize themselves into a line on the heavily wooded battlefield. Confusion reigned. The attack had been so sudden and so violent that the Federals were still unsure what had happened. They didn't even know where their interior lines were. The situation was illustrated when Confederates captured a Union colonel who rode into their lines carrying a white flag. The colonel's purpose had been to find out if the men he heard in the woods were Confederates or Federals. He took a chance and lost, though he gamely tried to talk his way out of capture by suggesting the white flag entitled him to his freedom.

Elsewhere in the woods, Union soldiers heard someone occupying the same stretch of log works they were moving into. In the dim light, it looked like the other soldiers were facing the opposite direction. "Who's over there?" the Federals asked.

"Confederates," came the reply. "Who are you?"

"Federals," came the answer.

The Federals quietly moved back. Neither side fired on the other.

The Confederates sent out a foot patrol to try to figure out where the closest Federal lines were. As the skirmishers moved forward, a rider came down the Plank Road toward them. The Confederates held their fire, asking who the rider was. Union brigadier general Joseph Knipe, realizing he had stumbled into Confederate lines, wheeled his horse and shouted, "Don't fire. We're friends!" The Confederates held their fire momentarily, confused by the incongruity of a rider's coming from the direction of the Federals but declaring he was a friend. Knipe escaped a Confederate volley from a North Carolina regiment in Brigadier General James Lane's brigades. The Tar Heels' volley was answered by a Union volley not far away. Each side was feeling out the other's lines. They were very close.

Not far away was Jackson, who had been in a frenzy of activity since the battle was launched. He was beside himself with excitement. Against all odds, and to his great satisfaction, his corps had smashed the Union flank. Now, he had to keep the Yankees on the run to make the victory complete. If the Federals were allowed to re-form, they might not be so easy to break the second time.

Jackson mounted his horse. With staff in tow, he rode toward his outermost lines, toward the scattered shooting, as the day's light faded into darkness. Jackson had to know the strength of the Federals. He had to know if they were digging in or still running. He had to know if the time was right to launch a moonlight attack that would send the entire Federal army reeling back to the Rappahannock River. Even as most of his corps' regiments were re-forming in the darkness, Jackson told Lane to push ahead with his four regiments. Jackson himself rode off in the same general direction he had just pointed Lane. He rode at least two hundred yards in front of the last known Confederate battle line. He was in a no man's land between lines that had just fired blindly at each other. It was not the normal place for a corps commander to be.

"General, don't you think this is the wrong place for you?" asked one of his nervous aides.

"The danger is all over. The enemy is routed," Jackson replied. "Go back and tell A. P. Hill to press right on."

Jackson wanted the attack to continue. He had no evidence that the danger had passed. He either hadn't heard or was ignoring the scattered firing that had taken place just minutes earlier. Led by a scout who lived in the area and had hunted this same ground, Jackson rode along the road toward the enemy.

The Confederates finally pulled up when they heard wood being chopped. Jackson surmised that the Federals were forming log breastworks to resist night attack. He knew he would have to attack immediately if he was to keep the Federals moving. If he waited, the Federals would have good defenses. Jackson wheeled his horse and started back toward his own lines.

No one on Jackson's staff thought to ride ahead to warn the regiments that the corps commander and his staff were returning. Then Jackson himself made a dangerous mistake. Leading the way, he turned down a different road—he had left on the Mountain Road and was returning on the Plank Road. The Confederates who had seen the general and his staff ride toward the enemy would not be the same ones hearing horses riding toward them from the direction of the enemy. The men now hearing the horses were the same ones who had just fired at a Union rider on the same road. And they had just traded volleys in the darkness with men they knew to be Federals.

As the riders approached, the Confederates fired a volley, apparently without orders. Jackson's brother-in-law rode toward the lines and shouted, "Cease firing. We are friends! You are firing into your own men." It was almost the same thing that Knipe had said just minutes earlier to allow his escape.

Major John D. Barry of the Eighteenth North Carolina Regiment called out, "Who gave that order? It is a lie! Pour it into them, boys!" A second volley was fired at the horsemen.

Jackson was hit three times, the most severe wound breaking his arm near the shoulder. He was helped from his horse and moved off into the darkness. The Federals he had wanted to find were so close now that two stepped out of the brush and accidentally witnessed Jackson's being treated. They were quickly captured. As Jackson was borne away on a stretcher, one of the soldiers carrying it was hit by Union fire. He fell, and Jackson was dropped to the ground. He was then picked up and hustled off to an ambulance.

Jackson's wounds were not necessarily fatal. Scores of officers and men on both sides survived amputations. But Jackson, who had always believed he had a weak constitution, developed pneumonia, a problem almost unrelated to the amputation of his arm. Told that it was Sunday, May 10, 1863, Jackson smiled and commented that he had always wanted to die on the Sabbath. He did.

Lane's brigade was not punished for Jackson's wounding. It was no one's fault but his own. A lieutenant general had no business scouting between lines at night. It was the job of lower officers to find the enemy and then report its position to their commanders. Jackson, anxious to cut out the middleman, took on the job himself. He could just have easily been captured or shot by the Federal troops filling the woods that night.

It was also a mistake on Jackson's part to take a different road back. The men who shot him had no idea that their commanding general was riding a scouting mission. No one had told them. All they knew was that Federals had fired on them from the same direction just minutes earlier.

Finally, Jackson should not have been leading his column. If someone is going to get shot in the darkness, let it be lower-ranking couriers or other aides.

It is one of history's ironies that almost a year later and not far—perhaps three miles—from the same spot, another lieutenant general made the very same mistake that killed Jackson. This time, it was Jackson's alter ego, James Longstreet.

Born in South Carolina, Longstreet moved to Alabama as a child and later accepted an appointment to West Point. He graduated in 1842 close to the bottom of his class. Wounded in the Mexican War, he remained a professional soldier in the regular army until resigning to join the Confederate army on June 1, 1861, long after many other Southerners had sworn their allegiance. Research has suggested that he secretly agreed to join the Confederates but wanted to stay in the United States Army long enough to collect a few final paychecks. Longstreet, always a pragmatist on the battlefield, also lived that way in his personal doings.

Longstreet distinguished himself early in the war with his defense of Blackburn's Ford on Bull Run, a small engagement before the major battle that proved to the Federals that the Confederates would resist Union invasion.

Longstreet fought well under Joseph Johnston and won the trust of Lee during the Seven Days' Battles in June 1862. He was given command of the First Corps, a post he kept no matter how controversial he became during the course of the war.

The controversy that dogs Longstreet to this day revolves around his preference for defensive war. Cut from the same cloth as Joseph Johnston, Longstreet believed the South could only win the war by forcing the Federals to constantly attack while the Confederates sat behind formidable defenses. Such tactics worked well at Fredericksburg. Longstreet was not in favor of Lee's invasion of Maryland in September 1862. He believed the long march exposed Lee's army to endless opportunities for the Federals to attack. If caught in the open, the Confederates could be cut off from support, surrounded, and killed. Lee did not ignore such advice. He let it go in one ear and out the other. He knew Longstreet would obey his commands even if he did not agree with them.

It was at Gettysburg in July 1863 that Longstreet's desire to fight a defensive battle caused a rift with Lee. Longstreet wanted to swing around the Union army's flank and get between it and Washington. He reasoned that the Federals would make desperate, costly charges on ground of the Confederates' choosing in order to save Washington. Lee disagreed.

Ordered to attack as soon as practical on the second day, Longstreet dawdled, waiting for reenforcements. By waiting all day, he allowed the Union lines to be reenforced. The second-day attack failed to break the Federals, and Longstreet again suggested that the Confederates put themselves close to Washington. Lee listened to and then shelved Longstreet's advice. He pointed at the Federals on Cemetery Hill behind Gettysburg and said, "The enemy is there and that is where we will attack him."

It was men from Longstreet's corps who were chosen to attack on the third day. Longstreet, who had told Lee, "No 15,000 men can take that ridge," could not bring himself to give the order to make the charge across the mile-wide open field. He just nodded and waved his hand when Major General George Pickett asked if it were time to attack.

Though Lee could have relieved Longstreet for his disruptive, possibly destructive, performance at Gettysburg, he did not. Lee trusted his "Old War Horse" even when Longstreet questioned direct orders.

Longstreet was instrumental in winning the Battle of Chickamauga in September 1863. He then returned to the Army of Northern Virginia in April 1864 to help Lee face a new threat from U. S. Grant. Grant and Longstreet had been friends at West Point, Grant graduating one year behind the Confederate.

It was during the Battle of the Wilderness on May 6, 1864, that Lee almost lost his Old War Horse for good. It was one year and four days after Stonewall Jackson's wounding. It was near the middle of the afternoon when Longstreet ordered four brigades to make a flank attack against the Federals' left, which was aligned near the Plank Road, the same road where Jackson had been shot. When the Confederates attacked from a makeshift road hidden in the dense underbrush, the Union units rolled up like a scroll, some Federal regiments being hit by musket fire from three sides.

The Confederates drove the Federals all the way past the Plank Road, killing a Union general in the assault. The same scout who had found the hidden access to the Union left near the Plank Road located a similar access to more Federals along another road. Longstreet ordered him to lead the way. The battle was rapidly shifting from one front to another. Federal regiments were scattering and Confederates were chasing them. Gunfire was erupting from unseen regiments who were probably not even seeing clear targets in the tangled growth that was the Wilderness.

Longstreet then made the same mistake as Jackson. The lieutenant general, whose place was normally in the rear directing the placement of whole divisions, decided to ride to the front to see what was happening. One of the men who linked up with Longstreet was Brigadier General Micah Jenkins of South Carolina, an 1855 graduate of the Citadel. Jenkins's men were advancing through the woods. He rode alongside Longstreet and spoke as the two men galloped: "I am happy. I have felt despair of the cause for some months, but am relieved and feel assured that we [will] put the enemy back across the Rapidan [River] before night."

Jenkins felt safe. With him, he carried the broken top half of a sword that had been shattered by a bullet in a previous battle. Instead of throwing it away, Jenkins called it his "sword of prophecy." He believed that as long as he kept it by his side, another bullet would not find him.

Longstreet and his staff were riding on the Plank Road nearly opposite some regiments attached to Major General William Mahone's brigade. One regiment of Virginians had already crossed the Plank Road when its colonel realized that the rest of the brigade had halted some distance back, on the other side of the road. Not wishing to be isolated when he didn't know where the Federals were, the colonel reversed his march and rapidly returned to the Plank Road. The other Virginia regiments, not expecting to see a line of armed men marching their way, opened fire in the belief that Federals were coming out of the under-growth.

Riding at full gallop right into that volley came Longstreet and his men. One of Jenkins's brigadiers, Joseph Kershaw, cried out "Friends!"—nearly the same forlorn call heard when Jackson was hit. Two of Kershaw's staffers died instantly. Jenkins went down with a musket ball in his brain. He writhed on the ground for hours, sometimes issuing orders to unseen regiments, until he finally expired. His broken sword lay at his side.

Longstreet was struck by a bullet that passed through his shoulder and into his throat. It hit with such force that he was visibly lifted from his saddle. His men grabbed his horse and pulled him down. Longstreet sat with his back to a tree. In great pain, he still gave orders for the disposition of his corps and for the attack to continue.

When Longstreet was removed from the field, one of his men laid the general's hat across his face to shield him from the sun. Several soldiers misinterpreted the gesture and began to shout that Longstreet was dead. Hearing the cries, Longstreet left the field continually lifting his hat in salute to his men so they would know he was still alive.

Lee countermanded Longstreet's attack orders. He was afraid that the disorganized condition of the Confederates would not allow them to make a coordinated assault. By the time Lee judged it time to attack about four o'clock that afternoon, the Federals had reenforced and reorganized. The moment of Federal confusion that Longstreet had recognized but Lee had not was past.

Even strong supporters of Lee later wrote that it was a mistake to stop Longstreet's attack. "The time was ripe for it and the opportunity far more favorable than the one presented to Jackson [since Longstreet was attacking in daylight]. Longstreet intended to play his hand for all it was worth and to push the pursuit with his whole force," wrote Brigadier General Edward Porter Alexander, one of Lee's artillery experts.

Longstreet recovered from his wound over the rest of the summer and was back with the army by October 1, 1864, though his arm was stiff and sometimes in need of a sling. He stayed Lee's right-hand man on the march west from Petersburg. On April 6, 1865, some of Lee's staff officers asked Longstreet to discuss surrender with Lee. Longstreet replied that the army could still beat four times their number and that as long as that was true, he would not ask Lee to surrender. "I am here to back him up, not tear him down," Longstreet said.

Later that night, Grant sent a message to Lee suggesting surrender. Lee read the note and passed it to Longstreet, who said, "Not yet." He still thought there might be a way to get the army to Lynchburg or to North Carolina to link up with Joseph Johnston's men.

Three days later, the Union army closed in around Lee. On the morning of April 9, some of Lee's regiments tried to break out. The road to Lynchburg was briefly cleared of Federals, but it quickly filled with even more. Lee and Longstreet met later that morning for the last time of their careers.

As Lee mounted his horse to meet Grant, Longstreet called out, "General, if Grant does not give us good terms, come back and let us fight it out!"

Longstreet may have been too defense-oriented for the Army of Northern Virginia, the most offense-minded army in history. He may have sometimes been slow in deploying his forces on the battlefield. He may have been careless the day he rode into the fire of his own men.

But the man could fight. When Lee's supporters targeted Longstreet for blame in losing Gettysburg, Lee would not listen to or support them. He would not do anything to disparage his Old War Horse.

FORREST'S BIG BLUFF

Union colonel Abel D. Streight, commander of the Provisional Brigade of the Fourteenth Corps of the Army of the Cumberland, had a good idea in March 1863. Confederate cavalry had found great success over the previous two years in leading raids behind Federal lines. Now that the Federal cavalry had finally caught up in tactical skill, why not lead a Federal raid behind Confederate lines? Why not destroy the Army of Tennessee's railroad supply line running between Atlanta and Chattanooga? Why not destroy the Confederate cannon factory in Rome, Georgia?

The first answer Streight received when he proposed the expedition was that there were not enough horses to allow him to go riding off into northern Alabama and northern Georgia. But in Streight's view, the beauty of his plan was that he didn't need horses—he'd use mules! Streight would be traveling through hill country. Mules were more surefooted. They wouldn't trip and fall as easily as horses. Plus, they were more durable than horses. They would walk longer and carry more equipment.

Streight, a New Yorker, must not have had much experience with mules. He never thought that they might be stubborn, that they might make noise at inopportune times, that they would be slower than horses.

Depending on mules for a mounted raid was Streight's first mistake. Trusting Confederate brigadier general Nathan Bedford Forrest to tell him the truth in a face-to-face meeting was his second.

After listening to Streight, Union major general William Starke Rosecrans approved the plan. But he made a bureaucratic error. Though Rosecrans assigned more than seventeen hundred men in four regiments to go on the raid, he gave Streight only nine hundred mules. His reasoning was that the raid would be able to mount the walkers quickly by stealing horses and mules from Confederate farms in northern Alabama. Helping the Yankees find those farms would be two cavalry companies of Alabama farmers who had stayed loyal to the Union.

When he got his first look at what he would be riding, Streight found that unscrupulous contractors had sold the army hundreds of inferior mules. Many were sick, lame, or colts that had never even had a saddle thrown on them. When his men tried to ride the young ones, they were bucked off. Hundreds of mules broke out of their holding pens on the night Streight arrived at Eastport, Mississippi, the jumping-off point for the raid. He had to spend two days gathering them from the countryside.

The raid finally got under way on April 22, 1863, five days late. Then it started to rain. Mules dropped out, exhausted from walking through the mud. The soldiers who had to walk started mumbling about the parties who had thought up this crazy stunt. Streight took time to sort the fit men from the unfit, reducing his force to about fifteen hundred. Within a few days, they reached the mountains of northern Alabama, the bottom of the Appalachian chain. Streight knew his decision to use mules would come in handy as they climbed the steep hills.

On April 30, they began to climb into the mountains. The rain had stopped. The sun was shining. Things were looking up. Then the bullets started zinging.

Nathan Bedford Forrest had found them. Forrest had been ordered south from Spring Hill, Tennessee, to oppose an infantry column supporting Streight. When local residents told Forrest that a mounted column had passed heading east, he decided to ignore the enemy infantry and find out what mounted Federals were doing in northern Alabama.

For the next three days, Forrest's thousand men pursued Streight's fifteen hundred. Streight handled the situation well. As he advanced eastward after climbing out of the mountains, his men stripped the farms of horses, mules, foliage, and food, so there was nothing further for Forrest to commandeer. Streight's rear guard set up ambushes at regular intervals, smashing Forrest's lead riders regularly. In one such savage counterattack, Forrest lost two twelve-pound cannons, valuable pieces for any small force trying to shell a larger one.

Streight learned that embarrassing Forrest by capturing his cannons was not a way to prepare for one's inevitable capture. Most military commanders would have stopped fighting at night so their men could eat and sleep, but Forrest kept riding and fighting all night. Streight was forced to keep riding, too. At times, some of the Federals had to form a skirmish line to hold off Forrest long enough for the remaining mules and men to get a few bites to eat and a drink of water. Then the skirmish line would fall back so those men could switch places with the ones who had just eaten. For more than a hundred miles and three days, Forrest and Streight carried on a running battle. Streight would take advantage of what natural obstructions he could find, hold for a while, then fall back. Forrest pressed forward.

Once, the Federals set up a trap on the far side of a small river, hoping the Confederates would come charging across the bridge without checking. Forrest sensed the trap and rode to a farmhouse asking if there was a ford. A sixteen-year-old girl, Emma Sansom, volunteered to show him as soon as she got her horse saddled. Forrest said there wasn't time for that and pulled her up behind him on his horse. After she showed the Confederates a way to flank the Federals, Forrest returned her to her house and thanked her for her "gallant conduct." He took a lock of her hair as a souvenir. She remained a Forrest devotee for the rest of her life.

Onward Forrest pressed, never letting Streight's men rest a minute. Forrest was sure the Federals would collapse if he could keep the pressure on. Streight never took the time to try to count Forrest's men, so he was unaware that his soldiers outnumbered Forrest's, giving him the advantage in a stand-up fight.

About twenty miles from his original objective, Rome, Streight followed the west bank of the Chattooga River, crossed a bridge, and burned it. That done, he imagined he had finally bought some time from Forrest.

He was wrong. Forrest's men swam across, then rigged ropes to their two remaining cannons and pulled them along the bottom of the river. They built rafts to ferry the powder and shells across. Forrest then took a few moments to rest and take stock. He now had fewer than six hundred men. Almost half of his soldiers were scattered behind him walking or leading lame horses—or they were wounded or dead. The Federals still had at least twice as many men and still had their cannons. Forrest decided that the only thing he still had going for him was that the Federals didn't know how well off they were in comparison to their pursuers. He asked Streight to surrender.

Streight, personally meeting with Forrest in no man's land, refused. He held the high ground. And even if Forrest did outnumber him by at least three to one (Streight's belief at the time), Forrest's men would have to come uphill, always a disadvantage to the attacker. Forrest kept the conversation going, trying to persuade Streight that it was hopeless to resist. While Forrest was talking, Streight was looking over the Confederate's shoulder, watching cannon after cannon—actually, the same two cannons being pulled in a circle—pass along a narrow portion of the road before disappearing behind a rise.

Streight knew what Forrest was doing. He was bringing up his artillery to blast the Federals off their little hilltop. Streight asked that the guns be pulled back, and Forrest agreed, asking an aide to make sure "all the guns" comply. Soon, Streight was watching guns move all over the field. Finally, the tension was broken when he fairly shouted at Forrest, "In the Name of God! How many cannons do you have? I've counted 15 already!"

Forrest turned around and looked in the same direction. "Oh? That's all? Well, I guess that's all that have been able to keep up."

When Forrest turned back, he ordered one of his aides to position additional regiments around Streight's hilltop. These regiments existed only in Forrest's mind, but Streight could see them being positioned. At least he could see troops being marched back and forth from behind one hill to behind another. What he could not see was that the same troops were being marched in circles for his benefit.

The men parted and went back to their lines. Streight looked at the mules he had thought were unstoppable. All but about a dozen were lame. They had broken down much faster than Forrest's supposedly frailer horses. Streight broke the news to his regimental commanders that Forrest was ready to shell them into submission. When they heard that, the frightened commanders urged their colonel to surrender. Streight questioned a Confederate prisoner about how many men Forrest had with him. The sharp-thinking prisoner lied, saying that Forrest had his own brigade, Armstrong's, Roddey's, and so many others that he could not remember all the commanders' names. Finally, Streight learned from a messenger that the bridge to Rome that he hoped to cross was heavily guarded by Confederates. If he went farther, he would have to fight on two fronts instead of one.

Streight surrendered his command of more than fifteen hundred men. When he discovered that Forrest had fewer than six hundred, he made a halfhearted effort to unsurrender, but Forrest just smiled.

Forrest marched his prisoners into Rome, their objective anyway. The excited citizens decided to fire some cannons in a salute to General Forrest and his brave men. In the excitement, the battery's commander forgot to remove the cannon shells from the guns. Only bad aim prevented the Confederate gunners from killing the general they were trying to honor.

To their surprise, the Federals were invited to join in the victory celebration. The citizens of Rome explained that they did not mind feeding Yankees as long as they were not carrying guns. Forrest himself did not get to rest and eat. He led his men back into Tennessee to meet the next Yankee threat. For defeating Streight, he was promoted to major general.

Though easily fooled by Forrest, Streight proved to be a tough customer in Confederate prison. He and others dug their way out of Libby Prison in Richmond. He rejoined the army and was breveted a brigadier general just before he resigned from the service.

MAJOR GENERAL EARL VAN DORN, "THE TERROR OF UGLY HUSBANDS"

Confederate major general Earl Van Dorn died at age forty-two. He had survived a musket ball to the foot at age twenty-seven in the Mexican War. He had survived an arrow in the arm and another in his ribs at age thirty-eight while fighting Comanches in the Indian territory. Early in the Civil War, at age forty, he had survived a fall from his horse into a cold stream. He had survived camp fevers and chills at age forty-one.

The one thing Van Dorn could not survive in his twenty-one-year military career was the husband of a woman he knew too well.

Van Dorn was a Mississippian who won an appointment to West Point, where he graduated fifty-second in a class of fifty-six in 1842. Graduating that far down the roll meant the cavalry. He served eighteen years in Mexico and on the Indian frontier, working his way up to third in command of the Second United States Cavalry before he resigned to become a colonel in the Confederate cavalry. In Texas when the war started, he helped secure Brigadier General David Twiggs's surrender of all United States forces and equipment to the Confederacy.

Though Van Dorn had fought no major battles to prove his value to the Confederacy, he was jumped in rank from colonel to brigadier general in six months, then to major general in nine months. He was given command of the Trans-Mississippi Department, which stretched from west of the Mississippi River to New Mexico.

In Van Dorn's first major battle, Elkhorn Tavern (also called Pea Ridge) on March 7, 1862, he proved that an aggressive officer who likes to personally fight might not make a good army commander. Van Dorn's seventeen thousand men attacked Union major general Samuel Curtis's eleven thousand, who had dug in on Pea Ridge. Van Dorn tried the same tactic Stonewall Jackson would attempt just over a year later, a flank march designed to hit the enemy with a surprise attack. It was repulsed twice before it broke the Federal left. The Federal right also broke, but both flanks were able to fight back to their original positions. The next day, the Federals pushed hard in the belief that Van Dorn's men were running out of ammunition. They were. Van Dorn's army was crushed, and the Trans-Mississippi command was taken from him.

Later that year, Van Dorn was in charge at the Battle of Corinth, Mississippi. With equal forces of around twenty-two thousand men, Confederates and Federals fought to a standstill. Afterwards, Van Dorn claimed that most of his staff generals were incompetent. He relieved two of them. Van Dorn had now failed to win either of his two battles, which was enough for the Confederate war planners. They relieved him of command of the Army of Mississippi and put him in charge of that army's cavalry.

Van Dorn blossomed in this lesser role, which allowed him to personally lead his men. On December 20, 1862, he led a thirty-five-hundred-man cavalry raid on the Union equipment depot at Holly Springs, Mississippi. Van Dorn swept into town while most of the Federals were asleep. He captured more than fifteen hundred prisoners and burned almost all of the Federal supplies, which were being stockpiled for U. S. Grant's attack on Vicksburg. Grant had to delay his massive march on that city for several months thanks to Van Dorn's skill in handling his small command.

For the next five months, Van Dorn rode roughshod over the Union army. His men seemed to raid at will throughout Mississippi. Rightly considered a failure as an army commander, Van Dorn found great success as long as he had someone over him to plan strategy. Freed from administrative duties, he had time on his hands. And he started putting those hands where they did not belong—like on the bodies of other men's wives.

A twenty-four-year-old widow once counseled him, "General, you are older than I am, but let me give you some advice. Let the women alone until after the war is over."

The general answered, "My God, Madam! I cannot do that, for it is all I am fighting for. I hate all men, and were it not for the women, I should not fight at all. Besides, if I accepted your generous advice, I would not now be speaking to you."

A newspaper reporter following Van Dorn's exploits described him as "the terror of ugly husbands and serious pappas."

Van Dorn had been transferred to Spring Hill, Tennessee, by May 1863. There, he made the acquaintance of Jessie Peters, the twenty-five-year-old wife of George Peters, a prominent forty-nine-year-old doctor, real-estate speculator, and slave dealer. The general and the lady first exchanged pleasantries, then notes, then nods at the occasional party, particularly when the good doctor was out of town on business.

At some point, Van Dorn may have become intimate with the lady, although his staff denied it. Regardless, Peters discovered the state of affairs and came to believe the general had "violated the sanctity of his home." One story says the doctor confronted the general at gunpoint and demanded that he sign a statement saying Jessie was innocent of any relationship. The general agreed to write such a statement at his headquarters.

On May 7, 1863, Dr. Peters drove his buggy to Van Dorn's headquarters, walked in, and found the general poring over some papers. Peters later claimed that he demanded the statement and that the general refused to produce it and ordered him to leave. The doctor said he then drew a pistol and fired, intending to hit Van Dorn in the forehead, but that a "convulsive" movement of the general's caused the bullet to enter his head in the left rear. The doctor may have lied about this, as Van Dorn's body was found slumped near a writing table, as if he was busy with his pen when the fatal shot was fired.

The truth of Van Dorn's relationship with Mrs. Peters is still murky. He certainly had a weakness for women, and he was seen flirting with Jessie, but whether he actually dallied with her is unclear. Jessie was capable of cheating. Peters himself said that he had caught his wife with another man on a different occasion, and that the only reason he stayed with her was for the sake of their children. In a strange twist, Peters left Jessie after the assassination but remarried her after the war.

Some writers believe that Van Dorn was the victim of an assassination plot. There is speculation that Dr. and Mrs. Peters were double agents who took the opportunity to kill Van Dorn in exchange for Federal favors. The only evidence of this is that Peters's property was returned to him after the war, and that he did remarry his cheating wife.

The Mexicans, the Indians, the Yankees, and disease could not kill Earl Van Dorn. Most likely, the thing that killed him was what Shakespeare called "the green-eyed monster."

"I WILL TAKE MY DIVISION . . . AND GET THOSE SHOES": HENRY HETH BRINGS ON GETTYSBURG

Confederate Major General Henry Heth must have been a charmer. He certainly was not a student. He graduated from West Point in 1847 at the bottom of his class. Neither was he an outstanding officer in the prewar army. In fourteen years of service, he advanced only two ranks, to captain, while fighting Indians on the frontier.

Still, he had something that appealed to his commanding officers. Even when he blew his first opportunity at independent command and was soundly defeated at Lewisburg, Virginia, early in 1862, Heth kept the confidence of his superiors. President Jefferson Davis once considered promoting Heth from colonel of a Virginia regiment all the way to major general with responsibility for all of Missouri. Heth humbly told Davis he was not ready for such a command. But at Davis's urging, he did accept a brigade under Lieutenant General Edmund Kirby-Smith when Kirby-Smith invaded Kentucky.

Even General Robert E. Lee, a man supposed to be able to spot command talent, saw something in Heth that few others did. Lee had Heth transferred back east and gave him senior brigadier ranking over several officers who chafed at being passed over by this outsider. They need not have bothered complaining to Lee. Tradition has it that Lee referred to all his subordinates by their formal military rank and last name, such as "General Jackson." Lee called only one man by his first name, and that was "Harry" Heth.

Some would call Heth's way with his superiors an easy familiarity. Others might interpret it as a propensity to bootlick.

While Heth was successful in presenting the image of an upstanding officer, he lied to his superiors on one occasion. Another time, he ignored Lee's direct orders, an error in judgment that led to the war's largest battle. But according to Henry Heth, it was not his fault.

In January 1863, when he was commander of the Department of East Tennessee, Heth may have authorized a mass murder.

Eastern Tennessee was a difficult command because many, if not most, residents were Unionists. This mountainous region had little flat land on which to raise the labor-intensive cotton that supported other areas of the South, so slaves were a rare sight. Most residents scratched out a living plowing the hillsides. They saw no need to fight a war of secession when their own lot would little improve. To the people of eastern Tennessee, it was a "rich man's war and a poor man's fight."

Eastern Tennessee was a magnet for Unionists escaping other Southern states. The phrase "going over the mountain" became a popular expression for North Carolinians threatened with Confederate conscription. They climbed over the ridges separating the two states to join the Union army. Such disloyalty to the Southern cause must have irritated a Virginia aristocrat like Heth.

In early January 1863, he learned that a band of men he presumed to be Unionists had broken into a Marshall, North Carolina, storehouse to steal salt. The salt had been supplied by the Confederate government so loyal families could cure meat for the long mountain winters. While in town, the men also broke into the home of Colonel Lawrence Allen, commander of the Sixty-fourth North Carolina Regiment. In fact, some of the men in the raiding party were deserters from the Sixty-fourth. Allen was not home, but his wife and two children, sick with scarlet fever, were. The bedclothes of the children were taken, more out of spite than need.

Allen and his lieutenant colonel, James Keith, were enraged. They immediately left to see Heth in his Knoxville, Tennessee, headquarters. They asked permission to lead a raid into the mountains north of Marshall, a section that shared its name with the creek that ran through it, the Shelton Laurel.

There is speculation that Allen and Keith, professional men with little formal military training, misunderstood what Heth, a professional soldier, told them. According to Allen, who was backed up by two witnesses, Heth was quite clear: "I want no reports from you about your course at Laurel. I do not want to be troubled with any prisoners and the last one of them should be killed."

Allen and Keith took the general at his word. They returned to Shelton Laurel and split the Sixty-fourth into two forces, one sweeping down the valley and the other sweeping up. As they moved, some Confederates stopped off at mountain cabins to demand of the women the whereabouts of their men. Some women were tortured for their answers. As the two columns met, they captured fifteen men and boys, who fought a skirmish with the Confederates before giving up. The captives were told they would be marched to Knoxville and put on trial for stealing the Marshall salt, although it is unclear if any of them admitted being part of the raiding band.

The next day, thirteen prisoners (two had escaped during the night) started marching. They had gone barely more than a mile when Keith halted the column. He herded the prisoners—one age thirteen—into a clearing, where they were unceremoniously shot and buried on the spot. The boy had to be shot several times before he died. The action became known as the Shelton Laurel Massacre.

Though the murdered men were Unionists, Confederate North Carolina was shocked. Governor Zeb Vance vowed to bring Keith and Allen to justice, a promise he was unable to fulfill.

Attention turned to Heth and his orders. As he would do less than six months later in a much bigger affair that also turned on the interpretation of orders, Heth denied responsibility for the Shelton Laurel killings. He claimed he had told Allen and Keith that "those found in regular arms ought not to be treated as enemies [meaning uniformed Union soldiers] and in the event of an engagement with them to take no prisoners as I considered that they had forfeited all such claims." Heth said he "had not used any remarks which would authorize maltreatment of prisoners who had been accepted as such or to women or children." Heth's claim turned on a fine point. He had assumed the Unionists would die on the battlefield but had not meant for captured prisoners to be murdered in cold blood.

It was a standoff. Allen and Keith insisted that Heth had made it clear that they were to take no prisoners under any circumstances. Heth insisted that Allen and Keith, inexperienced in understanding military language, had not understood what he meant.

Heth escaped further scrutiny when the transfer he had applied for in November 1862 came through in February 1863. He was then able to join the Army of Northern Virginia, headed by his old friend and mentor, General Robert E. Lee. Lee even engineered Heth's promotion to major general and gave him a division in A. P. Hill's corps.

Lee did not invade Pennsylvania the last week of June 1863 with one monolithic army. He split his forces into their three corps, which were at times separated by as much as thirty miles. It was easier to move a large army this way, since it could take advantage of the forage and foodstuffs in different parts of the state.

It was also dangerous. If the entire Army of the Potomac, which Lee supposed was still on the south side of the Potomac River, caught up to the Army of Northern Virginia, it could fight each of the South's vastly outnumbered corps in turn. A nervous Lee kept in constant contact with corps commanders James Longstreet, Richard Ewell, and A. P. Hill so he could order them to concentrate at one point when the time came.

It was a spy working for Longstreet who brought word to Lee that the Union army had crossed the river and was in pursuit of the divided Confederate army. Lee was shocked. He had ordered his cavalry under Major General J. E. B. Stuart to keep watch on the Federals and to report the instant they crossed the Potomac. Lee had heard nothing from Stuart in over a week. In fact, he had no idea where Stuart was. All he had was the word of a spy. It would have to do. The three corps of Lee's army started concentrating where the roads they were on led them—a small town called Gettysburg.

Longstreet's spy also told Lee that the Union army was as scattered as the Confederates. That nugget of information gave Lee his battle plan. If he could concentrate his army and hit the unsuspecting Federals as they came up the roads from the south, he could defeat them in pieces. His whole army would overwhelm and smash each Union corps as it came onto the field.

Such a plan required cooperation from his battle-hungry generals. Lee specifically ordered his corps commanders not to bring on "a general engagement" until all three corps were in place at Gettysburg. Those orders were passed down the chain of command to division commanders like Heth, then down to brigade commanders, even down to regimental colonels. Lee wanted his army to remain invisible in the

Pennsylvania woods until it was time to smash forward. Simple orders—if only his generals would abide by them.

The commander of Lee's Third Corps was Ambrose Powell Hill, called Little Powell by his friends but remembered by historians as A. P. Hill, a sickly man who was nevertheless a fighter. When Hill knew he was going into combat, he often doffed his formal military coat and changed to a bright red battle shirt. Normally, Hill could be counted on to follow Lee's orders. But at Gettysburg, he seems to have treated such mandates cavalierly.

Heth was in command of the lead division of Hill's corps. He heard a rumor that Ewell's corps had discovered a supply of shoes in Gettysburg when it had passed through town the previous week. Since many of his men were barefoot, Heth ordered a brigade of North Carolinians into town to see if they could find the shoes. The brigade commander, Brigadier General James Johnston Pettigrew, was more mindful than Heth of Lee's orders. He took his brigade to investigate but pulled back when he saw some blue-coated men in the woods west of town.

Pettigrew reported back to a decidedly peeved Heth, who was angry that Pettigrew had not even exchanged shots with the Federals. Heth took Pettigrew to Hill and asked that he describe again what he had seen. Hill shrugged when he heard Pettigrew's description of the Federal soldiers. "The only force at Gettysburg is cavalry, probably a detachment for observation," said Hill.

Heth then made his fateful comment: "If there is no objection, I will take my division tomorrow and go to Gettysburg and get those shoes."

"No objection in the world," was Hill's incredible reply. Hill must have thought about his vague agreement overnight. The next morning, he gave Heth an admonition: "Do not bring on a general engagement."

Had Heth suggested that a company return to Gettysburg to scout out the story of the shoes, he would probably have obeyed the spirit of Lee's orders not to bring on a general engagement. Instead, he took his entire division, in excess of seventy-five hundred men. That many troops were hard for the Federals to ignore.

The Federals—two cavalry brigades armed with breechloading carbines—did not ignore the gray ranks coming over the rise. Heth's leading brigade, commanded by Brigadier General James Archer, marched straight down the road toward Gettysburg, not even bothering to send scouts or skirmishers in front to see what lay ahead. As the men crested a hill, they came under immediate fire from the dismounted cavalrymen.

The vastly outnumbered—but not outgunned—cavalrymen slapped hard at Heth's men, even capturing Archer. Heth's attack was slowed so much that the leading elements of the Union army's First Corps, attracted by the gunfire, came on the scene at double-quick. Heth's attack was finally slowed to a crawl.

When Lee rode through a mountain pass between Gettysburg and Chambersburg later that morning, he was puzzled to hear gunfire. Who was fighting? He had given precise orders that could not be misinterpreted.

He found Hill at Cashtown, a few miles west of Gettysburg. Lee demanded to know what was happening. A chagrined Hill admitted he did not know anything more than that Heth's division had marched out that morning. Lee was probably stunned to hear *division*.

"In the absence of reports from General Stuart, I am in ignorance of what we have in front of us here. It may be the whole Federal army, or it may be only a detachment. If it is the whole Federal force, we must fight a battle here. If we do not gain a victory, those defiles and gouges which we passed this morning will shelter us from disaster," Lee said to one of his generals.

He rode ahead to Herr's Ridge, where he could see Heth's division regrouping in front of him. In the distance, Federals were still streaming onto the field. Heth rode up and asked Lee if he could attack again. Lee at first refused, repeating that he did not want to bring on a general engagement. He changed his mind when he saw Confederates on the left enveloping the Federals on that front.

Heth was unhorsed in the attack when hit in the head by a shell fragment. His head might have come loose from the rest of his body had he not been wearing a hat appropriated from a Pennsylvania shopkeeper. Since the hat was too big for him, Heth had stuffed several newspapers into the sweatband to make it fit. The folded newspaper absorbed much of the shell fragment's force. After Heth's wounding, his division was taken over by Pettigrew.

The savage fighting went on until dark. The Federals finally broke and retreated to the high ground in back of town. More than eight thousand Confederates—equivalent to a whole division—had been killed, wounded, or captured. Lee would miss those men over the next two days.

Heth, the man who started the Battle of Gettysburg before Lee was ready, would not share much glory for the three-day battle. His division, under Pettigrew, went all the way to the stone wall on July 3 in what history knows as Pickett's Charge, more properly called the Pettigrew-Pickett-Trimble Assault (after the three divisions that took part).

If Lee admonished his old friend "Harry" for bringing on the battle, it was done in a gentle way. Lee did not like to condemn his generals, as evidenced by the way he treated J. E. B. Stuart when the cavalry commander finally arrived on the battlefield. Stuart had left Lee's army blind, an offense that might have resulted in his removal from command or arrest. Lee simply admonished Stuart and ended the dressing down by saying, "Let me ask your help now. We will not discuss this longer. Help me fight these people."

After the war, Heth shifted blame for the premature battle brought on by his search for shoes. He faulted his commander, Hill. Heth speculated that if Stonewall Jackson had been in command of the Third Corps instead of Hill, the battle would have ended differently.

As usual, Henry Heth's mistakes were someone else's fault.

THE CRUISE OF THE FLOATING BROTHEL

Soldiers throughout history have enjoyed the favors of "professional ladies." In doing so, they have run a very real risk of picking up life-threatening health problems. The maladies suffered by soldiers stationed near urban areas during the Civil War included not only the expected dysentery and fevers associated with drinking polluted water, but a wide variety of venereal diseases that came from consorting with "Cyprians," as they were called at the time.

The common soldier was not the only one to suffer pain following in the wake of short-term lust. Most historians believe that Confederate major general Ambrose Powell Hill, the leader of Lee's famed "Light Division" and later a corps commander, suffered from gonorrhea he contracted while a cadet at West Point in 1844. Some historians believe Hill's condition had so deteriorated by 1865 that he would have soon died had he not been killed by Federal soldiers that April.

Harlots were such a problem in Nashville, Tennessee, that Union commanders tried to throw them all out of the city. Nashville was the first Confederate capital to be captured by the Union, falling in February 1862 after Forts Henry and Donelson were taken. The city offered Union soldiers temptations in the form of women and opium, both of which could be found along "Smoky Row." By July 1863, the problem of soldiers infected with venereal disease was so bad that Brigadier General James D. Morgan decided it was within his power to "seize and transport to Louisville all prostitutes found in this City." He called it a "preemptory remedy."

Morgan gave the job of handling the prostitutes to Lieutenant Colonel George Spalding, who took his mission to heart. Spalding went looking for a riverboat that would accommodate all the ladies. He walked down to the Cumberland River wharves and selected the *Idahoe*. Spalding never recorded how he chose the boat, which had been built just three weeks earlier. He didn't even tell the captain of the *Idahoe*, which was contracted to the Federal government to move men and supplies, what his next cargo would be.

The first thing Captain John Newcomb knew about his part in this bold mission was when Colonel Spalding showed up on his gangplank with a hundred hookers in tow. Spalding handed Newcomb a simple order that said he was to take the "passengers" to Louisville, and that he was to allow "none to leave the boat before reaching" that city.

When Newcomb protested that his brand-new boat would get the reputation of being a floating whorehouse, he got no sympathy from the colonel or the general, who pointed out that the *Idahoe* was under contract to the government to haul cargo, and cargo was what he now had.

The *Idahoe* sailed up the Cumberland River on July 9. Along the way, the ladies of the evening came out in the daytime long enough to smash furniture and vandalize the ship's wall paneling in protest at the way they were being treated. Newcomb tried to land at several points along the river but was turned back by guards who were under orders not to let the women set foot on land.

The inability to land did not keep the ladies from lying on the deck. They made the best of a bad situation by waving at men on shore and in rowboats, sometimes taking their dress tops off to make clear what they were selling. Newcomb wrote that he was unable to stop the prostitutes from plying their trade with the civilians along the river and even with his own crew. He counted 111 prostitutes on board, far too many to monitor. Actually, the women did not sell anything to the crew. Everything was on the house.

By July 14, a relieved Newcomb reached Louisville, on the Ohio River. That did not mean his journey was over. Brigadier General Jeremiah T. Boyle, the military governor of Kentucky, did not appreciate General Morgan's gift of the ladies. Boyle refused to let Newcomb land. He ordered him to proceed with his cargo to Cincinnati.

Two days later, armed policemen met Newcomb's ship at the dock at Newport, Kentucky, across the river from Cincinnati. They, too, refused to let the fallen angels off the riverboat.

Newcomb finally was able to get a telegram to Secretary of War Edwin Stanton in Washington asking him what to do. Stanton, an attorney, was quite familiar with loose ladies. He had once defended New York politician Dan Sickles, who had murdered his wife's illicit lover in broad daylight across the street from the White House. This case marked the first time "temporary insanity" was used as a courtroom defense.

Stanton settled the matter of the *Idahoe* quickly and in a manner that would allow him to get at political enemies in Tennessee, like Governor Andrew Johnson. Stanton saw no need for Tennessee hookers to be off-loaded in Ohio. He ordered them back to Nashville and reprimanded Morgan for thinking of the scheme in the first place.

By August 3, the love boat's three-week voyage was over, and the ladies were back at work in Nashville. Brigadier General Robert S. Granger, who had replaced Morgan as military commander of the city, settled on a simple solution to the problems brought by prostitution. He legalized it. The general had the women inspected, licensed, and treated for the diseases of the profession.

It was a full year before Captain Newcomb was paid for feeding the women while they were on board his ship. The *Idahoe* never escaped her label of being a floating whorehouse. She sank in a river accident in 1869.

And Newcomb's crew? It is unknown how many were treated for disease after their three-week encounter. But as long as they were members of his crew, the captain made them wipe the smiles off their faces whenever they reminisced about that strangely satisfying voyage of July 1863.

THE BATTLING BUCK-NAKEDS

No soldiers like to be caught with their pants down on the battlefield, figuratively or literally. It happened in a literal sense several times during the Civil War.

For more than a year and a half, the Federals occupying coastal North Carolina had been keeping their eye on one major objective, the railroad bridge over the Roanoke River at the small town of Weldon. The bridge was the terminus of the Wilmington & Weldon Railroad, one of the longest continuous lines in the state, and the most important. Every cargo of food and ammunition that was off-loaded from blockade runners in Wilmington was put on railroad cars and sent to Weldon. From there, the supplies crossed into Virginia, where they were carried to the army in the field.

The Weldon bridge was one of the most important in the Confederacy, and both sides knew it. If it could be destroyed, the Confederate supply line would be disrupted. If it could be captured and held—an unlikely possibility, since it was deep within the Confederacy—it could be used as a back-door invasion route into Virginia. Even if the bridge could be constantly threatened by the Federals, the Confederates would have to assign troops to protect it. The more Confederates guarding the bridge, the fewer Union soldiers would have to face on other battlefields.

The way to Weldon was well known by the Federals. Going up the Roanoke River was out of the question. It was mined, and there were too many places where the Confederates could stage ambushes. The only alternative was to load men on transports, cruise up the Chowan River from the Atlantic at least as far as the small town of Winton, North Carolina, then march overland the rest of the way. Several expeditions had tried this more than a year earlier.

On July 26, 1863, five regiments of infantry landed at Winton. Instead of marching for Weldon right away, they waited for several regiments of cavalry being sent south on transports from Federal-held Fort Monroe, Virginia. The next day, the cavalry forces, under the command of Colonel Samuel Spear, arrived. Ferried across the Chowan, they rode hard for Weldon.

Confederate scouts had seen all the activity and alerted headquarters in Richmond. Within hours, two regiments were riding the trains south to Weldon. Brigadier General Matt W. Ransom, who happened to have a plantation within a few miles of the Weldon bridge, was ordered south to take command of the situation at a defensive position several miles east of the bridge. His job would be to slow the Federals so other defenses could be thrown up at the bridge.

Ransom was disappointed when he arrived at his station. There was not much to command. The natural point of defense was at a place called Boone's Mill, just east of Ransom's plantation. Behind the millpond, Confederates had dug trenches extending into the swamp on either side, but Ransom had only two cannons and two hundred men of the Twenty-fourth North Carolina Regiment. He ordered them to dig more trenches and be prepared to pull up the bridge in a hurry if the Yankees arrived.

Ransom then rode east to see if he could detect any activity. Riding back, he heard "a great shout" behind him. Charging him were several hundred Federal cavalrymen. Ransom spurred his horse to Boone's Mill. He charged over the bridge and ordered his men to pull up the planks after him.

Almost all of his men were skinny-dipping in the millpond. It was a hot day, and none of them had expected trouble. Nobody made a move to jump out of the water.

An exasperated Ransom started shouting orders for them to throw on their cartridge and cap boxes, grab their muskets, and fill the trenches. There was no time for the soldiers to throw on anything else—like pants, shirts, and shoes.

As the buck-naked men of the Twenty-fourth North Carolina scrambled to their positions, they heard Ransom shouting orders to other regiments. They were puzzled at first. Only a few companies of the Twenty-fourth were stationed at the mill. Then it dawned on them. Ransom was shouting to phantom regiments, and he wanted the Federals to overhear.

His gambit worked. The Federals hesitated before attacking when they heard orders being shouted to what amounted to several thousand enemy soldiers. They might also have been stunned to see two hundred naked men crawling out of a swimming hole in order to shoot at them.

Spear unlimbered six cannons and tried blasting Ransom's men out of their trenches. Ransom and his two cannons responded as best they could. For more than five hours, Spear's cavalrymen tried to find a way around the entrenched nudists of Boone's Mill, but the swamp was too vast. The Federals would have to go over the Confederates.

The Federals almost got lucky. Ransom was standing behind an oak tree when a solid shot from a Union cannon slammed into the trunk and bounced back. Had the tree not been there, what would have been left of Ransom's head could have been mopped up with a towel.

For some unexplained reason, the Federal infantry regiments back at Winton were never brought up to attack. After the Forty-ninth North Carolina arrived to help the Twenty-fourth, Spear began to fear that the Confederates were amassing heavy reenforcements. The cavalrymen retreated toward Winton at nightfall.

Casualties were light on both sides for the five hours of fighting that took place. The Federals lost at least six killed and twenty-five wounded. The Confederates lost only one killed and several wounded.

The significance of the battle was great. Ransom and a few hundred men—counting the reenforcements who arrived late—had protected the bridge against a combined force of more than five thousand Federals. The Federals never even saw the bridge they had traveled so far to capture. Supplies for Lee's army continued to flow for another year and a half over that bridge. There were no more serious attempts by the Federals to capture it, as the strategy settled on destroying the Confederate armies in the field. Had the buck-naked Confederates allowed the Federals to slip past their position, the Civil War might have been over two years sooner.

Ransom returned many times to the scene of his victory. After the war, he put a fence around the tree that had saved his life. He fertilized it and watered it during periods of drought. He called the tree his good friend. Ransom became one of North Carolina's most successful and popular politicians. He spent more than twenty years in the United States Senate.

And the naked heroes of Boone's Mill? They went on to fight the rest of the war wearing their uniforms.

Fighting the Yankees nude was not only done in the Eastern theater. Brigadier General John Hunt Morgan's cavalrymen also fought well in the buff.

On July 2, 1863, Morgan and two thousand cavalrymen began their month-long raid into Indiana and Ohio by crossing the rain-swollen Cumberland River in Kentucky. The muddy, fast-moving river was a half-mile wide in some spots. Anxious to get across before Federal patrols discovered their intent, Morgan's men lashed rafts together and rolled their four precious cannons on board. They piled their gun belts onto the rafts and wrapped them in blankets to keep them dry. Some men found old dugout canoes, which they lashed together with fence rails. Most of the men took off their uniforms to keep them dry and clean. Those who could not swim tied themselves to their horses or grabbed the animals' tails to get across the raging river.

A few dozen men were across when a Federal patrol riding along the shore saw hundreds of men in the river. They started firing, unaware that some Confederates were already ashore. The Federals also did not see an old flatboat edge ashore around a bend. On board were some of Morgan's raiders, including Bennet H. Young. "Those who had clothing on rushed ashore and into line. Those who swam with horses, unwilling to be laggard, not halting to dress, seized their cartridge boxes and guns and dashed upon the enemy. The strange sight of naked men engaging in combat amazed the enemy. The Union pickets didn't know what to think of soldiers fighting as naked as jaybirds," Young wrote.

He was right. As hundreds of naked men started swimming ashore and shooting at them, the amazed Union patrols retreated into the woods.

For the next month, Morgan and his men fought a skirmish a day. Eventually, the command was shattered, and only a few hundred of the two thousand escaped into West Virginia to complete the raid. They escaped by swimming the Ohio River just ahead of a gunboat sent downstream to shell them. This time, all the men who escaped were uniformed. They hadn't found time to take their clothes off.

A BOASTFUL CONFEDERATE GIVES UP CUMBERLAND GAP

Confederate brigadier general John Wesley Frazer may have done the right thing when he surrendered. He may have avoided needless bloodshed in the face of an impossible situation.

Or should he have at least tried to carry through on his own boastful promise? Confederate politicians thought so.

Frazer came a long way home to join the Confederacy that would later reject him. He was serving as a captain in the Washington territory when the war started. Resigning his commission, he headed home, where he was named a lieutenant colonel in an Alabama regiment. Frazer served well during the fall 1862 invasion of Kentucky, well enough that he was promoted to brigadier general in May 1863.

He made his mistake that summer by taking command of four regiments on top of Cumberland Gap, the famous mountain pass between Kentucky and Tennessee. Military thought suggested that anyone holding the high ground had a distinct advantage over those attacking from below. Those on high could see the enemy coming, fire cannons down on the enemy, hide behind rocks, and generally act like a much bigger force. So certain was Frazer of the advantages of holding the high ground that he boastfully promised he could "hold Cumberland Gap for a month under siege."

He was certain, that is, until he came to believe that his twenty-five hundred men had been hung out to dry, offered as sacrificial lambs to buy time for the rest of the Confederate army. Frazer figured he would not be reenforced by the Confederates then forming to lure the Union army into a trap being set up in northern Georgia along Chickamauga Creek. There were already too many Federals between Cumberland Gap and Chickamauga, and now Union major general Ambrose Burnside was in Knoxville marching his twenty-five-thousand-man force toward Cumberland Gap. Burnside could not let Frazer's pesky little force operate in his rear. He would clean it out—but good. Having no intention of dying or sacrificing his men, Frazer surrendered rather than live up to his promise, made on the assumption that reenforcements would come to help him in any battle with the Federals.

Taken prisoner, Frazer was sent to Fort Warren, an old stone fort in

Boston Harbor. He likely expected to spend a few weeks there and come back south.

That did not happen. The Confederate Congress was outraged that Cumberland Gap had been surrendered. The members of that august body, wealthy civilian slave holders who had found ways to avoid field service themselves, expected Frazer to fight to the last man. They wanted Cumberland Gap to be bathed in Southern blood, held to the death like the Greeks had done in ancient times. When Cumberland Gap was surrendered, they revoked Frazer's appointment as general and probably sent word through prison channels that he would not be exchanged. He spent more than two years at Fort Warren, an uncommonly long time for a captured general.

Frazer's two years at Fort Warren were probably pretty comfortable as prison stays go. While most Civil War prisoners on both sides suffered terrible conditions, those sentenced to Fort Warren did not. Only twelve Confederates died at the prison.

During his imprisonment, Frazer may have come to dislike his countrymen for their criticism of him and come to like Yankees for his kind treatment. After the war, he moved to New York City. He stayed there the rest of his life, dying in 1906, long after most of his tormentors. It is not known if he made any promises as a businessman that he could not keep.

THE CHARMED LIFE OF AN ACCIDENT-PRONE GENERAL

General in Chief Ulysses S. Grant was not a blunderer by nature, but he narrowly avoided disaster on so many occasions that he must have felt like he'd stepped out of a *Perils of Pauline* reel. Other than that, for a man who ordered thousands of Federal soldiers to their deaths by marching into the guns of the Confederates, Grant led a pretty safe life.

His biographers all say Grant showed a fascination with horses as a boy. When wagon teams came to his father's leather shop, young Hiram (his real first name) would hold the reins and talk to the horses while their owners went inside the shop. He would stroke them and study their form. He learned to ride early. When Grant was five, his father looked up one day to see the youngster standing on top of a horse and leading it back from a creek, balancing himself with the reins. At West Point, the shy cadet drew horses on a sketch pad when he was not riding them.

Grant started what proved to be a charmed life on the battlefield in 1846. Though he labored behind the lines as a quartermaster during much of the Mexican War, he did make it onto the battlefield, where he won two brevets for his courage. After the war, Grant resigned from the army and tried private business, for which he was not suited. When war flared again in 1861, he returned to the army and secured an appointment as colonel of an Illinois volunteer regiment.

First brought to national attention when his men captured Fort Donelson, Grant continued to rise in the public eye when he saved his army from disaster at Shiloh. It took another year and the capture of Vicksburg to win over his many detractors. Soon given command of all forces in the West, Grant lifted the siege at Chattanooga. By the spring of 1864, he was ready to come east to take care of Robert E. Lee.

It's a wonder Grant lived long enough to fight Lee. On two occasions, he had come close to being killed or paralyzed by the animals he loved.

On the night of April 4, 1862, Grant heard that Confederates had attacked one of his outlying picket posts. He rode out himself in a driving rainstorm to check conditions. On the way back, his horse slipped in the mud and fell. Grant's leg was severely bruised, and his ankle was wrenched. The leg swelled so much so quickly that his boot had to be cut off.

Grant hobbled around on crutches after the accident, but he did not feel any great need to get well quickly, as nothing was happening. "I have scarcely the faintest idea of any attack being made upon us," he wired his boss, General Henry Halleck.

Two days after the accident, the Battle of Shiloh opened when Confederate troops overran Grant's camps in a surprise assault.

The second accident came more than a year and a half later. In September 1863, Grant took a steamboat down the Mississippi to New Orleans to be guest of honor at a banquet Major General Nathaniel Banks was hosting. The trip was uneventful—if you discount the rebel sniping that wounded several people on Grant's boat.

Early on the evening of the party, Grant set out to review some troops. He rode to the review site as hard as he could, taking pleasure in the speed of the nearly unmanageable horse which had been selected for him. He rode so fast that most of the other officers were left in his wake.

After the banquet, Grant and the other officers were riding back to New Orleans when he again took off, leaving his staffers behind. He was riding at full gallop down a road paralleling a railroad track when a locomotive came around the bend and gave a warning whistle. Grant's horse reared, lost its footing, and fell with a crash on the general's left leg. He was knocked unconscious.

Grant was taken to a roadside inn, where he regained consciousness, probably from the pain shooting through his body. His leg swelled from knee to thigh, and his left side was very tender. "The swelling, almost to the point of bursting, extended along the body up to the armpit. The pain was almost beyond endurance. I lay at the hotel something over a week without being able to turn myself in bed," Grant wrote. He would need crutches for more than a month.

While the accident did not kill him, it started anew the rumors that Grant was drinking. One not-so-loyal general even claimed that Grant had been drinking so much that he actually fell off his horse, a claim that has never been considered credible. Many tongues were wagging, but the one that mattered, Lincoln's, never made anything of the accident.

Grant didn't let the accident slow him. When he visited Chattanooga, a Union-held city besieged by Confederates, he had to be lifted into his saddle and taken off like a child. Once, while riding to a river where the Union would later force a crossing in order to get supplies to the city, a party of high-ranking Union generals was startled to find itself in plain view of Confederate pickets on the other side of the river. Instead of taking advantage of the best opportunity they ever had of shooting the general who was defeating them, the Confederates saluted Grant. He returned the salute, then carefully moved out of sight and range.

Grant retook Chattanooga, one of the feats that brought him to Washington in March 1864 to meet President Lincoln and take command of all Union armies. While in town, Grant went to the studio of Mathew Brady to have his photograph taken. All pictures in those days were made with natural light, so studios were outfitted with large skylights. At some point during the preparations for Grant's photograph, one of the photographer's aides was sent to the roof to uncover a shade over one such light. The man stumbled and shattered the skylight, sending dozens of shards of two-inch-thick glass crashing down around the general. Miraculously, none of them hit him. Grant, who had once remarked that he didn't fear death since it would only happen once, didn't even get angry about the accident. Brady later said that Grant's only reaction was to glance up at the sound of the breaking glass, then back down once all the shards had fallen. He patiently sat for the pictures and left unpunctured.

On August 9, 1864, Grant was relaxing at his headquarters at City Point, Virginia, a giant staging area and supply depot on the James River below Petersburg. An aide had just finished warning him that something had to be done about the spies rumored to be hanging around the camp. At that moment, an ammunition barge tethered not far from Grant's headquarters blew up, the work of a Confederate spy who had planted a time bomb containing twelve pounds of gunpowder. On the wharf, more than 40 men were blown to bits and another 126 were wounded. Body parts were found more than a quarter-mile away. Three of Grant's staff were hit by wooden splinters or other debris.

"Such a rain of shot, shell, bullets, pieces of wood, iron bars and bolts, chains and missiles of every kind were never witnessed. It was terrible," wrote one of the general's aides. Grant noted that "every part of the yard used as my headquarters is filled with splinters and fragments of shell."

The spy who planted the bomb did not hint that Grant was a target of the attack. He just saw an opportunity and took it, partly in retaliation for the mine the Federals had used to blow up Confederates at the Crater just ten days earlier.

Grant continued to lead a charmed life despite a faultless ability to get into physical danger. Not long after the war, he was invited to attend a play in Washington. He turned down the offer because he had other business. He returned to the hotel, picked up his wife and children, and left Washington to go to Philadelphia. At midnight, when the Grants finally arrived at their hotel, the general was handed a telegram.

President Lincoln had been shot while attending a play at Ford's Theatre. Had Grant accepted the president's invitation, he would have been in the box. Mrs. Grant later recalled that she had noticed a dark man with a mustache watching her eat in the hotel earlier that day. She had seen the same man as she and the general took a carriage to the train station. Her description fit that of Lincoln assassin John Wilkes Booth.

General Grant had no more accidents as long as he lived. An incessant cigar smoker, he died of throat cancer.

THE BUCKLAND RACES

Major General James Ewell Brown (J. E. B.) Stuart, commander of Confederate cavalry in the Army of Northern Virginia until his death on May 12, 1864, loved banjo music, his children, his wife, innocent flirting with ladies, a good joke, fighting Federals, and hunting.

He was happiest when he could pack all his loves into a single day. At least once, he was able to combine what he called "fox hunting" and a good joke in one battle.

Stuart was born in 1833 on the family estate in Patrick County, Virginia. He was a natural horseman, and there was never any question that he wanted to be a cavalryman when he graduated from West Point in 1854. He spent most of his six years in the regular army on the Kansas frontier fighting Indians. By the time the war started, he was ready to follow his old regimental commander, Robert E. Lee, into Confederate service.

Stuart saw combat at First Manassas, where he frightened Union infantry with his First Virginia Cavalry, the "Black Horse Cavalry." During the Seven Days' Battles on the Virginia peninsula, Lee asked the cavalry for information on the location of McClellan's flanks. Stuart stretched his orders by riding around McClellan's entire army. He lost only one man. Such boldness brought Stuart continual attention. He was named a major general at age twenty-eight in 1862.

For Stuart, boldness was both a strength and a flaw. He frequently ignored orders—he called it "expanding orders"—to go adventuring. The cavalry's duties were to be the eyes of the slow-moving infantry, to scout where the other army's infantry was, and to report that information to the commanding general. When Stuart left on Lee's invasion of Pennsylvania in late June 1863, he neglected those goals. Lee had not heard from Stuart in more than a week and had already fought two days at Gettysburg before Stuart rode into the Confederate camp.

One of the best aspects of Stuart's character was that he kept a sense of humor when everything around him was exploding in war. On August 22, 1862, he raided a railway station at Catlett's Station, Virginia, near the Federal lines, which were building for an attack near the old Manassas battlefield. Stuart hit at Catlett's Station in hopes of retrieving valuable information. By chance, Union major general John Pope's headquarters wagons were there when Stuart struck. In one of the wagons was Pope's dress uniform coat. Stuart grabbed it and rode away. Earlier that month, Federal mounted soldiers on patrol in northern Virginia had surprised Stuart, forcing him to flee without his hat. Stuart now had a prisoner. He sat down and wrote Pope a letter that went, "General: You have my hat and plume. I have your best coat. I have the

honor to propose cartel for a fair exchange of prisoners. Very respectfully, J. E. B. Stuart." Pope, soon to be thrashed by Lee at Second
Manassas and relieved of command, did not appreciate the humor.

Another time, Stuart captured a Federal wagon train and a telegraph
station. He sent a message directly to Abraham Lincoln: "The last draw
of wagons I've just made are very good, but the mules are inferior quality, scarcely able to haul off empty wagons. If you expect me to give
your lines any further attention in this quarter, you should furnish better stock."

In an engagement near Warrenton, Virginia, on October 19, 1863,
Stuart was able to capture more than two hundred Federal cavalrymen
and kill around a hundred by playing a military joke on them.

By then, the Federal cavalry had finally caught up with the Confederates in tactics and quality of horses and riders. For the first two years
of the war, the Confederates, mostly young men familiar with horses
from their life on farms and plantations, had run rings around the
Federals, many of whom were from the urban Northeast. Time and training had finally begun to pay off for the Federals. Now, they were more
often besting the Confederates, who were beginning to feel the strain of
too many battles.

On October 14, Lee was withdrawing his army after a disastrous engagement at Bristoe Station. Thanks to the rashness of Major General
A. P. Hill, who thought he was pursuing a Union force in full retreat,
two brigades had been cut down when an entire Union corps waiting in
ambush rose up from behind a stone wall and fired into Hill's unsuspecting men. Lee was now going back the way he had come. He needed
Stuart's cavalry to cover the retreat.

Federal cavalry, which had beaten Stuart back in June at Brandy Station, was now following Lee's army. Stuart and a supporting column under
Lee's nephew, Major General Fitzhugh Lee, were trailing the infantry
and trying to think of a way to trap the Federals into a stand-up fight.

As Stuart spent the night at Buckland Mills, an idea slowly formed.
He knew the Federals were aware of his division, but he was fairly certain they were unaware of Fitz Lee's men, who were some miles away. If

Stuart could get Fitz Lee's help, he might be able to defeat the Federals by using his own men as bait to attract the Federals into a trap set by Lee.

The next morning, the Federals caught up with Stuart at the creek where he was camped. As a skirmish was raging, a courier arrived from Fitz Lee with a message that suggested something along the same lines Stuart had been thinking. If Stuart could hold the Federals for a while, Lee would find a likely ambush site down the Warrenton Pike. Stuart would then abandon his position and ride in a fake panic down the road with the Federals in pursuit. Once Stuart had ridden past Lee's hidden position, Lee would fire on the Federals, Stuart would reverse his flight, and the Federals would find themselves in a fight for their lives.

Stuart purposely left the bridge over Broad Run Creek standing as he limbered his cannons and sent them speeding down the road. There was no need for the Yankees to get their feet wet, and besides, making them ford the creek would slow down their pursuit. Stuart then had all his troopers ride as hard as they could, as if they were frightened of their fate if the Yankees caught them.

The plan worked as expected. The leading Federal division was headed by Major General Judson Kilpatrick, with Brigadier General George Armstrong Custer's brigade showing the way. The Union army did not have two more reckless, impulsive men in its service. Both Union generals were flamboyant. Custer liked to wear flaming red bandannas, and Kilpatrick affected huge muttonchop whiskers that flew in the wind.

For five miles, the jubilant Federals chased the hard-riding Confederates. Their focus was on the cloud of dust and the fleeing men in front of them. Not a single Union trooper noticed that the woods were getting thicker beside the road. None suspected he was riding to his death, wounding, or capture.

Two miles short of Warrenton at a place called Chesnut Hill, the Federals were surprised to hear, see, and feel the explosion of artillery shells in their ranks. There were cannons in the woods. Confederate cannons. Up ahead, Stuart's cavalrymen were braking their horses and wheeling them.

A Federal officer described what happened rather dryly: "Stuart, who had hitherto retired before us quietly, now turned about and advanced upon us with terrible determination. Scarcely had we time to recover our sense from the first shock of attack upon our rear and front, when General Gordon [James Gordon of North Carolina], with a third division of cavalry, until now concealed behind a low range of hills and woods on our left, appeared with a furious attack, which threatened to sever our two small brigades."

There was nothing for the Federals to do but turn around and ride for their lives. Some plunged their horses into a rain-swollen creek, where many men and horses drowned. Those who stayed on the road took off over the same five miles they had just ridden. All along the way, Stuart's laughing troopers made sport of pulling Federals from their horses and dumping them on the ground. While this was preferable to being shot, it didn't make the humiliation of riding into Stuart and Lee's trap much more palatable.

Both Custer and Kilpatrick escaped. While Custer would improve as an officer—at least until he caught up with several thousand Indians in the next decade—Kilpatrick would habitually find himself surprised by Confederate cavalry.

Stuart could not contain his laughter when he caught up with General Robert E. Lee to report on "the Buckland Races." Stuart said the battle reminded his boys of the fox hunts they used to enjoy before the war. Things had not been going well for the Confederacy since the summer defeat at Gettysburg, so any humorous diversion was appreciated.

Neither could Stuart help teasing the Federals in his official report: "It is remarkable that Kilpatrick's division seems to disappear from the field of operations for more than a month, that time being necessary, no doubt, to collect the panic-stricken fugitives."

It had been a good week for Stuart and his cavalry. He had captured more than fourteen hundred Federals, killed several hundred, and lost a total of only four hundred men himself. What Stuart did not know was that the Buckland Races was the last major victory he would score against the Federals. He was mortally wounded less than eight months later when a Federal cavalry raid led by Major General Phil Sheridan caught the Confederate cavalry leader and his command near Richmond at a place called Yellow Tavern. Brigadier General James Gordon, Stuart's subordinate, died less than a week later in the same Union cavalry sweep around the Confederate capital. Fitz Lee was wounded so badly at Third Winchester in September 1864 that he remained out of uniform most of the rest of the war.

Though the Confederate cavalry found itself on the wane after the Buckland Races, that battle brought laughter to Confederate campfires for the remainder of the war. Confederate cavalry veterans told and re-told the story at reunions for years to come. Union cavalry veterans never saw the humor in it.

THE BLOODIEST DRESS PARADE

What was Major General U. S. Grant to do? Court-martial officers who could not stop their men? Imprison the men—all twenty-five thousand of them—for ignoring their officers? Or congratulate both officers and men for turning a simple "demonstration" into a major victory that changed the fortunes of the Union army?

By late November 1863, Grant had finally broken the Confederate siege of the Federal troops trapped in Chattanooga, Tennessee. He had retaken the town but now found himself in a valley with the Confederates holding the high ground in front of him on Missionary Ridge. In the Confederate center, in plain sight on the top of Missionary Ridge, was General Braxton Bragg's headquarters.

On November 23, Grant was ready to feel out Bragg's lines. He ordered a "reconnaissance" in front of Bragg's forces at Orchard Knob, a small hill in front of the main Confederate line on Missionary Ridge.

This reconnaissance was nothing short of a spectacle. There was no tree cover on the plain before Orchard Knob. The ground was virtually flat, like a mile-wide parade ground. The Federal soldiers had no cover under which to prepare their lines for the charge, so no attempt was made to hide their assembly. Regiment lined up on regiment, brigade on brigade. For most of the men and officers, it was the largest assembly of troops in one spot they had ever seen. "It was an inspiring sight. Flags were flying, the quick, earnest steps of thousands beat equal time. The sharp commands of hundreds of company officers, the sound of drums, the ringing notes of the bugles, companies wheeling and countermarching and regiments getting into line—all looked like preparations for a peaceful pageant, rather than the bloody work of death," wrote one Federal lieutenant colonel.

The Confederates on Missionary Ridge and Orchard Knob thought it was a parade. Bragg, watching through binoculars from his headquarters, declared that it was probably a dress parade in honor of Grant's arrival in Chattanooga. Dozens of Confederates leaned their rifles against trees and walked forward to get a look at the sea of bluecoats marching to and fro.

Bragg, his officers, and the rest of the Army of Tennessee went bug-eyed at one-thirty that afternoon when the parade started marching at double-quick for Orchard Knob. This was no dress parade. This was an all-out attack by five divisions of Federal veterans of Chickamauga out to prove something.

The Confederate pickets were so astonished that they stood in their tracks before it sunk in that this blue wave of humanity was heading their way. The first line of rifle pits got off only one volley before the first of the Federals reached and captured them. The cannons on Missionary Ridge were not much help. The gunners there, too, were surprised by the sudden attack. Orchard Knob, a fine little area of raised land from which to observe Missionary Ridge, was captured.

Two days later, on November 25, Grant was ready to take on Bragg again. Mindful of the more than one hundred cannons he knew were near the center of Missionary Ridge, Grant expected Major General William T. Sherman on the left and Major General Joseph Hooker on the right to push up both flanks. Those plans failed. Sherman ran into Confederate major general Patrick Cleburne's men, who refused to budge an inch. Hooker, too, was delayed. Sherman finally asked that Grant order an attack on the Confederate center in hopes that Bragg would pull some troops from Cleburne.

Grant was reluctant to do that. The twenty-five thousand men he had in the center were from the Army of the Cumberland, the same men who had been chewed up so badly at Chickamauga two months earlier and who had just been relieved from the siege. He didn't think they were up to attacking. He also didn't think Major General George Thomas, their commander, was up to it. He did not like or really trust Thomas, a Virginian who had stayed loyal to the Union. It didn't matter that Thomas was "the Rock of Chickamauga," the man who had covered the retreat of the Army of the Cumberland from Chickamauga to prove his loyalty.

Still, Grant knew he had to do something to help Sherman, who had been repeatedly repulsed on the rocky slopes of Tunnel Hill, several miles to the north. The terrain was so steep in that direction that Sherman's men were constantly dodging boulders dislodged by playful Confederates.

Grant turned to Thomas and asked if he wanted to attack the rifle pits at the base of Missionary Ridge, a mile past Orchard Knob. Thomas acted as if he did not hear. He wanted Grant to specifically order him to make the charge. He didn't like Grant any more than Grant liked him. Grant finally did order the movement.

The Confederates appeared surprised at the Federal attack, as they had been two days earlier at Orchard Knob. They finally started firing their cannons, but by marching rapidly, the Federals gained the base of Missionary Ridge within minutes. The Confederate cannons could not be depressed enough to fire on the base of the ridge.

Grant had ordered that the rifle pits be taken. They were, but the Federal soldiers ignored their officers' orders to stay in the pits and kept climbing Missionary Ridge, chasing Confederates who scrambled up ahead of them. Realizing no one was listening to them, the officers started clambering up the slope after the men they were supposed to be leading.

Puzzled, Grant watched his army climb away from him. He turned to Thomas. "Thomas, did you order those men up that slope?"

"No, I did not," Thomas answered, as surprised as Grant.

Grant turned to Major General Gordon Granger, who also denied giving any order. Granger came close to being insolent, however, adding, "When those fellows get started, all hell can't stop them."

Granger probably wished he hadn't said that when Grant replied that if the unauthorized charge failed, someone would suffer the consequences. What worried Grant was the unknown. If Bragg met those men at the top of Missionary Ridge with canister-loaded cannons, they would come streaming back down and there would be no reserves to hold back a Confederate counterattack.

Had that happened, Grant would probably have had to deal harshly with Major General Phil Sheridan, who was in the thick of the fighting. When he was almost to the top of Missionary Ridge, Sheridan impulsively saluted a battery of Confederate guns with a silver flask before taking a long drink. When the cannons fired, narrowly missing him, an angry Sheridan declared, "That is ungenerous! I will take those guns for that!"

In a few minutes, he did. Sheridan leaped astride a captured Confederate cannon still hot from firing. The little general twirled his cap in glee as he rode the gun like a horse. Brigadier General Charles Harker, one of Sheridan's brigade commanders, figured what was goofy enough for Sheridan was goofy enough for him. He, too, leaped astride one of the just-captured cannons but was instantly sorry he had. Harker's cannon must have seen more action than Sheridan's. Harker's buttocks were burned so badly that he couldn't sit in the saddle of his horse for two weeks.

Grant couldn't believe his eyes. He had ordered nothing more than a simple charge on some gun pits at the base of Missionary Ridge. Instead, his men had captured the fortified center of the Confederate line and almost taken two Confederate generals, Bragg and John C. Breckinridge. In two days, the Federals had captured more than four thousand Confederate soldiers and forty-one cannons, a third of the guns that had frightened Grant so much just a few hours earlier. The Confederate army was running in disarray.

Granger, the Union general who had come close to insubordination with Grant, rode his horse up to Missionary Ridge and playfully shouted to the soldiers that they would soon be court-martialed for disobeying orders.

Bragg blamed the defeat on his men, claiming they had run. He took no responsibility for the placement of his troops or guns, which had not been located in positions that allowed them a full range of fire on the Federals climbing up to them.

Bragg abandoned hope of retaking Chattanooga, and the Army of Tennessee moved into Georgia. Grant would soon head east to take command of all Union armies. Sherman would take over for Grant in the West. From Chattanooga, he would march south toward Atlanta.

The sudden change in Federal fortunes all started with a nice dress parade.

1864

"We have five times *as*

many generals here as we

want, but are greatly in

need of privates. Anyone

volunteering in that capacity

will be thankfully received."

–HENRY HALLECK
AS JUBAL EARLY'S TROOPS MARCH
TOWARD WASHINGTON

STALE AIR AND ELBOW GREASE:
THE ATTACK OF THE CSS *HUNLEY*

The *Hunley* showed just how desperate and inventive the Confederates could be in fighting the wealthier, better-equipped Federals. It was late 1863 when the growing effectiveness of the Union blockade finally forced Confederate officials to realize they had to do more than just build blockade runners that could outrun Federal ships. They needed something that would sink Federal ships. Building huge, expensive, terrifying ironclads like the *Tennessee*, the *Albemarle*, and the *Manassas* was one way to do that. Building small, inexpensive, almost-invisible submersibles was another.

The latter was the idea of Horace L. Hunley, a forty-year-old lawyer and bureaucrat who was living in New Orleans when the war started. By March 1862, he and several mechanical engineers and investors constructed the *Pioneer*, a stubby, hand-cranked submarine. They planned to collect bounties as privateers, sinking Federal blockaders and collecting money from the Confederate government for each ship sunk. The Union's sudden capture of New Orleans killed plans for that submarine. Hunley sank the *Pioneer* himself, successfully hiding her existence from the Federals.

Fleeing to Mobile, Alabama, Hunley and his partners designed a second submarine, the *American Diver*, which foundered during testing but provided her inventors with ideas they could use in a third effort. Their next submarine, eventually named after Hunley, started as a twenty-five-foot-long boiler. The builders added stabilizing fins, diving planes, and a propeller powered by a hand crank running down the middle of the boiler. On top, they added two hatches, one fore and one aft. Later, they attached a long wooden spar to the bow. From the end of the spar dangled the *Hunley's* only weapon, a waterproofed keg containing ninety pounds of black powder.

The key to success for the submarine would lie in staying below the surface of the water, unseen by the lookouts aboard its targets. The crew would remain on the surface until the *Hunley* got close to the target, get a final bearing, close the hatches, fill the ballast holds, submerge, and crank to the target. The men would either ram a wooden ship or place the torpedo under her keel, reverse the propeller to back away a safe distance, then pull a lanyard to set off a percussion cap.

The *Hunley* intrigued General P. G. T. Beauregard, who believed in the concept so much that he had the submarine shipped by rail to Charleston, South Carolina, to help in breaking the blockade. The engineering behind the boat was ingenious for the time. The boat was equipped with seacocks to let in water for ballast to sink the boat and pumps to remove it so the submarine could rise back to the surface. Even slight changes in the angles of her diving fins changed her ascent or descent. A mercury gauge registered depth, which would preferably be only a few feet under the surface—just enough to avoid detection. The power came from brawny, nerveless volunteers who sat on a bench and cranked the propeller.

The placement of the crew may have been one design flaw. While the final plans have not been found, drawings indicate that all the men sat on the same bench. If true, that would have required a ballast tank on the other side to balance their weight. The submarine may have been carrying more water than necessary to keep her on an even keel, unnecessary weight that would have tired the crew. Accidents showed that the hatch cylinders were too short. Heavy waves could sweep over them. And the method of determining oxygen levels was nothing more than a lit candle. Once it went out, the sub's commander knew his supply of oxygen was gone.

A string of disasters began upon the submarine's arrival in Charleston. The crew jumped in and started heading toward the blockading squadron on its first cruise. Before the hatch was closed, a swell poured water into the crew compartment. The sub sank like a rock. Only the commander, who had left the hatch open, and two others escaped. The rest of the men sitting in the cramped quarters could not pull themselves out from under the hand crank.

Hunley and Lieutenant George Dixon were brought up from Mobile to master the vessel. They worked on the *Hunley* until they declared her problems solved. The next time the submarine went out, Hunley was at the helm. Unfamiliar with piloting the submarine, he dove her too fast by allowing too much water into the ballast tanks. He apparently forgot that he had control of the seacock and thus never closed it. The compartment flooded, and all the crew—including the submarine's namesake—were killed. It took nearly a week to raise the *Hunley*.

And there may have been more. Some historians claim there were a couple of other training accidents that claimed more crews. Beauregard was reluctant to continue backing the *Hunley*, but Lieutenant Dixon insisted that she could be a valuable weapon. He pointed out that previous crews had been lost because of human error, not any design flaw. Dixon himself took command, determined not to let his friend Hunley and those other crew members die in vain.

Dixon and some amazing men—a crew recruited knowing that their friends had drowned in a dark, dank, cramped boiler—labored to make the submarine work. Learning from the other accidents, Dixon perfected the submarine. Once, to determine how long the submarine could stay submerged, he and the crew stayed on the bottom of a shallow creek for more than two hours. By the time the sub surfaced, she had been down so long that guards assumed yet another crew had drowned. After several successful training runs, Dixon was convinced it was time to go to war.

The USS *Housatonic*, a twelve-hundred-ton sloop of war mounting thirteen cannons, was the target of choice, probably because her station lay closest to the *Hunley's* base on Sullivan's Island. On the night of February 17, 1864, the crew cranked into Charleston Harbor toward the target, which lay more than four miles away. The *Hunley* probably stayed on the surface with the hatches open as long as possible. The moon was a quarter full, providing just enough light to navigate but little enough to make objects on—and under—the water difficult to see.

Just before nine o'clock, a lookout on the *Housatonic* reported something in the water. At first, it seemed to be a plank of wood. But then it was seen to be moving toward the ship. All hands were called to stations, but it was too late to get under way and too late to fire on the object. An explosion shook the ship, partially from the torpedo but mostly from the *Housatonic's* magazine, which was set off by the torpedo. Whether by chance or aim, the *Hunley* had placed her charge right where it would do the most harm. The *Housatonic* went down immediately, but only 5 men of her 160-man crew lost their lives. Most of the rest grabbed onto loose lines or climbed into the rigging. The shallow harbor allowed the ship to settle with her sails still flying in the air.

At least one Union seaman perched in the rigging reported seeing a small vessel lying at an angle off the starboard side. It could only have been the *Hunley*. She had survived the concussion and must have surfaced to survey the damage. That seaman in the rigging proved to be the last person to ever see the submarine afloat.

What happened to the *Hunley* has been debated for more than 130 years. Historians of the time assumed she became lodged in her prey and went to the bottom with the *Housatonic*. But searches carried out later did not find her near the Union ship. Most historians now believe something happened on her way back. A Confederate sentry on Sullivan's Island said he saw a light on the water, a prearranged signal from the submarine for a bonfire to be lit so she could find her way home. The bonfire was indeed lit, but the submarine never returned.

The theories have narrowed to a few possibilities. The submarine may have developed a slow leak from rivets popped by the concussion.

She may have been swamped when the captain opened the hatches for fresh air. Another tantalizing theory is that she may have been accidentally run down by a Union ship rushing to help the *Housatonic*.

The truth may be known in the near future. In 1994, a team headed by Clive Cussler, a novelist whose hobby is finding lost ships, undertook the discovery of the *Hunley*. Using sophisticated electronic equipment, members of the team located something that matched the submarine's length on the bottom of Charleston Harbor not far from the *Housatonic*. They dove on the spot and dug away enough silt to find one closed hatch cover and some glass portholes, a description that matched the submarine.

Using what clues he had, Cussler wrote a fictionalized account of the last moments of the submarine. He speculated that the *Hunley* was run down by a rescuing ship which buckled the submarine's iron plates, filling her with water within seconds. The *Hunley* would have been so buoyant and the rescuing ship in such a hurry to reach the *Housatonic* that such a collision might have gone unnoticed by the rescuing ship's crew.

Plans are under way to raise and preserve the submarine. Once that is accomplished, researchers will look for signs of a collision or loose rivets to solve the mystery of why she sank. Historians are anxious to see what the submarine really looks like. Photos of the sunken wreck suggest that the *Hunley* may have been more bullet-shaped than previously thought.

When the submarine is raised, there will be a delicate issue to resolve. The bones of nine men may be inside. Once the crew is recovered, the spirits of the last of Horace L. Hunley's brave men will finally be at rest. It will be fitting if these last men are buried beside their comrades in Charleston's Magnolia Cemetery—specifically, that part of the cemetery called "the Hunley Circle." When Hunley's wealthy family learned of his death, and further learned that his crews were volunteers, it paid for the burial plots of all of the men.

Hunley died in his invention, as did at least twenty-one other men. Strictly speaking, they were failures, but their sacrifice led to the design of more efficient submarines that helped win two world wars.

"Crazy Bet" and the Spies in Richmond

Both sides set up elaborate spy networks during the Civil War. There was a Confederate saying that anything mentioned in Washington would be heard in Richmond within twenty-four hours. Though details are tantalizingly few, the same might have been said about leaks heading from Richmond to Washington. The Confederates had dozens of spies in Washington, but they probably saw few documents firsthand. Most of what they passed on were rumors and secondhand information. The Union had a much better system. It placed at least two spies in the Confederate White House.

One of them was William Jackson, a coachman for President Jefferson Davis. What he heard and what he was able to report has been lost to history, but it is known that he had occasional contact with Union agents operating in Richmond.

Someone who might have done more damage was Mary Elizabeth Bowser, a black house servant in the Confederate White House. Bowser's direct contributions remain shrouded in mystery, but it is known that once she gained the trust of Jefferson and Varina Davis, she had free run of the house to pick up after the president's meetings. Jefferson Davis probably felt free to speak his mind around her and to leave important documents on the table. After all, Bowser was a slave in a slave state. He assumed she couldn't read.

She could. Bowser had been educated in a Northern school. She trained herself to scan Davis's desk and memorize important information, which she later wrote on bits of paper to be passed to outside contacts.

Perhaps the most noteworthy spy in Richmond was Elizabeth Van Lew, a forty-something spinster known as "Crazy Bet" to her neighbors. Van Lew liked to dress in bizarre fashions and loudly proclaim her love of the Union. She intentionally kept her hair and clothes unkempt and talked to herself out loud when she knew others were looking, all in order to emphasize her "craziness." She believed that if her Confederate neighbors figured her to be loony because of her Unionist activities, they would never suspect her of actually spying. The plan worked.

Richmonders knew Crazy Bet was all for the Union. She even made a bed for Major General George McClellan to use when he captured Richmond in early summer 1862. When Lee turned McClellan back during the Seven Days' Battles, she left the bed made up and told her neighbors McClellan or some other Union general would be coming back one day.

Van Lew hated slavery. She made her feelings known in her journal, writing, "Slave power is arrogant, is jealous, and intrusive, is cruel, is despotic, not only over the slave, but over the community." She freed her family's slaves when her father died and made it a point to track down the relatives of her former slaves, buy them, and set them free also.

Still, knowing slaves had its advantages. It was Van Lew who placed Mary Elizabeth Bowser in the Davis White House. Why Varina Davis accepted a recommendation from an avowed, if slightly daft, Unionist who freed her own slaves is unknown, but it happened.

Van Lew's spy network around Richmond was so extensive that she sent regular dispatches to nearby Union forces at least three times a week. Her couriers were so adept at eluding capture that none of her reports was ever intercepted, something that could not be said of famed Confederate spy Rose Greenhow, who was captured within days of starting her career. That is not to say the Confederates didn't eventually suspect Van Lew of spying. They just could never catch her at it.

Van Lew later became even more bold in her Unionist activities. She began visiting Federal officers in Libby Prison. Oddly enough, whenever any of those prisoners happened to escape, chances are they would never be seen again. Rumors were that the Van Lew mansion had secret passages and hiding places. One suspecting hiding place was the thick, hollow, open porch ceiling stretching over the front entrance.

The quality of Van Lew's information was considered very good by the Union. The man who headed the Bureau of Military Information credited her with being "all that is left of the power of the United States government inside Richmond." Late in the war, Grant was receiving messages from Van Lew and flowers cut from her garden daily.

Though a thorough spy, Van Lew probably never passed along any critical news, such as alerting the Union command to out-of-town trips by President Davis or the precise movements of troops in distant theaters. Most of her information dealt with the disposition of troops around Richmond and Petersburg, the strength of the region's forts, and how much food was left in the cities. The bulk of her contributions came in the last year of the war, when the tide had already turned for the Union.

Although never proven, there is speculation that Van Lew was the Richmond contact for the Kilpatrick-Dahlgren Raid in 1864. Union colonel Ulric Dahlgren was killed when his small band of cavalrymen was caught after trying to ride into the city. On his body were papers that vaguely described the raid's goal of killing the Confederate president and his cabinet. If the raid had been successful, Van Lew might have been suspected of being part of an assassination plot. Had that happened, she probably would have been executed as a spy. To be fair to Van Lew, it must be noted that the authenticity of the papers was never confirmed. The Union denied the existence of an assassination plot and charged Confederates with forging the papers.

One of the riskier acts Van Lew and her Richmond ring performed was to dig up the body of young Dahlgren and send it north to his father, Admiral John Dahlgren. Van Lew was not afraid of death, dying, and the bloody business of war in general. In her journal, she described in detail how Dahlgren's body had deteriorated, even mentioning that it had sprouted some mold.

Though they might not have liked her, the citizens of Richmond accepted Crazy Bet for who she appeared to be, a cranky old Unionist who would not be happy until the Stars and Stripes flew over Richmond again. And that is just what happened. When Richmond fell, Elizabeth Van Lew was the first person in the city to fly her American flag. When a crowd gathered to complain, she shouted that she knew them all and that she would make sure the Union army retaliated against them if something happened to her or her family.

After the war, Van Lew was rewarded for her service by being named postmistress of the city, a gift from a grateful Ulysses S. Grant. She lived until 1900. Though her neighbors never forgave her once they found out she was a real spy and not a crazy woman, she lived out her life in Richmond. She is buried there.

"COMMISSARY" BANKS AND THE RED RIVER CAMPAIGN

Nathaniel Prentice Banks was a prime example of how a hard-working, self-educated man could become a success. Born into poverty, he was forced to work as a child in Massachusetts textile mills. Without wealthy parents, an expensive education, and the political connections that come with such advantages, Banks steadily rose in politics to become a United States congressman, Speaker of the House, and governor of Massachusetts.

When the war started, Banks hoped to build a battlefield reputation that might carry him to the highest office in the land. Instead, he became one of the Union's most incompetent generals, a favorite of Confederate soldiers for always providing them fresh supplies, and an embarrassing danger to Union men because he killed hundreds of them in poorly planned assaults.

Banks's crowning fiasco would come in the Red River Campaign of March 1864, a campaign noted not for brilliant maneuvers but for nature's assault on the Union navy.

Banks, a career politician with no military training, never should have been appointed major general of volunteers at the start of the war, but Lincoln felt he had little choice. The president had asked for seventy-five thousand volunteers. When the governor of Massachusetts offered to be one of them and to raise troops and equipment, he could not be turned down.

Banks did more than get his feet wet in learning how to be a general.

He fell in up to his armpits. During May and June 1862, he battled crafty Confederate major general Stonewall Jackson in the Shenandoah Valley of Virginia. Actually, *battled* is too charitable a term. Jackson ran rings around Banks, sending the Federal soldiers into an uncontrolled panic at the First Battle of Winchester in May 1862. Banks left behind so much Federal equipment that the Confederates called him "Commissary" Banks.

Lincoln felt uneasy at how badly Banks was beaten by Jackson's rag-tag little army. Still, Banks was a politician who wielded considerable influence in Washington, so he was not replaced. Two months later, Banks got a measure of revenge on Jackson at the only battle in which he could *almost* claim victory. This was the Battle of Cedar Mountain, Virginia, on August 9, 1862, when Jackson rushed in to attack without knowing much about the ground or his opponent. Banks was able to counterattack and crush the Confederate left. Jackson personally had to rally his troops. When he did, the Confederates charged back and pushed the Federals from the field. Banks thus lost another battle, but at least he could—however briefly—lay claim to being competent.

Later that year, Banks was transferred to New Orleans to relieve another political general, Major General Ben Butler. Before Banks even unloaded his troops in New Orleans, he sent some of them upriver to recapture Baton Rouge, which Butler had abandoned. It was then that Banks started studying Port Hudson, a Confederate stronghold on the Mississippi twenty-five miles above Baton Rouge reportedly reenforced with heavy guns and twelve thousand troops. With a long-range assignment of helping U. S. Grant capture Vicksburg, Banks knew his first task would be to take Port Hudson. It would be a pleasure, since it would erase the stain of being a loser.

Banks besieged Port Hudson in June 1863. Once, he stopped firing long enough to offer the Confederates a chance to surrender before they would suffer "unnecessary slaughter." When the Confederate commander refused, Banks mounted a full-scale assault. At the end of the attack, he counted nearly eighteen hundred killed, wounded, and missing. The Confederates lost forty-seven. It was slaughter, but not the way Banks intended.

Some of the Federals killed themselves when they failed to correctly use a new weapon under experimentation. Hand grenades were then as now small, hand-thrown bombs. The 173rd New York first fused them too long, then failed to react quickly when the Confederates developed what may have been the first recorded use of the "beach-blanket toss." Confederate lieutenant Howard C. Wright described what happened:

> When these novel missiles commenced falling among the Arkansas troops, they did not know what to make of them, and the first few which they caught and not having burst, they threw them back upon the enemy in the ditch. This time many of them exploded and their character was at once revealed to our men. Always equal to any emergency, they quickly devised a scheme by which they turned this new style of warfare against the parties who introduced it. Spreading blankets behind the parapet, the grenades fell harmlessly into them, whereupon our boys would pick them up and hurling them with much greater force down into the moat they would almost invariably explode.

Over the month, Banks lost more than 4,000 men out of his 30,000. That did not count another 4,000 felled by disease and sunstroke during operations along the sweltering Mississippi. The Confederates, protected by a hundred-foot cliff on the river and extensive earthworks and obstacles on the land side, lost fewer than 650 of the 7,000-man garrison at Port Hudson.

Banks finally decided that there would be no more attacks; besieging would have to do. In the end, the Confederates surrendered on July 7 when Banks sent them proof that Vicksburg, a hundred miles north along the river, had surrendered on July 4. Banks had finally won a victory. He even won the "Thanks of Congress," but that was hardly the glory he needed for his future political career.

It was nearly a year later that Banks embarked on a campaign he hoped would make him president. The basic idea was to go up Louisiana's Red River with a combined navy and army force to capture Shreveport. The strategy was to capture control of western Louisiana and eastern Texas, prime cotton-growing country. Capturing and then "protecting" the cotton land would guarantee the growers that their crops would not be destroyed, but would be bought by Northern mills. Instead of being hostile to the Union invaders, the cotton growers would renounce their Confederate leanings in order to sell their crops.

Banks loved the idea. It would ingratiate the mill owners back home in Massachusetts to him. As every national politician knows, it never hurts to have wealthy businessmen on your side. And this plan came right from the top. President Lincoln was thinking forward to the 1864 presidential elections and prematurely counting the electoral votes of Louisiana, Arkansas, and maybe Texas if those states could be brought back into the Union with puppet governments under his control.

Military men did not like the Red River Campaign one bit. Grant did not see the point. He thought the next big objective should be the capture of Mobile Bay, an important blockade-running port, not a little inland river town like Shreveport. Admiral David Porter did not like the idea either. Commander of the naval forces to be used, Porter was nervous about taking his twelve ironclads and two gunboats so far up an unfamiliar, twisting, small river dominated by high banks on both sides. Those banks could hide Confederate artillery that the Federal ships' guns could not be raised to meet. Porter's worst nightmare was imagining what would happen if spring rains did not come and the river started falling. His whole fleet could ground in the middle of Confederate territory. He checked the history of the river and found that on at least two previous occasions, on nine-year cycles, spring rains had not come and the Red River had fallen. Spring 1864 marked the close of another nine-year cycle.

Still, Banks pushed on, with Porter following on the river. At Mansfield, Louisiana, Confederates under Major General Richard Taylor, the son of former United States president Zachary Taylor, made a stand and routed Banks's men. Suddenly, the entire expedition to Shreveport was in retreat. It was like the Shenandoah Valley two years earlier—Banks's men ran so fast for the rear that they left all manner of equipment behind. Taylor captured more than twenty cannons and two hundred wagons. The next day, Taylor pressed the retreating Federals too hard and was beaten back at Pleasant Hill.

All the way back down the river, Porter's ships were under cannon and musket fire from Taylor's pursing soldiers. During one skirmish, the admiral himself had to take over the wheel of his flagship when his helmsman and all the other men in the pilothouse were shot. Each hour, it looked more and more like Porter was going to be the first admiral in history to lose his entire fleet to enemy cavalry and mother nature.

Then Porter faced what at first looked like a disaster. When he got to the falls at Alexandria, a shallow spot in the river that had given him trouble on the way up, he discovered that the depth was barely three feet. His ironclads needed at least seven feet to float over the falls. The fleet was stuck.

That was before a former Wisconsin lumberjack, Lieutenant Colonel Joseph Bailey, came forward with an idea he had used to get logs down shallow rivers. He proposed constructing wing dams to raise the water level. Porter was skeptical, but he still had his sense of humor. "If damning had helped, we would be floating now," he said. Then Porter was told that his soft-handed sailors could sit on their boats and watch ditch-digging soldiers try to solve the problem. The prospect of not working appealed to the admiral, so he told Bailey to give it the old army try.

For a week, Bailey's men constructed wing dams from each bank reaching toward the center of the river. Thanks to the artificial narrowing of the river, it started to rise. When it was finally deep enough, the ironclads were launched through the narrow opening. The lightest was able to make it through while the heaviest waited—waited too long, as it turned out. One of the dams burst, and the artificial lake built up on the river started to drain. Three ironclads threw caution to the wind and pushed off, hoping to surf the rushing water downriver. One shot the gap in the broken dam and plunged down the artificial falls, disappearing from view in the foaming water. The ironclad slammed into the bottom of the river, then popped back to the surface with a dent in its bow. Six ships that could not get under way in time to catch the rushing water were left above the broken dam.

Banks was contemplating leaving those ships to their fate when the lumberjack colonel got to work again. Using the breached dam to direct water and act as a buffer, he built another dam downstream within three days. Soon, there was enough water to float the ironclads past the falls. Porter, who had bitterly laughed at the scheme when it was first proposed, praised the lumberjack, gave him an ornate sword, and made the unusual move—for a navy man, anyway—of suggesting Bailey be promoted to brigadier general. Bailey, who had joined the army out of patriotism rather than any vision of political advancement, found himself a brigadier general. He also received the rare "Thanks of Congress."

One week later, the two-month Red River Campaign was over. The gunboats went back to the more predictable Mississippi River, and Banks was shuttled aside. He was not dismissed or replaced. His power in Massachusetts was still too great for that to happen. But Grant made it clear that Banks would not be leading any more expeditions with his troops.

Lincoln, too, lost. The plan to make cotton planters feel a debt to the North never happened. Porter had apparently never been clued in to the political aspects of the Red River Campaign. When he found cotton bales on shore, he first stamped them C.S.A., drew a line through it, then restamped them *U.S.A.* Military regulations allowed the confiscation of Confederate military supplies, and Porter saw nothing wrong with making believe that private cotton belonged to the Confederacy.

Banks had done little more than waste two months. About the only thing accomplished was that the United States Navy discovered a civil-engineering genius among the officers of the United States Army. Porter learned a lesson. He had no intention of ever sending his ironclads up a shallow Confederate river again. He much preferred the open water of oceans and bays. He would find deeper water that summer when he attacked Mobile Bay.

Banks's military career and his dreams of the presidency ended on the Red River, but his political career continued until his death. After the war, he returned to the United States House of Representatives. He later ran for his state senate, then had himself appointed a United States marshal. The old politician who answered to the textile-inspired nickname "Bobbin Boy" lived to be seventy-eight.

An Unlucky Ricochet Finds
Charles W. Flusser

"Flusser was a cool and daring officer. He was always found to be where fighting was going on. He was a terror to the marauding troops of the enemy. He seemed to delight in making explorations where little was to be gained except hard knocks." These were the admiring words Admiral David D. Porter used in his *Naval History of the Civil War* to describe Lieutenant Commander Charles W. Flusser.

Porter also acknowledged that while "Flusser had no superior as a gallant and energetic officer, his arrangements for meeting the ram were certainly ill-judged."

The ram in question was the CSS *Albemarle*, a 154-foot-long iron-clad with 4 inches of armor over 16 inches of wood planking and mounting two 6.4-inch Brooke cannons, the finest made in the Confederacy. The ship was designed to do one thing: sail down North Carolina's Roanoke River and destroy the entire Federal fleet stationed at the river's mouth in Roanoke Sound.

Flusser spent his entire Civil War career in North Carolina, first winning notice for shelling the Confederate forts on Roanoke Island on February 8, 1862, followed the next day by a smashing attack on the Confederate "Mosquito Fleet" at Elizabeth City.

On July 9, Flusser was embarrassed not by the Confederate navy but Confederate cavalry. He led three small wooden gunboats and a hundred sailors far up the Roanoke River to Hamilton, a small town he hoped to capture. About two miles below town, his gunboats came under musket and pistol fire from Rainbow Bluff, a high spot in the river where Fort Branch was later constructed. For more than two hours, his men were under fire. He lost two sailors dead and ten wounded to a ragtag bunch of cavalrymen.

Flusser continued his service in North Carolina through 1864, eventually winning command of the naval contingent stationed in Albemarle Sound.

It was around three o'clock in the morning on April 19 of that year when Flusser met his odd—and messy—end at Plymouth, North Carolina.

It was then that the *Albemarle*, the most feared Confederate ironclad since the *Virginia*, came steaming full speed down the Roanoke. She passed Fort Gray without even pausing, though the fort fired every cannon it had at her. A sailor inside the *Albemarle* reported that the cannonballs hitting the ship sounded "no louder than pebbles thrown against an empty barrel."

As the ironclad passed the fort, her captain saw two Federal "double enders"—sidewheelers with rudders at both bow and stern so they could quickly change direction. These were the USS *Southfield* and the USS *Miami*, Flusser's command ship. The two were loosely chained together in hopes that they could slip to either side of the *Albemarle* and trap her between them. Flusser apparently then planned to board the ironclad and drop kegs of gunpowder down her stack. It was a clever, risky strategy that would have been difficult to pull off even under ideal conditions.

The *Albemarle*'s captain, instantly understanding what the Federals were planning, pulled hard toward the left bank of the river, then hard right until he was aimed at the side of the *Southfield*. He then opened his throttle and rammed the Federal ship with his iron prow, opening a huge hole. The *Southfield* started sinking, carrying the *Albemarle* with her until the Federal ship struck bottom and the Confederate ironclad popped free.

Now the *Miami* and the *Albemarle* were within yards of each other. Flusser ran to a hundred-pounder Parrott rifle and pulled the lanyard. The solid ball bounced off the Confederate ship's armor. He ran to a second cannon and pulled its lanyard. That ball also bounced away. He ran to a third cannon, an eleven-inch Dahlgren (identified in some reports as a hundred-pounder Parrott rifle), and pulled its lanyard. This cannon was loaded with an explosive shell designed to fragment once the fuse burned into its interior. Unlike the others, this shell did not bounce away. It bounced back aboard the *Miami* and landed at Flusser's feet. Witnesses said Flusser never let go of the lanyard. He just watched the hissing shell at his feet until the fuse ran out. A doctor's report said

Flusser had at least nineteen pieces of shrapnel in him and one arm blown off. It described him as "horribly mangled." He was the only man killed aboard the *Miami*.

The *Miami's* executive officer—and new captain—cut the ship loose from the *Southfield* and hightailed it down the Roanoke, accompanied by the other two surviving gunboats. The *Albemarle* stayed at Plymouth to shell the Federal fort, which had been keeping back a force of Confederate soldiers. The ironclad played a major role in the capture of the town, which netted twenty-five hundred Federals, twenty-eight cannons, and more than five thousand muskets.

Flusser, the Federal navy's golden boy of Albemarle Sound, was honored for his brave death. He was also blamed, probably rightly, for the *Albemarle's* swift victory. As Porter noted, "Had the four [Union] vessels been properly disposed, the *Albemarle* herself could have been rammed while endeavoring to ram others. Tying two vessels together gave the enemy the very opportunity he desired. Either of the two gunboats was twice as fast as the ram, and there were chances of crippling her that were not improved."

Lieutenant Commander Charles W. Flusser, aggressive and brave, was too quick on the trigger. Had he thought about what might happen when he fired his cannons point-blank at four inches of armor with a base of wood sixteen inches thick, he might have lived to be a commander.

THE MIGHTY *NEUSE* GROUNDS ON HER FIRST MISSION

The CSS *Neuse* would not only control the river after which she was named, she would cruise to New Bern, North Carolina, and crush the North's wooden fleet, which had held the town since March 1862. This Confederate ironclad might even be able to join forces with her sister ship, the CSS *Albemarle*, operating on the Roanoke River, to push all Union forces from the Tar Heel State.

The *Neuse*, equipped with two 6.4-inch Brooke rifled cannons, a prow for ramming ships, and four inches of rolled iron plate over three layers of wood planking, should have been a formidable weapon. She should have struck fear in the hearts of Union seamen as they watched her chug down the river toward them. Even if there had been Union ironclads in North Carolina to fight her, she should have been difficult to dent, much less sink.

This best-designed of all Confederate river ironclads would probably have worn the mantle of the "mighty" *Neuse* had someone not over-looked one very large detail. Either her draft of eight feet was too deep or the Neuse River was too shallow. The *Neuse* was too big for her river. It was the Civil War equivalent of building a sailboat in the basement, then discovering the door is too narrow to take it outside.

The *Neuse* was planned to be the savior of the South, probably even more important than the Confederacy's first major ironclad, the *Virginia*, the 263-foot-long, 51-foot-wide ship that fought the *Monitor* to a draw off Hampton Roads, Virginia, in March 1862. The *Virginia* had a draft of nearly 22 feet, making her too big to operate in the Southern coast's shallow waters. But the *Virginia's* basic design had proven effective in sinking two Federal wooden warships. War planners in Richmond believed that if the Confederacy could build smaller, lighter, shallower-draft ironclads that could operate from the safety of the South's numerous rivers, the Federal blockade could be broken.

By the summer of 1862, at least eighteen ironclads were planned for construction along Southern rivers in North Carolina, Alabama, Georgia, Mississippi, and Louisiana. In North Carolina, the *Albemarle* started to take shape at Edwards Ferry on the Roanoke River and the *Neuse* at the small town of Whitehall (present-day Seven Springs) on the Neuse River.

The *Neuse* was almost destroyed before she was even recognizable as an ironclad. In December 1862, Major General John G. Foster, the commander of Union forces in North Carolina, got wind of the ironclad under construction at Whitehall. Since he had already planned an expedition to the Goldsboro bridge to draw Confederates from reenforcing Fredericksburg, Foster added the destruction of the ironclad to his goals. His men found the *Neuse* and shelled her wooden keel and hull repeatedly from a distance of less than a mile, but the damage was superficial and repairs were easily made.

Once the 158-foot-long ironclad was finished enough to float, plans called for her to move down the Neuse to Kinston, where it would be easier to outfit her. At least that was the theory.

Bureaucratic infighting between the Confederate army and navy and between old-line wooden-fleet navy men and those who believed in ironclads held up construction for months. The major problem was the procurement of iron plating, which was frequently rolled from old railroad rails. Even when rails could be found, transporting them to and from the South's few rolling mills on the overburdened rail system was often difficult. The Confederate army's quartermaster general frequently refused to give the navy railroad cars to transport the iron. Even during transport, it often was bumped to a siding for weeks in favor of sending food and weapons to the armies in the field.

Confederate major general William H. C. Whiting, the commander of Wilmington, North Carolina, once wrote a report saying, "So far the gunboats have caused more trouble, interfered more with government business and transportation, been bound up more and accomplished less than any other part of the service. Here I do not permit them to interfere any longer."

Whiting and Flag Officer William Lynch, the naval commander at Wilmington, strongly disliked each other and did everything in their power to hamper each other's work. It finally took an order from the Confederate secretary of war to force Whiting to cooperate in moving material to the *Neuse*.

Lynch himself did not go out of his way to push the cause of ironclads. He hated the idea. A seagoing, world-traveling, wooden-ship sailor for forty years, he believed the Confederacy should be building more ocean raiders and blockade runners instead of ironclads that would not leave the rivers and coastal bays.

Whether Lynch and Whiting agreed or not, the completion of the *Albemarle* and the *Neuse* was a top priority at the highest levels of the Confederate government. Robert E. Lee wrote a letter to President Jefferson Davis on January 2, 1864, suggesting that he wanted to attack New Bern, since winter weather was preventing him from doing anything in Virginia. He suggested all he would need were two brigades, which he would command himself, if he could get help from the *Albemarle* and the *Neuse* in capturing or destroying Union troop transports and shelling Union defenses around the town.

Davis answered Lee two days later: "The progress on the boats on the Neuse and Roanoke is slow and too uncertain to fix a date for completion, but your suggestion is approved."

A disappointed Lee wrote on January 20, "I regret very much that the boats on the Neuse and Roanoke are not completed. With their aid I think success would be certain. Without them, though the place may be captured, the fruits of the expedition will be lessened and our maintenance of the command of the waters in North Carolina uncertain. I think every effort should be made now to get them into service as soon as possible."

Even Lee could not stop Whiting and Lynch from interfering with the ironclads' construction. On one occasion, Lynch used his power as naval commander of North Carolina to move the *Albemarle* to another shipyard, a move that her contractor, Gilbert Elliott, considered harassment. "Lynch is universally looked upon in this state as incompetent, inefficient, and almost imbecile," Elliott wrote North Carolina governor Zeb Vance. "His management of the Roanoke Island fleet convinced the people in my district of his utter incapacity."

Lee went ahead with an assault against New Bern, though it was led by Major General George Pickett rather than himself. Supported by just a few Confederate launches and hampered by Pickett's poor organization, the attack failed. The supplies Lee had hoped to capture for his depleted army stayed in Federal hands.

Finally, by April 1864, both ironclads were ready to leave their moorings.

On April 19, the *Albemarle* made her place in Confederate naval history when she came barreling out of the night toward three Union gunboats at Plymouth, North Carolina. She rammed one to the bottom and sent the other two scurrying downriver. She then shifted her attention to shelling the Federal forts around Plymouth. Her accurate fire forced the Federal commander to surrender more than twenty-five hundred men. Confederate soldiers could not have captured the town without the *Albemarle*.

The *Neuse* was completed less than a week after her sister ship. Her mission on the Neuse River would be almost a copy of what the *Albemarle* had done on the Roanoke. She was to proceed down the Neuse to New Bern to help Major General Robert Hoke. Hoke's plan was to use the *Neuse* and the *Albemarle* to do what Pickett had been unable to accomplish three months earlier—pound both the Federal wooden fleet and the earth forts surrounding the city.

On April 27, 1864, the *Neuse* was under way, probably on a shakedown cruise, since Hoke was busy contemplating an attack on Federal-held Washington, North Carolina. She had gone less than a half-mile downriver when she ran aground. Within hours, the falling river left her bow more than four feet out of the water. One officer wrote that it would take a "freshet" of hard rain to move her and noted that such weather did not normally come to the region until midsummer.

President Davis himself was informed of the grounding. When convinced that the *Neuse* was stuck fast, he ordered that the *Albemarle* be sent to Hoke's aid. She tried but could not fight her way past a phalanx of Federal ships. Her smokestack was so shot up that the captain threw in the cook's supply of bacon and every piece of wooden furniture on board to raise steam to make it back to port. Hoke attacked New Bern anyway and was on the verge of taking the city with land forces when he got an urgent message to return his men to General Lee in Petersburg.

The *Neuse* was finally freed after spending more than a month on the sandbar. Carefully, she made her way back upriver to Kinston. By this time, Hoke and his men had returned to Virginia and all hope of retaking New Bern had been abandoned.

The *Neuse* was now a ship without a mission. True, she could try again to go downriver to New Bern to attack the Federal fleet, but now she had no hope of infantry support. Even if she battered the Federal fleet, there were no troops to reoccupy the town and give her shore support to hold the mouth of the river. Worse, if the ironclad grounded closer to Federal lines, she would probably fall into enemy hands.

She had taken more than two years to build, soaking up thousands of man-hours of labor and thousands of dollars in precious iron plating that might have gone to other uses, such as laying more railroad rails. Now, she was bottled up on her river for no other reason than that the Neuse had not been eight feet deep the week it needed to be.

The *Neuse* finally went into combat in March 1865 when the Union army marched for a second time on Kinston. She chugged downriver close enough to the Federal lines to lob a few shells their way. Certain she was about to be captured as they moved back upriver, her crew set her on fire, believing the powder magazine would be set off and she would blow up. She did not. Instead, she sank almost intact in the river. Most of her machinery was salvaged and her armor removed. Her guns apparently were removed by the Union army after the war. For years, she lay in the river, more a nuisance to boaters than a curiosity. Then, in the 1960s, a private organization raised her, and the state of North Carolina eventually built a museum around the ribs of her hull. She rests today in Kinston, not far from the spot where she ran aground on her one major mission in life.

There are questions about the *Neuse*. How much checking was done to determine that the river was deep enough to float such a vessel? Could dredging have eased her way downstream? Could she had been redesigned to draw less water? Why didn't the same rains that swelled the Roanoke seventy miles to the north at almost the same time make it to the Neuse?

All history will remember about the *Neuse* is that the Confederacy invested a lot of time, money, and effort in building a marvelous ironclad that sailed a half-mile from its moorings before it ran aground on a sandbar.

"THEY COULDN'T HIT AN ELEPHANT AT THIS DISTANCE"

Everyone in the United States Army seemed to like Major General John Sedgwick. An 1837 graduate of West Point, he had served in the Seminole Indian Wars, the Mexican War, the Mormon expedition, and the Indian wars on the plains. In an army in which generals were not always respected by the men who did the fighting and dying, Sedgwick answered to the affectionate label of "Uncle John." His men liked him because he did not place them in danger that was not necessary to win the battle. And he was always right there with them on the front lines. His men respected that and followed him because of it.

If he had a blind spot, it was keeping up with the Confederacy's military technology.

Sedgwick was one of those Union officers who knew practically every general on the other side. In his West Point class were Braxton Bragg and Jubal Early. In the following class were P. G. T. Beauregard and Edward Johnson. When Sedgwick was appointed major of the First United States Cavalry, the two colonels above him were Robert E. Lee and William J. Hardee.

When Lee and Hardee resigned to join the Confederacy, Sedgwick was appointed commander of the unit. His obvious skills soon brought him a brigadier general's commission and a divisional command during the Peninsula Campaign in the late spring of 1862.

Sedgwick was both a magnet and a sponge when it came to Confederate bullets. No matter where he stood, he attracted gunfire. But no matter how many bullets hit him, he absorbed and recovered from them. During the Seven Days' Battles in June 1862, he was wounded at Frayser's Farm. He stayed out of action only a few weeks and returned to the field with a promotion to major general. At the Battle of Antietam in September 1862, his division was hit on three sides and Sedgwick himself was hit by three different bullets. He was carried from the field unconscious. Still, Sedgwick could not be stopped.

After a recovery lasting several months, he was given command over the Sixth Corps. By May 1863, he was part of Hooker's army facing Lee at Fredericksburg. Hooker left Sedgwick to demonstrate on the north side of the Rappahannock River while he took the bulk of the army west to cross the river near Chancellorsville. Lee discovered the ploy and left Early's men to demonstrate in front of Sedgwick so the bulk of the Southern army could meet Hooker. Sedgwick's men were assigned to look like the whole Army of the Potomac, while Early's men were assigned to look like the whole Army of Northern Virginia. When Sedgwick finally discovered the true situation, he crossed the river and chased Early back to Salem Church. There, Lee met and defeated Sedgwick in a furious battle.

During the following year, Sedgwick fought solidly and retained the confidence of Hooker, Meade, and finally Grant, who reduced the number of corps in his army from five to three. When Grant started his Wilderness Campaign, Sedgwick was right in the middle of it with another corps command.

As the fighting moved out of the tangled undergrowth, it shifted southeast to the small settlement of Spotsylvania Court House. On May 8, 1864, Sedgwick and his staff arrived on the field, and he immediately began to personally place his troops. That night, the major general did not even bother setting up a tent. Instead, he slept on the grass like a common soldier.

The next morning, he was idly watching some troops file into line when one regiment proceeded to lie down right in front of a battery of cannons. Sedgwick walked toward the guns to order the infantry to another position.

Martin McMahon, Sedgwick's chief of staff, pointed to the cannons and said, "General, do you see that section of artillery? You are not to go near it today [during battle]."

Sedgwick, who loved to play practical jokes on and tease his staff, reacted with mock indignation: "McMahon, who commands this corps? You, or I?"

Playing along, McMahon replied, "Well, General, sometime I am in doubt of that myself, but seriously, General, I beg of you not to go to that angle. Every officer who has shown himself there has been hit, both yesterday and today."

Sedgwick replied, "Well, I don't know that there is any reason for my going there."

Within a few minutes, consumed by the details of preparing for a major battle, both men forgot the conversation and walked to the battery. As Sedgwick and McMahon ordered the infantry away from the artillery, Confederate sharpshooters located probably a mile away opened up. The Union troops cringed.

Sedgwick laughed. "What? What? Men, you are dodging this way for single bullets! What will you do when they open fire along the whole line? I am ashamed of you! Why, they couldn't hit an elephant at this distance." He believed that the Confederates used only short-range rifles.

At that instant, a man walking in front of the general heard a bullet come whistling his way and dove to the ground.

Sedgwick, who still stood in the same position, gently touched the man with his foot and repeated what he had just said: "Why, my man, I am ashamed of you, dodging that way. They couldn't hit an elephant at this distance."

The man stood up, saluted, and said, "General, I dodged a shell once, and if I hadn't, it would have taken my head off. I believe in dodging."

The general laughed and said, "All right, my man, go to your place."

For the third time in less than a minute, the same whistling sound came toward the battery. This time, McMahon heard a dull thud. The Confederates may not have been able to hit an elephant, but a steady sharpshooter armed with a British-made Whitworth sniper rifle equipped with a telescopic sight had just hit a Union major general with a hexagonal .45-caliber bullet.

McMahon was about to resume the conversation with Sedgwick when the general turned toward him. A hole under his left eye was spurting blood in a steady stream. Sedgwick fell into McMahon's arms, and both of them fell heavily to the ground.

When they rolled him over, Uncle John was dead. A smile was on his face. As the surgeons futilely worked on Sedgwick, McMahon noticed that the entire infantry line was on its knees looking at the fallen commander. That afternoon, a bier of tree branches was built in the open behind the lines. Men filed by to mourn the loss of their leader.

Grant could have used Sedgwick the rest of that week as he pounded Lee in some of the most fierce fighting of the war, culminating in two Union attacks on a Confederate line that curved back on itself. History remembers it as "the Mule Shoe." It was just the kind of fighting Sedgwick liked—close, personal. It was a shame that he died from a bullet fired by a man too far away to distinguish much more than a shape standing next to a cannon. He probably would have liked Uncle John.

"I FIGHTS MIT SIEGAL!": LINCOLN NAMES MEDIOCRE FOREIGN-BORN GENERALS

President Abraham Lincoln knew the danger and power of naming generals. He realized that some appointees—like Ben Butler and Nathaniel Banks of Massachusetts, Daniel Sickles of New York, and John C. Fremont of Missouri—hoped to ride military careers into the White House. But Lincoln also knew that appointing generals could be an opportunity to put certain men—men he would never have to worry about running against him for president—and their constituents forever in his debt.

That's why Lincoln appointed so many foreign-born generals. He knew that these generals had immigrant admirers and that the Constitution forbade them from running for president. And if they won a few battles along the way, so much the better.

Some of the foreigners did well.

Russian-born colonel Ivan Vasilovitch Turchinoff was almost thrown out of the army for burning Huntsville, Alabama, before torching Southern cities became standard procedure. His wife appealed to President

Lincoln, who promoted Turchinoff to brigadier general. "The Russian Thunderbolt" later went on to a good career in the Western army.

Swedish-born colonel John Stolbrand ably commanded a brigade of forty-six cannons during Sherman's march through Georgia and the Carolinas, doing so well that he was named a brigadier general late in the war.

Irish-born brigadier general Thomas Meagher founded the most famous brigade in the Union army, the Irish Brigade. A close friend of his was Brigadier General Michael Corcoran, who once refused to parade his regiment in honor of that hated Englishman, the Prince of Wales. Corcoran bravely handled his immigrants at First Manassas but was captured. Later freed, he raised the Irish Legion, but he never got another chance to prove his mettle in battle. His horse fell on him and killed him in the winter of 1863.

Of all the Prussians Lincoln favored, the oddest had to be August Von Willich. Lincoln probably never bothered to ask his politics. The man was a card-carrying communist who counted Karl Marx as one of his personal friends.

Willich was actually one of the few European officers who didn't embarrass Lincoln. Appointed a colonel of Indiana troops, he worked his way up to brigadier general in just over a year. While most battlefield generals drilled their men to listen to the commands of their majors and captains, Willich taught his to respond to Prussian bugle calls, which were unlikely to be duplicated by other Union regiments or imitated by Confederates trying to confuse the enemy. Captured once and wounded once, Willich survived the war.

Though he had been chased out of Germany for his communist leanings in 1848, Willich returned to offer his services during the Franco-Prussian War. He was turned down. While in Europe, he could not resist looking up his old friend Marx and attending several of his public lectures, which seems a strange activity for a breveted major general in the United States Army. He died in Ohio, never having seen his dream of communism crossing the Atlantic to the American continent.

Most of the president's forty-three foreign-born generals were inferior to these men. But Lincoln was too good a politician to publicly announce that he regretted appointing so many foreigners to command. He just allowed most of them to be quietly replaced. He might have been wrong about at least one of them. Hungarian-born brigadier general Julius Stahel was relieved of command in the spring of 1864 for being inefficient. But in June, he performed well enough in action to be later awarded the Congressional Medal of Honor.

Most of Lincoln's foreign appointees were more the caliber of Louis Blenker, the leading German immigrant in New York State in 1861. Lincoln assumed Blenker had some military training, since he had taken part in the abortive German revolution of 1848. Actually, Blenker's experience was mainly as a jeweler's apprentice and a winemaker, but his standing in the German-American community was enough to get him a colonel's commission of volunteers. After proving his mettle at First Manassas, where he helped cover the retreat, Blenker was appointed a brigadier general in August 1861. He was charged with recruiting Germans.

In April 1862, Blenker's division of Germans was ordered to western Virginia to help trap Stonewall Jackson. Trying to move fast, Blenker left his division's tents and heavy coats and most of his food supply wagons behind. A freak April snowstorm trapped his men in the mountains. Blenker fell from his horse and was severely injured. His men grew hungry and broke ranks to ransack farms for food. Another Federal unit had to be sent to guide them to safety.

In Blenker's only major battle—at Cross Keys, Virginia—his division was routed and suffered heavy losses.

Someone in Washington must have taken note of all this, because Blenker was transferred back to Washington. Within seven months, he died of complications from the fall from his horse.

Lincoln was not about to give up on Germans. In Blenker's place, he sent Brigadier General Franz Siegal, a former German soldier who had recently been teaching school in Missouri. Siegal started his career in the West and did so well against inferior Confederate generals in that theater that Lincoln brought him east. He didn't do so well against Jackson in the Shenandoah Valley or against Lee at Second Manassas. Still, he had a certain value. In the German immigrant community, a common phrase about the war was "I fights mit Siegal!" He brought thousands of volunteers into the Union army.

Siegal was trounced at the Battle of New Market, Virginia, in May 1864. Most embarrassing to the German were the cadets from Virginia Military Academy manning the center of the Confederate line. The teenage boys, not yet soldiers, captured several Union cannons. Siegal was relieved of field command shortly thereafter.

Prince Felix Constantin Alexander Johann Nepomuk Salm-Salm, a thirty-three-year-old Prussian hero of several European conflicts, had a great name and a pushy American-born wife named Agnes who somehow got him an audience with President Lincoln. Salm-Salm's major problem with securing a generalship in the Union army was that he didn't speak English. But that didn't stop Lincoln from making him a colonel and chief of staff for Blenker. Agnes lived with her husband in the field, working as a nurse and probably interpreting for him.

Whether by luck or a desire among other generals to keep an untested officer who couldn't speak English out of the way, Salm-Salm didn't get any major commands during the war. The only conflict he actively participated in was the Battle of Nashville in December 1864. As a reward for this little bit of service, he was appointed "military governor" of Atlanta.

After the war, Salm-Salm went to Mexico to fight with Emperor Maximilian, but he was captured by the rebels. He barely escaped execution thanks to the fast-talking Agnes, who somehow got to the leaders of the rebels and convinced them to let her husband go. Salm-Salm's luck ran out in 1870, when he was killed during the Franco-Prussian War. Agnes never returned to the United States.

Brigadier General Alexander Schimmelfennig was a hard-luck general in a hard-luck corps. A Prussian who had fled the German revolution in 1848, he was working for the United States government when the war started. Assigned a colonel's commission, he set about recruiting other immigrants to his Pennsylvania regiment. That's when his trouble started.

First, he fell from a horse. Then he suffered a bout with smallpox. His command was transferred to the Eleventh Corps, which was where most of the German regiments were concentrated. Schimmelfennig's men were on the far right at Chancellorsville when Stonewall Jackson's flank march surprised them and sent the immigrants fleeing. The Eleventh Corps broke again at Gettysburg on the first day. In trying to rally his men from their flight, Schimmelfennig was struck down by a gun. He never learned whether it was one of his own men. When he awoke, he found himself behind Confederate lines. He crept into a pigpen, where he held court with the porkers for the rest of Gettysburg. It was not until July 4 that he emerged and reported to his commanders. They held their noses and agreed to his request for a transfer from the Eleventh Corps.

Before Schimmelfennig made the move, he came down with malaria. He recovered in time to return to the army just before the surrender. Back on duty, he discovered he was suffering from tuberculosis. He died in September 1865 at age forty-one.

Despite the fair performance of some foreigners appointed generals in the United States Army, Schimmelfennig's troubles seem a symbol for them all.

THE UNTIMELY END OF A BISHOP MAJOR GENERAL

Perhaps the most dramatic death of a Civil War general was that of a man who had faith that God would protect him.

Leonidas Polk did not spend much time in the United States Army after graduating from West Point in 1827. Instead of finding a military career, he found God. Polk resigned his commission almost as soon as he got it and entered an Episcopal seminary. By 1841, he was bishop of Louisiana. By 1860, he played a leading role in founding the University of the South at Sewanee, Tennessee.

When the war started, Polk's old friend Jefferson Davis (West Point, class of 1828) appointed him a major general in the Confederate army, though the bishop had been out of the service for more than thirty years and had never ranked higher than second lieutenant. Perhaps realizing that Polk needed seasoning, Davis put him in charge of building up defenses in Mississippi. When it became obvious that the Union was targeting that state, Davis replaced his friend with another of Polk's old buddies, General Albert Sidney Johnston.

Polk finally found his niche as a corps commander in the Army of Tennessee under General Braxton Bragg, who praised his performance at Perryville, Kentucky, so much that Davis pushed his friend up to lieutenant general. But Bragg never got along with any subordinate for long. He threatened Polk with court-martial for poor performance at Chickamauga. Davis saved his friend again by transferring him away from Bragg.

By mid-1864, General Joseph Johnston had taken over the Army of Tennessee, and Polk's Army of Mississippi was reenforcing him as the Confederates slowly retreated south before Union major general William T. Sherman's push into Georgia.

It was June 14, 1864, when Johnston, Lieutenant General William J. Hardee, and Polk rode their horses to Pine Mountain, Georgia, to get a look at the advancing elements of Sherman's army. The three generals were warned that the enemy was close and had zeroed in on the mountaintop with rifled cannons. The generals ignored the warning and trained their binoculars on the Yankees, who could see them perfectly, too.

Sherman himself spotted the three generals and ordered that a cannon battery force them off the top of the mountain. After the first round, Johnston realized they were in danger and ordered everyone to leave. The second round landed closer. Johnston and Hardee scrambled, but Polk ambled behind at some distance, in no hurry. Witnesses said he walked with his hands clasped behind his back, seemingly deep in thought or prayer. The third cannon shell from a ten-pounder rifled Parrott passed entirely through Polk's side before exploding. The bishop of Louisiana, who had taken off his general's uniform from time to time to preach and perform weddings for officers, was dead before his mangled body hit the ground. He was fifty-eight years old.

There is speculation that Polk, a chunky man, didn't have the wind to run as fast as the thinner, fitter Johnston and Hardee, so he walked so as not to embarrass himself. If so, the old injunction "Walk, don't run" may have killed him that day.

"He Did Not Show Me a Fair Fight": Old Beeswax Bristles at Losing the *Alabama*

Captain Raphael Semmes, commander of the feared sea raider CSS *Alabama*, captured sixty-four Union merchant or whaling ships and sank one Yankee warship in just over two years. Though considered a pirate by many in the Federal government, he always believed himself a sailor at war. He never murdered the crews of the ships he captured. Semmes usually tried to win Union ships by showing his vessel's superior speed. When he did have to attack, he was always a gentleman about it. He believed in a fair fight.

Thus, in the fight that sank the *Alabama*, Semmes became livid at what he considered unfair tactics. Though that may have been the case, he should have been more practical. Semmes lost the battle partly because his opponents were better prepared—but mostly because of his own previous success.

Semmes might have been one of the most accomplished nineteenth-century men to sail the sea. After joining the navy at the relatively late age of seventeen, he worked his up through the ranks to captain. Between cruises, he planned for a future away from the sea by studying law and writing.

Though the navy played a minor role in the Mexican War of 1846, it almost proved the end of Semmes. His ship capsized in a gale and he narrowly avoided drowning. The navy held a board of inquiry to see if his actions had endangered the ship and her crew. The board eventually confirmed Semmes had done all he could, but the experience embittered him. When not at sea, Semmes used his legal training to defend other officers who had run afoul of the naval powers.

Though a native of neutral border state Maryland, Semmes considered Alabama his home. When it seceded, so did Semmes, in February 1861. Over the next few months, he traveled the North buying naval equipment for the war everyone knew was coming.

Semmes was a visionary in the fledgling Confederate navy. He recognized that one effective way to slow the proposed blockade of Southern ports was to cruise the oceans attacking Union merchantmen. He took over a fast merchantman, renamed her the CSS *Sumter*, armed her with five cannons, and set to sea. In six months, he captured eighteen Federal merchant ships. His cruise caused dozens of other ships to stay in port or add days to their voyages rather than risk capture. In January 1862, three Union warships finally caught up to the *Sumter* at Gibraltar. One of the ships involved in the chase was the USS *Kearsarge*, commanded by an old navy friend of Semmes's, John Winslow, a North Carolinian who had remained loyal to the Union. Outnumbered, Semmes wisely walked away from his ship to fight another day.

In just six months, Semmes had built a worldwide reputation. He cut quite the figure of a man. Thin, erect, and stern, he looked like a ship's captain was supposed to look. He twirled his mustache until the ends defied gravity and stood several inches to either side of his face. His nickname was "Old Beeswax."

Instead of returning him to America, the Confederacy sent Semmes to England to supervise the outfitting of the *290*, a ship designed to be the fastest ocean raider the world had ever seen. The 211-foot-long vessel, powered by a screw and three masts, was armed with six 32-pounders, a 68-pounder, and the real terror, a 110-pound rifled cannon. History would call her the *Alabama*.

From the end of July 1862 until June 19, 1864, the *Alabama* struck terror in the hearts of captains in all the world's oceans. Semmes took her in the North and South Atlantic, the Indian, and the Pacific Oceans. Though she never circumnavigated the globe as her fellow raider *Shenandoah* did, the *Alabama* cruised more than seventy-five thousand miles. The total value of her prizes was more than six million dollars, a tremendous sum in the days when a sailor was paid ten dollars a month. The *Alabama* never entered a Confederate port, and few of her international crew other than her officers even knew much about the Confederacy. They did, however, understand that they got a cut of the prize money when a captured ship and her goods were sold.

On June 11, 1864, the *Alabama* pulled into Cherbourg, France, for much-needed repairs. Semmes, writing in his postwar *Memoirs of Service Afloat*, noted, "The poor old *Alabama* was not what she had been. She was like the wearied foxhound, limping back after a long chase, footsore, and longing for quiet and repose. Her commander, like herself, was well-nigh worn down." Semmes knew from newspapers captured from Union ships that the Confederacy was suffering one disaster after another back home. "Might it be, that, after all our trials and sacrifices, the cause for which we were struggling would be lost?" he pondered.

Winslow, Semmes's old Mexican War shipmate, heard that the *Alabama* had run to Cherbourg. He rushed the *Kearsarge* to France and lay off the port. He wanted the *Alabama* to know she would not get away again. She would have to fight her way out.

Convinced that his ship could fight anything that came before her, Semmes had every intention of doing battle. In January 1863, in history's first battle between steamships, the *Alabama* had sunk the USS *Hatteras* in a thirteen-minute engagement off the Texas coast. Being the gentleman he believed all captains should be, Semmes had put his lifeboats to sea to rescue men from the Union ship. Only a pair of Federal sailors lost their lives. The 121 survivors were put ashore in Jamaica as the *Alabama* returned to her prowling.

Semmes loaded his ship with coal and made what repairs he could during the week at Cherbourg. He may have been able to run past the

Kearsarge on a moonless night, but Semmes was a fighting sailor who wanted to test his warship against the enemy. He did have some reservations, he later wrote, about the lack of practice his men had firing cannons. Since Semmes could never be sure of resupply of powder, balls, and shells, he rarely let his men practice. That proved a mistake when his mercenaries were matched against the well-drilled gun crews of the Union navy.

On paper, it looked like a fair fight, the *Alabama*'s eight cannons against the *Kearsarge*'s seven. Semmes later pointed out that the two eleven-inch Dahlgren cannons on the Union ship were more than a match for his 110-pounder rifled cannon. Those two guns were mounted on pivots so they could be swung to either side of the ship. And the *Kearsarge* had something extra that Semmes could not see through his telescope.

The *Alabama*, escorted out of the harbor by a French ship to make sure the two antagonists fought in international waters, met the Union ship about seven miles off the French coast. Both held their fire until they were within three-quarters of a mile of each other. They then started sailing in circles. Semmes wrote that he suspected something was wrong with the *Kearsarge*: "Perceiving that our shell, though apparently exploding against the enemy's sides, were doing him but little damage, I returned to solid-shot firing, and from this time onward alternated with shot, and shell."

The engagement took a little more than seventy minutes. Though the match went totally in favor of the Union ship from the beginning, the Confederates came agonizingly close to winning by a lucky shot. A cannon shell from the *Alabama* lodged in the stern of the *Kearsarge* but did not explode. Had it gone off as designed, the Union ship's stern would have been blown off and she would have sunk like a rock. When Semmes finally tried to steer the badly damaged *Alabama* for the coast of France, he could make no headway, as water coming in from several holes found the ship's boilers. Within minutes, she slipped beneath the waves.

In reality, nothing about the *Alabama* made her equal to the *Kearsarge*.

The *Alabama* was slower than she should have been thanks to two years of active campaigning in rough seas. She was also hampered by old, damp gunpowder and gunners who were used to having merchant ships surrender to them, not warships fire at them. And at some point either during the battle or after the war, Semmes discovered something about the *Kearsarge* that he considered unfair. Captain Winslow had draped all his spare anchor chain on both sides of his ship in a line with his boilers and engines. He had then covered the chain with a layer of wood to disguise the fact that he had done anything to protect his wooden ship. Semmes was outraged:

> He did not show me a fair fight. His ship was iron-clad. It was the same thing, as if two men were to go out to fight a duel and one of them, unknown to the other, were to put a shirt of mail under his outer garment. The plain fact is, without any varnish, the *Kearsarge*, though as effectually protected as if she had been armed with the best of iron plates, was to all appearances a wooden ship of war. But, to admit this, would spoil the victory, and hence the effort to explain away the cheat as far as possible.

Nine men on the *Alabama* were killed and twenty-one wounded by cannon fire. Additional men drowned in the English Channel as the crew of the *Kearsarge* watched, making no effort to rescue them. That, too, angered Semmes. He wrote that he had saved the entire crew of the *Hatteras* during a night engagement, but that the *Keursarge* "in broad daylight" was "only 400 yards distant and ten of my men were permitted to drown."

Semmes tried to give his old friend the benefit of the doubt by citing Winslow's official report, which noted that the *Alabama* sank without warning. Still, Semmes did not really believe it: "I had known and sailed with Winslow in the old service and I knew him then to be a humane and Christian gentleman. What the war may have made of him, it is impossible to say. It has turned a great deal of milk of human kindness to gall and wormwood."

Semmes and most of his officers were rescued by a British ship and carried to safety in England. Semmes never again sailed for the Confederacy, but he did serve. Appointed a brigadier general in the Confederate army, he ended his war career guarding a minor ford on a small creek above Greensboro, North Carolina, far from the ocean where he had won his fame.

Could Semmes have waited Winslow out? Probably not. Within days, other American ships would have arrived. Could he have made better repairs during the week in Cherbourg? His ship had been to sea so long that she needed a major overhaul, not just minor repairs. Could he have better trained his gunners? Yes, but at the cost of reducing his small store of shells.

Ironically, Semmes's downfall may have been his sinking of the *Hatteras* sixteen months earlier. The *Hatteras* had not been designed as a warship. The chief worry of her captain was that her machinery and boilers were vulnerable to shell fire because they were in the open. After the *Alabama* sank the *Hatteras*, Union captains began discussing what they could do to protect their engines. One suggested draping spare chain over the ships' sides. That remedy would be as close as they could get to transforming their vessels into ironclads if they, too, ever had to face the terrifying *Alabama*.

LIEUTENANT OLIVER WENDELL HOLMES INSULTS THE PRESIDENT

It takes a man who knows he is destined for greater days to call the president of the United States a fool to his face. What spared him from a potentially career-ending—or even life-ending—blunder? Perhaps it was only the fact that he was right.

Oliver Wendell Holmes, Jr., was a Massachusetts-born patriot who quit Harvard in April 1861 just before graduation when President Lincoln called for seventy-five thousand volunteers to put down the rebellion. Awarded

with a commission as second lieutenant in the Twentieth Massachusetts Regiment, Holmes went to war earlier than most and was wounded
earlier than most, taking a hit in October 1861 at the small but disastrous Union defeat at Ball's Bluff, Virginia.

Holmes recovered and rejoined his regiment, only to be wounded a
second time at Antietam in September 1862. It was after this battle
that Washington politicians, exasperated with the slow pace of the war,
replaced Major General George McClellan with Major General Ambrose
Burnside. While the War Department thought that replacing McClellan
would result in more fighting, soldiers like Holmes only became depressed. Holmes thought the time had come to let the South go. "I've
pretty much made up my mind that the south have achieved their inde-
pendence & I am almost ready to hope spring will see an end. The army
is tired with its hard and its terrible experience and & still more with
its mismanagement & I think before long the majority will say that we
are vainly working to effect what never happens—the subjugation of a
great civilized nation," he wrote. Holmes shrugged off his doubts about the
army's leadership and stayed, eventually getting a promotion to captain.

In the second week of July 1864, a force of nearly fourteen thousand
Confederates under Major General Jubal Early executed a rapid march
to the outskirts of Washington. What had started out three weeks earlier as a diversionary raid to force Grant to take soldiers from the siege
of Petersburg to reenforce Washington had turned into an attempt to
capture the city itself. Though Early was held up nearly a full day by
fighting at Monacracy, Maryland, he still thought he had a chance at
bulling his way through Washington's extensive ring of outlying forts.
He had visions of rushing the White House and capturing Lincoln himself.

On July 11, Early and his ragged, straggling force, which numbered
no more than ten thousand, marched to within a thousand yards of the
large, earthen Fort Stevens, located about six miles from the White
House and the Capitol. Indeed, Early used his spyglass to study the unfinished dome of the Capitol.

By the time all of Early's men made it onto the field that day, it was
growing dark. They were too tired to try a night assault. Though Early

could see Federal reenforcements coming up behind Fort Stevens, he decided to wait until the morning to try an attack. He knew that such an assault would probably be pointless, since more Federals would be rushing north to protect the capital city. Still, he did not want to leave Washington without at least trying an assault.

What Early did not know was that the capital was in a fine panic, scared to death of his ten thousand boys, half of whom were barefoot. Answering a request from a brigadier offering his services in protecting the capital, Union major general Henry Halleck said, "We have five times as many generals here as we want, but are greatly in need of privates. Anyone volunteering in that capacity will be thankfully received."

Late that night, Early received intelligence that large numbers of regular troops had arrived from Grant's army around Petersburg, perhaps as many as twenty thousand men. He canceled orders for a dawn attack on Fort Stevens. He wanted daylight to see for himself if Fort Stevens had been heavily reenforced.

What Early did not know was that Abraham Lincoln himself was planning to visit Washington's ring of fortifications that morning to show support for the troops and prove to panicked citizens that he had full faith in the defense of the capital. In fact, Lincoln would be dragging along reluctant, gun-shy secretary of state William Henry Seward, who preferred to wage war from the safety of his office.

That afternoon, the Federals in Fort Stevens were still waiting for the Confederates to attack when Lincoln showed up. Major General Horatio Wright casually asked Lincoln if he would like a tour of the fort, expecting the president to say that he had better things to do. To Wright's shock, Lincoln accepted. And before Wright could stop him, Lincoln jumped up on the fort's rifle parapet so he could see the field in front of him.

The field was filled with Early's sharpshooters, who were feeling out the defenses of Fort Stevens. The parapet had been constructed with the average soldier in mind, a soldier who stood around five foot seven. Lincoln stood six foot four, still the tallest president to have ever served. On that day, he wore his trademark black stovepipe hat, which probably added another six to eight inches to his height. As Lincoln peered over the parapet at the Confederates beyond, the men in gray saw someone who, at nearly seven feet, stood almost a foot and a half taller than any other target behind the wall. One wonders if any rifleman using a telescopic sight recognized the Washingtonian famous throughout the country for that ugly black hat.

Wright, touching the president's sleeve, tried politely inviting the commander in chief to stand down from the parapet. Lincoln, intent on seeing his first live Confederates, did not answer. At that moment, a Federal officer standing less than a yard from Lincoln fell mortally wounded.

That was all it took for Captain Oliver Wendell Holmes, Jr., who was standing nearby. He looked up at the president and shouted, "Get down, you damn fool, before you get shot!"

Lincoln, accustomed to the deference of aides and legislators, turned and looked down at Holmes. General Wright was stunned speechless. Lincoln routinely signed death warrants for men found sleeping on guard duty. What would he do to a smart-mouthed officer who insulted him?

Lincoln grinned and stepped down to safety. He then sat down with his back to the parapet. The immediate danger was over. But as a Union brigade moved out from the fort to engage the Confederate skirmishers, he jumped up to the parapet from time to time to see how the Federals were faring. Holmes apparently never gave his president a second warning. If Lincoln was a fool, no amount of talking would change him.

The fighting continued until about ten o'clock that night, when Early was able to use the cover of darkness to pull his men out and put them on the march back to Virginia. To the rear guard he left to cover his retreat, Early said, "We haven't taken Washington, but we've scared Abe Lincoln like hell!"

Well, maybe. Lincoln never again went on an active battlefield, but he did go into Richmond before it was totally secured by Federal soldiers. Witnesses said Lincoln reacted coolly under fire at Fort Stevens and showed no fear when told the only protection he had in Richmond was his small naval escort.

Holmes was not demoted or transferred for his outburst. He stayed in the army, then returned for his interrupted degree from Harvard. He graduated from law school in 1866 and took up the profession. In 1909, he was appointed an associate justice of the United States Supreme Court. He served for more than thirty years, becoming one of the most famous justices in history. And with his huge, white handlebar mustache, he created the public's image of a justice. Beneath his robes, he bore three Civil War wounds. And he remembered forever the day he called the president of the United States an embarrassing—if true—name.

"IT MOUNTED TOWARD HEAVEN WITH A DETONATION OF THUNDER"

Brigadier General James Hewett Ledlie was almost certainly the worst general the Union army produced during the Civil War. During his four-year career, he was responsible for killing hundreds of soldiers, almost all of them marching under the United States flag. While his incompetence was demonstrated early in the conflict, it was not until the Battle of the Crater during the summer of 1864 that he was able to inflict real damage on his own army. And it was not until the war was almost over that the United States was able to rid itself of the man.

Ledlie was a well-connected civil engineer in New York who specialized in developing railroad lines and bridges. When the war started, he was appointed a major of an infantry regiment later converted to the Third New York Artillery. Without a day of military training, Ledlie may have never even seen a cannon up close before he was given command of a whole artillery regiment. And at a time when skilled soldiers were competing for the ranks of lieutenant and captain, Ledlie jumped from major to lieutenant colonel on September 28, 1861. He had never been on a battlefield.

The men assigned to Ledlie's artillery regiment gave early warnings of what to expect of the man and his command abilities. At the end of their normal enlistment, a number of Ledlie's soldiers mutinied. They went to prison rather than go onto the battlefield under him.

In December 1862, Ledlie took part in Major General John Foster's expedition from New Bern to Goldsboro, North Carolina. The first objective was to clean out the rebels in the town of Kinston. The first test of Ledlie's artillery skills was not exactly auspicious. A soldier from a Massachusetts regiment wrote, "We were obliged to pass under the fire of one our own batteries; of course we felt perfectly safe in doing this, not supposing that we would be shot by our own men, when to our unspeakable horror, the first shot from the battery carried away half the head of a man in Company D, killing him instantly, and the regiment passed on. Company K, which comes next behind us came up in season for the next fire, and had several men wounded, and this from our own gunners."

After Kinston was taken, Foster's expedition moved northwest along the Neuse River to the town of Whitehall (modern-day Seven Springs), where the ironclad CSS *Neuse* was being laid. Reports indicate the 154-foot-long ship was probably little more than a wooden keel with part of the hull in place. Foster's intention was to destroy the ship. To do that, he either had to shell it or send soldiers across the river to burn it. Ledlie's cannons were unlimbered on Confederates hiding behind hastily thrown-up breastworks consisting mostly of logs intended for the *Neuse*. His artillery apparently could not hit stacked logs, which must have resembled the broad side of a barn. Neither could the cannoneers hit a ship a few hundred yards from their position.

The next morning, Ledlie's men wrestled ten cannons to a high bluff south of the river and parked them wheel to wheel. The Confederates were now a half-mile away and below the Federals. This was great ground for artillery. Ledlie's cannoneers, acting on his orders, short-fused many of the shells they flung toward the Confederates. Instead of exploding on the north shore of the Neuse River, the shells burst over the heads of the Federal troops on the south side, sending dangerous fragments of metal slicing into their ranks. As the colonel of the Ninth New Jersey

Regiment put it, "If Colonel Ledlie . . . perform[s] anything credible before this war lasts, the good citizens of New York state will have reason to be thankful."

From Whitehall, the soldiers marched to Goldsboro, where they attacked a railroad bridge. Ledlie's shells could neither knock the bridge down nor set it on fire, so Foster had some volunteers rush forward to ignite the bridge by hand. That accomplished, they got safely out of the way and allowed Ledlie a free field to shell the far bank. This time, he didn't kill any Federals.

One of the unsolved mysteries of the Civil War is why dangerous officers were rarely punished for their behavior. On at least two occasions on the expedition, Ledlie fired on and killed Federals troops. That should have brought him dismissal or at least some sanction. Instead, Foster praised him. Whether Foster, a career military man from New Hampshire, feared the New Yorker's political connections is not known. Foster might have also thought he could get rid of Ledlie by—in the time-honored tradition of all bureaucracies—"kicking him upstairs." Whatever Foster was thinking, he suggested a promotion. Within a few days, Ledlie was appointed a brigadier general. Some whistleblowers tried to stop the appointment, but Congress ultimately confirmed it.

In May 1864, Ledlie was transferred to the Ninth Corps and given command of a brigade and later a division of infantry. His career in the artillery was thankfully over, but now he had the opportunity to create even more havoc in his new job. Again, most of the men Ledlie killed in his new job fought for the Union. His day of everlasting infamy came on July 30, 1864, at the Battle of the Crater in Petersburg, Virginia.

By the summer of 1864, the action around Petersburg had become a siege. Frustrated Union forces faced dug-in Confederates who had devised a system of trenches and forts with overlapping fire that made a frontal assault suicidal. One day, a lieutenant colonel of the Forty-eighth Pennsylvania Regiment overheard a comment from one of his men that all they had to do to destroy a Confederate fort 150 yards away was tunnel under it and blow it up. The colonel instantly knew the man was right. It could be done by his regiment. The Forty-eighth was recruited from coal miners.

Major General Burnside approved digging the tunnel, and work began. Developing new technologies—such as using a stove to create a draft that drew fresh air to the diggers—the men took more than three weeks to construct a horizontal shaft over five hundred feet long. The chamber at the end lay twenty feet directly underneath the Confederate lines. It was packed with four tons of black powder.

Union generals began to plan an attack by four divisions, three white and one black. The whites were experienced fighting men. The black division, under Brigadier General Edward Ferrero, had been used mostly for guard duty. It was determined that it was their turn to lead the way in battle. Told about the large explosion that would come, the blacks practiced for their role in a shock-assault style of attack. The theory was that the Confederates would be so stunned by the blast that they would be unable to mount a defense. The black soldiers would pour through the breach in the lines.

Less than twelve hours before the attack, Generals Meade and Grant reversed the permission they had earlier granted to Ferrero's division. The army commanders feared that if the attack stalled and the black regiments were badly mauled, they would be charged by abolitionists with being racists who intentionally sent black soldiers to their deaths.

Burnside was stunned. The blacks had trained hard to spearhead the attack, and his white regiments knew only that they were following the blacks. He would have to rearrange the whole nature of the attack. Burnside was so upset by the change in plans that he could not settle on which of his three white divisions should take the black division's place. His three brigadiers chose by lot. The winner—or loser, depending on one's perspective—was Ledlie.

When the mine exploded at 4:44 A.M., its effect looked like that of a bomb made infamous in Japan in 1945. A Federal officer wrote, "Without form or shape, full of red flames and carried on a bed of lightning flashes, it [the explosion's dust cloud] mounted toward heaven with a detonation of thunder and spread out like an immense mushroom whose stem seemed to be of fire and its head of smoke."

When Ledlie's men saw the ground heave in front of them, they had a predictable reaction—they ran to the rear. Their officers got them turned around and headed in the right direction. The soldiers advanced for 150 yards and then stopped. The blacks had been told to march around the crater in case its sides were too steep to climb. The undrilled whites marched down into the hole and stopped. They were in awe. What had been solid ground only moments earlier was now a thirty-foot-deep pit that ran for two hundred feet along the Confederate lines. At the bottom were nearly three hundred dead and wounded Confederates.

As Ledlie's men piled into the crater, his line officers began to look around for their commanding general to ask for orders. He was not there. Ledlie had quietly slipped away. He was in the rear in a bombproof taking deep drafts from a bottle of rum. It was the way he always bolstered his courage.

Though Ledlie's men already filled the crater, the following two white divisions—under Brigadier Generals Orlando Wilcox and Robert Potter—joined them at the bottom of the giant hole. The Confederates, finally recovering from the blast, recognized the opportunity in having a big hole shaped like a barrel with Federals at the bottom of it. Confederate cannons loaded with canister soon found the range.

The black division marched around the crater as it had been taught, but by now the Confederates were rushing back to the line. The three white divisions were still in the bottom of the crater and could do nothing to help when the blacks came under fire. Within minutes, the black division lost a fourth of its strength. The blacks then made their first major mistake. They fell back and went inside the crater also. Now the Confederates had more than ten thousand Federals to shoot at. Confederate infantry came up to the edge of the hole to rain fire on the massed Federals.

By noon, it was all over. The Confederates had lost three hundred killed in the explosion and less than a thousand wounded. The Federals had lost four thousand killed, wounded, captured, or missing.

Brigadier General Ledlie, lying drunk in a bombproof, was not among them. He was not immediately court-martialed for cowardice or drinking. Allowed to go on sick leave, he did not officially leave the army until January 23, 1865. One Union wag noted that Ledlie's removal from the field "was a heavy loss to the enemy." After the war, he returned to a successful civil-engineering career.

Ledlie was not alone in his bombproof. In fact, he may have been learning to waltz. Sharing his safe haven—and probably his bottle of rum—was Brigadier General Edward Ferrero, commander of the black division slaughtered along with Ledlie's men. Before the war, Ferrero had been a West Point dance instructor.

What qualified Ferrero to be a general other than teaching the two-step to cadets is hard to determine. His only military training came as commander of a New York militia unit prior to the war. In those days, such units were less military organizations than social clubs given to parading around in fancy uniforms, then stopping to take a nip.

Ferrero obtained a rank of colonel of the Fifty-first New York Infantry, a unit assigned to the North Carolina expedition under Burnside, then Foster. It was probably during this assignment that Ledlie and Ferrero became friends. Ferrero saw more fighting than Ledlie in 1862 and 1863. *Saw* is probably the operative word, as reports seem to fault his command abilities at battles both in the East (at Antietam and Fredericksburg) and the West (at Knoxville). Still, he was given command of a division of black soldiers when he transferred back east. They spent most of their time guarding railroads until the ill-fated Battle of the Crater.

How culpable Ferrero was in the disaster is hard to determine. He at least was on the battlefield long enough to send his troops into the breach. But as soon as he issued the order, he apparently sought safety with Ledlie. His proper place was with his men. Major William H. Powell, an aide to Ledlie, wrote after the war, "Had any one in authority been present when the colored troops made their charge, and had they been supported, there would have been a possibility of success, but when they fell back and broke up in disorder, it was the closing scene of the tragedy."

It was a tragedy that might have been less severe had Ledlie and

Ferrero tried to save their men. Powell observed the Confederates massing their troops for a counterattack on the crater. He went looking for Ledlie, "whom I found seated in a bomb proof with General Ferrero." In Powell's view, there had to be "some means . . . for withdrawing the mass of men from the crater without exposing them to the terrific fire which was kept up by the enemy; that if some shovels and picks could be found, the men in an hour could open a covered way by which they could be withdrawn. Not an implement of any kind could be found. Indeed the proposition was received with disfavor."

Powell's charge was that Ledlie and Ferrero actively resisted efforts to extricate the men they were too afraid to lead. Powell had given both generals at least two hours' notice that the Confederates were going to attack, but they had done nothing to prevent the shooting and capture of thousands of men.

A court of inquiry confirmed that Ferrero had abandoned his troops. That was not even enough to keep him off the promotions list. In December 1864, he was promoted to major general. But at least he was shuttled off to a command guarding a part of Virginia that had already been captured.

After the war, Ferrero owned and operated a number of dance studios in New York. He must have been good at it. The man tap-danced around charges of cowardice that, had he been a private in his own division, would have put him at the deadly end of a firing squad.

Not every Union general who sent his men into the crater was a coward. Brigadier General William Francis Bartlett had demonstrated his bravery early in the war. He was so brave that he returned to the army after losing his leg, so brave that the Confederates refused to kill him when they saw the one-legged general riding his horse, so brave that he didn't mind leading his men on foot in a battle so fierce that his commanders hid in a bombproof.

Bartlett could have sat out the first months of the Civil War until he graduated from Harvard in 1862, but he left college on the day the war started and signed on as a private. His intelligence was soon recognized. His regiment elected him captain, though he had no military training. What he had was courage, even after he lost a leg at the siege of Yorktown in the spring of 1862.

Bartlett likely noted the irony of losing his leg in the fashion he did. He had complained about his company's being assigned picket duty: "It is very unpleasant duty. No glory in being shot by a picket behind a tree. It is regular Indian fighting." Several days later, a Confederate picket shot him in the knee.

After taking time off to heal and learn how to walk again with the aid of an expensive, lightweight artificial leg made of cork, Bartlett returned to combat as the colonel of another regiment. A Massachusetts native, he soon found himself in the command of a former governor of Massachusetts, Major General Nathaniel B. Banks, who had been ordered to take over command of New Orleans in the summer of 1863. During the long siege of Port Hudson, Bartlett made it a point to stay with his men under the heaviest of fire, a quality that brought him two wounds. Even then, he did not abandon his regiment, but had himself tied in the saddle. Officers on horseback made tempting targets, but Confederate officers instructed their marksmen to let the one-legged Yankee live. He was too brave to kill.

Mustered out after his regiment's enlistment expired, Bartlett transferred back east, where he was assigned a brigade under Ledlie, a general even worse than Banks. Bartlett was wounded for the fourth time during the Battle of the Wilderness in May 1864. After fighting at Cold Harbor, he was promoted to brigadier general but still assigned to Ledlie's division. That assignment would prove embarrassing to the brave Bartlett.

On July 30, 1864, Bartlett then did the dumbest thing he had ever done in his life. He led his men into the crater rather than marching them around it, as the original division that trained for the attack had been told to do. Bartlett didn't know any better. Ledlie hadn't issued his brigade commanders instructions on what to do once the explosion occurred.

As the men of Bartlett's brigade milled around in the crater, the Confederates recovered from the shock and started targeting cannons loaded with canister into the bottom. Riflemen came to the edge to shoot into the mass of men. Bartlett was trying to rally his soldiers when there was a loud thud. The general tottered and fell. His officers crowded around, thinking he was dead, probably shot in the head, judging from the sound of the bullet.

That was discovered not to be the case when Bartlett shouted, "Put me any place where I can sit down!"

"But you are wounded, General. We have to take you to the rear!" said one of his aides.

"No, my leg is just shattered to pieces," the general replied.

"Well, then, you can't sit up. You'll have to lie down until we can get you out," the aide persisted.

"Oh, no! It's only my cork leg that is shattered," came the reply.

Bartlett's aides did not get him out of the crater. But his high rank must have been noticed by the Confederates, since they did not kill him, as they did almost half the men unlucky enough to find themselves at the bottom of the hole that night. Instead, Bartlett was captured and exchanged within a few weeks, as generals always were.

Bartlett got some satisfaction after he returned to service. He was given Ledlie's old job of commanding the First Division of the Ninth Corps. Wounded five times during the first three years of war, Bartlett stayed out of harm's way the remaining ten months.

Bartlett did not hold hard feelings against the Confederates. He lived for a while in Richmond and worked at the reopened Tredegar Iron Works before moving back to Massachusetts. His many wounds probably played a role in his early death in 1876 at the age of thirty-six.

After his experience with what a bullet could do to a cork leg, one wonders if Bartlett experimented with an iron replacement during his stint at Tredegar.

WILLIAM DWIGHT, THE GENERAL IN THE LUNCH LINE

Brigadier General William Dwight must not have been the studious type. That is suggested by his discharge from West Point for "deficiency in studies" just months before his planned graduation in 1853.

One thing that is known about Dwight is that he liked to eat. Even in the middle of a battle, he never missed lunch.

Dwight was probably pushed into the service by his well-to-do, image-conscious Massachusetts family, which had been in the country for nearly two hundred years before he was born. For the eight years prior to war, he was a successful manufacturer in Boston and Philadelphia. When war broke out, it rekindled whatever military drive Dwight had at West Point. Some pulled strings brought him a lieutenant colonelcy of the Seventieth New York Regiment. Sent to the Battle of Williamsburg, the opening battle of McClellan's Peninsula Campaign, Dwight proved a brave man. His regiment was devastated by a casualty rate of more than 50 percent, and he was wounded and left for dead on the field.

Captured and saved from death by the Confederates, he was soon exchanged. Dwight's bravery was recognized by his superiors, and he was promoted to brigadier general in November 1862. At last, he had reached the same status as his West Point classmates, an illustrious group that included Major Generals James B. McPherson, John Schofield, and Phil Sheridan. And he never had to sit in class those last few boring months to do it!

Dwight was transferred west, where he participated in the siege and capture of Port Hudson, Louisiana, and the Red River Campaign of Major General Nathaniel Banks.

Dwight got into trouble during the Red River Campaign, but it had nothing to do with his bravery on the battlefield. Part of the strategy of the campaign was to capture and/or buy vast stores of cotton from Louisiana and Texas planters. This cotton would be shipped to the cotton mills of the North, which were sitting idle. Dwight, a mill owner himself, seems to have used the cotton to reward and punish his friends and enemies back in Massachusetts.

Rather than discipline him, the Federal commanders transferred Dwight away from the temptation of the cotton fields. He was given command of a division in the Nineteenth Corps, which was fighting in the Shenandoah Valley.

At the Third Battle of Winchester on September 19, 1864, Dwight's old classmate Sheridan opened the action at dawn by marching his divisions down a narrow valley toward the Federals. Since the Union men could not spread out in battle lines, their advance was slow. This gave the Confederates time to organize a counterattack with two divisions of their own. When the Confederates hit back, Dwight's division and one under Colonel Cuvier Grover crumbled and retreated. Dwight blamed Grover for not stopping his panicked men from falling back on Dwight's division.

Instead of ignoring Dwight, Grover dropped a bombshell. He said that the reason Dwight's men ran was that their commander was in the rear eating lunch instead of leading his men into combat. Dwight was immediately arrested, but no charges were formally prepared.

Dwight's old friends were now suspicious of him. Still, they gave him the benefit of the doubt—at least for another month. On October 19, 1864, his division was among those surprised and routed at daylight as Jubal Early's Confederates came charging across Cedar Creek, Virginia. Dwight joined his division and ran to the rear, as did most of the Federals that morning. It would be the end of the day before Sheridan arrived to rally his men to counterattack and drive back the Confederates. Dwight could have done it, but he missed his chance.

Dwight stayed in the army until 1866, but he was never given other important jobs. After the war, when many brigadier generals were given honorary promotions to major general, his name was not on the list. Though he had made himself a hero at Williamsburg, he had tarnished his name during the Red River Campaign. And for the want of a sandwich at Third Winchester, he had ruined his military reputation.

Bloody Bill Anderson Rides into a Trap

Bloody Bill Anderson liked his nickname and didn't mind living up to it, though he doubtless would have preferred being remembered for bloodying his enemies and not himself. But when you are the sole man nervy enough—or stupid enough—to charge an entire column of Federals, you tend to be the only target.

Missouri was anything but neutral during the war. More than a thousand engagements ranging from small skirmishes to large battles to wholesale massacres took place within its borders. It hosted more engagements than any other state that remained loyal to the Union. Among the Confederate states, only Virginia and Tennessee had more recorded battles than Missouri.

The saddest part about most of these engagements is that they were not fought by opposing armies that moved on to fight elsewhere once the smoke cleared. Most of the fighting in Missouri was guerrilla action, small engagements between angry, bitter men. Battles were fought by the same men over the same ground again and again. If they failed to burn the opposition's barns and crops one night, the riders came back another night. If they succeeded then, they might return to kill the stock. The next time, they might kill their enemy's entire family. War in Missouri was vicious, never-ending. It was just the type of action twenty-one-year-old William Anderson would come to enjoy.

By the summer of 1863, Union brigadier general Thomas Ewing, commander of the District of the Border, had grown so weary of Confederate guerrillas that he settled on a novel tactic. If he could not capture the guerrillas harassing him, he could easily capture their wives, mothers, and children. It was illegal—a fact Ewing knew, since he had been chief justice of the Kansas Supreme Court before he resigned to be a general—but it was effective.

In August 1863, Ewing wrote a letter to his commanding officer suggesting that "two-thirds of the families on the occupied farms of that region [Missouri bordering Kansas] are kin to the guerrillas, and are actively and heartily engaged in feeding, clothing, and sustaining them. The presence of these families is the cause of the presence there of the guerrillas. I can see no prospect of an early and complete end to the war on the border, without an increase of troops, so long as those families remain there." In other words, if the women and children were removed from their homes, their husbands and fathers would follow.

Ewing rounded up the women of some of the more notorious guerrillas and put them in a three-story, brick Kansas City jail until he could decide where to ship them. On August 14, the prison, so dilapidated that the general had been warned it could collapse if occupied, caved in, killing four women and severely injuring several others. The Union general denied rumors that he had intentionally weakened the structure by knocking out supports necessary to hold up the floors. He did not help his credibility when he claimed the women had caused the cave-in themselves by trying to build an escape tunnel.

When word of the disaster reached the Confederate guerrillas riding with William Clark Quantrill, they went wild with rage. One of the women killed was the sister of a thin young man who liked to wear his black hair long and unkempt. Until then, Quantrill had counted Bill Anderson as just another of his riders. But when he heard the news of the Kansas City jail collapse, the quiet Anderson seemed to explode with energy and leadership skills. It might have also driven him over the edge into insanity. Whatever happened in the mind of the young man, it led him to start living up to the nickname "Bloody Bill."

Ewing must not have been given to thinking things through to their conclusion. Though Missourians and even loyal Kansans were up in arms over the collapse of the jail, Ewing pressed on with his plan to move the families. On August 18, he announced he would issue General Order Number 11, which would call for the removal of virtually everyone from four counties along the Kansas-Missouri border.

It did not take long for Ewing to hear from Quantrill, who wanted revenge for General Order Number 11, and his sidekick Anderson, who wanted revenge for his sister's death. At dawn on August 21, more than

450 guerrillas rode into Lawrence, Kansas. Quantrill's orders to his men were simple: "Kill every man big enough to carry a gun." In two hours, more than 150 men and boys died. Not a single one of Quantrill's men was shot. Demonstrating the strange civility of the Civil War, the same raiders who shot down twelve-year-old boys did not harm a single woman.

Among the few adult men to survive was one of the raid's primary targets, United States senator James Lane, a Kansas Jayhawker who had led similar antislavery raids into Missouri. Lane, clad only in a night-shirt, hid in his cornfield.

Not long after Lawrence, Anderson split from Quantrill. He formed his own company of guerrillas, which at various times numbered from fifty to a hundred. He raided all over Missouri and Kansas, wantonly killing whomever he found in a blue uniform. It did not matter if they surrendered. Bloody Bill killed. He also scalped.

While the perpetrators of such savage behavior are generally thought to be illiterate brutes, Anderson was a polite gentleman when writing letters explaining that the only reason he was fighting was to avenge the murder of his father and sisters. His letters must have sent chills up the spines of editors whose papers he didn't like. In a letter he sent to two newspapers, Anderson wrote, "In reading both your papers, I see you urge the policy of the citizens taking up arms to defend their persons and property. You are only asking them to sign their death warrants. Your doctrine is an absurdity and I will kill you for being fools."

One of Anderson's worst atrocities—and there were many--was the massacre at Centralia, Missouri, on September 27, 1864. He and his men captured the town and were sacking it when a train pulled into the station. On board were twenty-five furloughed Union soldiers. Anderson had them all strip naked. He then asked if any of them was an officer or a noncommissioned officer. A sergeant, expecting to be shot immediately, stepped forward. He was pulled out of line, and the rest of the men were pistoled to death. The sergeant was thrown on the back of a horse and taken along for a while when the raiders left town. He was later turned loose unharmed after being congratulated for his bravery.

A force of more than 130 Missouri militia took out after the raiders.

The militiamen came riding over the crest of a hill to find Anderson's raiders standing in a line by their horses. The militiamen dismounted and formed a battle line. Anderson's men then mounted their horses and rode full tilt into the militia's line. Almost all of the bluecoats were killed by Anderson's men, who aimed at their heads, just as they did when practicing by shooting pumpkins mounted at head level on sticks.

A month later, on October 26, Anderson and 70 of his men were tracked to the little town of Albany by 150 men of the Missouri militia, tipped to Anderson's presence by a woman living nearby. Half the militiamen were stationed in the woods. The other half formed across the road the raiders would use to leave the farmhouse where they were eating breakfast.

When Anderson rounded a bend in the road, he saw the seventy-five men kneeling in the road. An untrained guerrilla used to murdering men rather than fighting them in battle, he never thought that the heavy woods beside the road might make an excellent place to stage an ambush. He never thought of anything but what he saw right in front of him. With a maniacal scream, Anderson rushed forward, his men behind him.

Just then, the Missourians hidden in the woods opened fire. Those raiders who were not killed in the first volley forgot the charge and took to the woods on the opposite side of the road. Most did not stop to set up a battle line. They headed for safety.

Bloody Bill did not. Without looking behind him, he charged forward—alone. The militiamen in the road must have been stunned. A single, long-haired, screaming wild man with a pistol in each hand was charging seventy-five men armed with muskets and shotguns.

If period reports are to be believed, none of the soldiers hit Anderson until he had run through their line of battle. Perhaps the bulk of them had already fired at the guerrillas behind Anderson, and that was what he was counting on in getting away. After Anderson charged past the skirmish line, he pitched backwards off his saddle. Two musket balls were found in the back of his head. Besides the pistols Anderson had in his hands when he died, six others were in holsters on his saddle.

Those pistols discovered on his saddle said much about the success of guerrilla bands led by men like Anderson and Quantrill. Within Anderson's reach were eight loaded pistols, giving him a total of forty-eight rounds he could fire without reloading. At most, an average foot soldier could fire three rounds a minute with his musket. Standard issue for regular Federal cavalry was one carbine and one six-shot revolver. Thus, if Anderson's armament can be considered typical of his command, his men more than outgunned most of the Federal forces they encountered. Add to that the fact that Anderson's guerrillas were country boys used to riding horses and hitting what they aimed for. Thus, his fifty men were more than a match for larger Union units assigned to kill them.

Anderson's personal belongings came under close scrutiny. In his pockets were a gold watch, more than six hundred dollars in cash, and a lock of his wife's hair, proving that even homicidal maniacs can find someone to love. Braided into his horse's bridle was a human scalp. Scalping was a habit Anderson had picked up early in the war. When Confederate major general Sterling Price had met with Anderson and other guerrilla leaders, he made them throw away their scalps before he would talk with them. It was fine with Anderson if Price was squeamish about such matters—there was an abundant supply of unharvested Union scalps to replace those thrown away. At the time of his death, Anderson wore a fancy guerrilla shirt with ruffles and embroidery. Guerrillas' wives customarily made such fine shirts for their killer husbands. No one had the nerve to suggest that they might make the guerrillas look, well, a little sissy. Since Anderson was shot in the head, his shirt was not even stained when his body was propped up and his picture taken with his pistol-holding hands crossing his chest.

Reports vary as to how Anderson's body was treated after death. One story says his head was removed and displayed on a telegraph pole. This desecration would have been in retaliation for the Yankee beheadings one of his lieutenants liked to do.

Was Bloody Bill crazy to charge a Federal column? No. Just days earlier, the same tactic had won him a victory at Centralia. Did he know he was by himself? Probably not. His men had never deserted him before, and he had no reason to think they would that day.

Bloody Bill Anderson left one legend that outlived him. Riding with Anderson throughout much of his short, murderous career were two sets of brothers who were cousins to each other. One set was Jesse and Frank James. The other was Cole and Jim Younger.

1865

"It requires great

patience to deal with fools

and I have no patience to

spare."

–ADMIRAL DAVID PORTER
REFERRING TO BENJAMIN BUTLER

Ship Bombs and Naval Land Assaults: The Fort Fisher Debacle

Fort Fisher, the mile-long sand fort on the Atlantic Ocean beach twenty-five miles south of Wilmington, North Carolina, may have been the most formidable fort ever built on the North American continent. Certainly, it was the strongest Confederate fort the Federal army and navy ever encountered. Before it fell, this installation was responsible for the deaths of hundreds of Union soldiers and sailors and the embarrassment of several Union generals and admirals.

From 1862 through 1864, Fort Fisher kept Wilmington the South's most important blockade-running port. Situated near the mouth of the Cape Fear River, the fort's cannons kept Union warships from slipping into the river and running up to capture Wilmington. At the same time, those cannons protected the blockade runners moving into and out of the river. As long as Fort Fisher was occupied, the Federals were unable to totally blockade the port.

For most of the war, Union forces viewed Fort Fisher with a mixture of fear and awe. Modeled after a giant European earth fort that Confederate colonel William Lamb had read about in a book on the Crimean War, Fort Fisher was simple in design. It looked nothing like the brick-and-stone forts that had been built for coastal defense since the early

1800s. Brick forts had been rendered obsolete early in 1862 when Union naval forces pounded Fort Pulaski, located on the Georgia coast near Savannah, into fine red dust. Rifled cannon rounds shattered the bricks at the point of entry, burrowed inside, then exploded. Within hours, any brick fort's walls could be pounded to the ground thanks to the new rifled cannons.

Fort Fisher was not even an enclosed fort in the traditional sense. It was L-shaped, its longer side facing the Atlantic and its shorter side crossing from the ocean to the Cape Fear River. The guns on the shorter side faced northward up the Federal Point peninsula to protect the fort from land attack. The fort's walls and the forty-foot-tall mounds protecting the cannons were constructed entirely of sand. Timber-supported chambers were buried deep inside for use as black-powder magazines and casemates in which to hide during bombardments. The tons of sand surrounding the shells muffled explosions, limiting the damage. Maintenance of such a sand fort consisted of nothing more than using wheelbarrows to dump more sand on top.

Just looking at Fort Fisher scared off most Union forces until December 1864, when Lieutenant General U. S. Grant finally decided that it had to be taken. Grant reluctantly agreed to turn over responsibility for the expedition to Major General Ben Butler, a political appointee whose battlefield abilities left much to be desired. Butler put together a land force of sixty-five hundred soldiers and a naval force of more than sixty warships. The date of the attack would be December 23.

That was assuming there would still be a fort to attack. If things worked out as the Union planned, Fort Fisher and its garrison would disintegrate long before the first Union soldier set foot on the beach.

Butler's secret weapon, towed south with his invasion force, was the USS *Louisiana*, an old, 295-ton ship that had been doing duty off Fort Fisher as a blockader. All her masts were removed, and the vessel was camouflaged to conceal her identity from the sharp-eyed pickets of Fort Fisher. The *Louisiana* was made to look like a blockade runner. In reality, she was the largest seagoing bomb ever conceived. Packed inside her holds and on her deck were more than 200 tons of black powder.

Butler had been thinking for months about a way to destroy Fort Fisher using a bomb, much as had been done with the Confederate trenches at the Battle of the Crater. At some point, he made the acquaintance of self-proclaimed experts who assured him that truly large explosions create their own shock waves. If placed close enough to the target, a huge bomb would knock down and destroy everything in the path of the shock wave. One expert told Butler it was like a directed tornado.

Grant scoffed at Butler's proposal but agreed to let him try. All it would cost him was gunpowder, and he had enough of that to go around. Admiral David Porter, who would lead the Union navy on the expedition, also bought into the idea. An aide to the admiral asked him if he really believed such a scheme would work. "The names of those connected with the expedition will be famous for all time to come," was Porter's emphatic reply. It was an oddly supportive comment coming from Porter, who, like Grant, considered Butler an idiot. In discussing Butler, Porter once said, "It requires great patience to deal with fools and I have no patience to spare."

Butler's plan was to have a volunteer crew tow the *Louisiana* as close as possible to Fort Fisher, ground her on the sandy bottom, set off a slow-burning fuse, then run for the open ocean in case the gigantic explosion set off a tidal wave that could swamp the Federal fleet.

On the night slated for the bomb's detonation, Porter pulled a double cross on Butler, who had been detained from reaching Fort Fisher by Atlantic storms. Though the bomb was Butler's idea, Porter ordered the *Louisiana* towed into place in Butler's absence. His intention was clear: he wanted full credit for destroying Fort Fisher. After the explosion, he would land a force of marines to mop up any Confederates still alive. By the time Butler and his soldiers arrived, there would be little left for them to do. The United States Navy would have captured Fort Fisher. Though a latecomer to the scheme, Porter totally believed in the awesome power of a directed blast. "I think houses in Wilmington [twenty-five miles away] and Smithville [six miles away] will tumble to the ground and much demoralize the people," he wrote.

With fourteen volunteers aboard, the *Louisiana* was towed close to the fort before her boilers were lit. Once she got up steam, the volunteers steered toward the fort. The leader of the expedition steamed to within what he thought was three hundred yards of the fort (actually around six hundred yards) and dropped anchor, afraid that he would be seen by the fort's pickets if he went closer. He and the others set several fuses, then abandoned ship to row toward a waiting rescue vessel.

The sixty ships of the Union naval contingent had set up watch twelve miles out. Porter had warned them that staying any closer would put them in range of the shock wave/tidal wave/tornado. He had brought along a number of reporters so they could send stories back to their newspapers about the brilliant admiral who had revolutionized warfare.

At about 1:45 A.M., a full half-hour after the explosion was expected, the *Louisiana* went up. Witnesses described the explosion as the greatest they had ever seen or heard. It rattled the masts and rigging of the Union ships and was extremely loud.

That was its total effect. It was a loud firecracker. The floating bomb did no damage to Fort Fisher, unless waking up the sleeping garrison counts. When Butler arrived, he blamed the failure of the bomb on Porter's not knowing how to light the fuses properly and how to direct the explosion. Butler likely considered himself lucky. His idea had been a giant dud, but he could legitimately blame someone else for it.

Porter refused to take the blame. Now that the army's bomb had failed, he insisted he would win the Battle of Fort Fisher the old-fashioned way. He would reduce it by naval gunfire.

His plan worked about as well as Butler's. The navy shelled Fort Fisher for twelve hours, firing more than ten thousand rounds at the fort without silencing its guns. Butler landed about a third of his force. His men advanced far enough to discover that even the wooden palisade around the sand walls was still intact, which would make it difficult for them to storm the fort.

Butler conferred with some captured Confederates, who told him all sorts of tall tales about the fort's strength and how there were hordes of Confederates hiding behind the sand dunes. They assured Butler that the fort was too strong for the Federals to storm. The general called off the attack with two-thirds of his men still on the transports and the other third almost touching the walls. Butler personally left the battle site so quickly with most of his transports that seven hundred of his soldiers were abandoned on the shore. They were rescued two days later.

An enraged Grant removed Butler from command and started planning an assault under the command of Brigadier General Alfred Terry, one of the few civilians to rise to the rank of general without being a professional politician. One difference between Butler and Terry was that Terry was an intelligent leader of men. He was a natural fighter.

Within two weeks, Terry was back at the fort with eight thousand soldiers. Also back was Porter. He had most of the same ships but a different strategy. During the December bombardment, the clever rebels had realized that the Federals were using the Confederate garrison flag as a sighting point, so they moved the flag to the far side of the fort. The Federal gunners had dutifully lifted their aim, and many of the naval shells had sailed over the fort and landed harmlessly in the Cape Fear River. Porter was determined to do better this time. He sent his ships in closer and ordered them to concentrate their aim on the seaward walls of the fort. When the second bombardment started on January 13, 1865, the new tactics worked much better. More of Fort Fisher's guns were taken out of action, and the palisade, almost unhit during the first bombardment, shattered after two days.

While Terry was planning a land attack for January 15, Porter approached him with an incredible idea. Concerned that history might only remember the ground soldiers at Fort Fisher, Porter proposed sending in a force of sixteen hundred sailors and four hundred marines to support Terry's men. This naval force would attack the fort where its sea face and its land face intersected. This also happened to be the point where the largest gun was placed, making it the strongest part of the fort. Porter figured the greatest glory would be won there. Porter further proposed that only the marines would be armed with rifles. His sailors would go ashore with Colt navy revolvers and cutlasses. In effect, he planned to "board" Fort Fisher like it was some giant, sandy, eighteenth-century pirate ship commanded by Blackbeard and his scurvy crew.

Terry likely thought Porter a fool. The Federals would be attacking a fort armed with cannons firing canister. Those cannons would be supported by riflemen armed with muskets accurate at four hundred to six hundred yards. By contrast, the pistol-wielding Union sailors would not be able to hit anything beyond thirty yards. And that was if they knew how to aim their seldom-used sidearms. Terry decided to say nothing. If Porter wanted to get his sailors killed, that was his business.

Porter had no real plans or tactics for his sailors. Soldiers were trained to form into companies, which formed into regiments, which formed into brigades. They were trained to march in varying formations to best use the lay of the land when attacking fortifications. Sailors were trained to stand on a pitching deck and to load and fire cannons. Porter's sailors would be little more than an armed mob.

He did issue one order that made sense. The sailors were to wait for the soldiers to attack Fort Fisher's land face near the Cape Fear River. Then, while the Confederates were distracted on the river side, the sailors would attack the sea side.

Things did not work out that way. When the army's attack was a half-hour late, the naval commander on the beach got tired of waiting in the woods. On his own, he ordered the attack on the sea face. His sailors were sent running across 1,200 open yards of sandy beach. After they had run about 600 exhausting yards and were slowing down, the garrison of Fort Fisher stood on its sand mounds ready to meet the attack. The Confederates had four cannons loaded with canister aimed up the beach. Their rifles already had the sailors in range. It would be another 570 yards before the sailors could use their puny pistols.

Colonel William Lamb, Fort Fisher's commander, watched the Federals close the distance. He ordered his men to hold their fire. Finally, when the Union men were just 150 yards away—still 120 yards beyond the effective range of their pistols—more than 500 Confederate riflemen fired the first volley into the 2,000 Federals.

Scores of seamen were cut down, falling face down in the sand. Hundreds more behind them were stunned to see what had happened. The naval officers got their men to their feet, urging them forward before the Confederates had time to fire a second volley. What the Federals did not know was that the men in Fort Fisher were already ready. They had handed their empty muskets to men behind them, who exchanged them for loaded weapons. The second volley came within seconds. With that volley, the firing became general as the Confederates fired at anything in blue that moved on the sand.

The sailors, unused to running on sand and totally unfamiliar with how soldiers were supposed to conduct themselves, dropped to the beach. Their only cover was the wooden palisade fifty yards in front of them, but many did not even try for it. The few who made it to the fence huddled behind it, rather than running around it to scale the sand mounds, as they had been ordered to do. Only one sailor climbed all the way to the top of the wall. He was shot and killed. Just one Confederate was shot by a sailor, who made it halfway up the wall before retreating to the safety of the wooden fence.

Officers tried to rally their sailors to continue the charge. They knew they outnumbered the Confederates more than four to one. If they could only get the mob of men to swarm the sand walls fifty yards away, they would win their objective.

The sailors would have none of it. As the officers rose and urged their men to charge, a handful of sailors turned and ran. The handful turned into scores, then hundreds. Soon, the entire contingent was running as hard as it could back up the beach. Most of the sailors had not even taken their pistols from their holsters. They hadn't gotten close enough to shoot at anything.

On the beach lay more than three hundred dead and dying sailors and marines. Some bled to death on the sand. Others who fell at the water's edge were swept out with the waves and were buried at sea.

The army had a better time of it. Terry's men were able to breach the fort's walls late in the afternoon. They slowly worked their way from near the river all the way to the sea face. It was brutal hand-to-hand, club-to-club combat that did not end until after ten o'clock that night. More than five hundred Confederates were killed or wounded in the second attack, compared to just a hundred in the first. Nearly a thousand Federals fell.

The fort was finally captured on January 15, but the death toll continued to mount the following day. The morning after the battle started out quiet and somber. The bodies of men on both sides still littered the fort. Activity increased as Federal soldiers, sailors, and marines began to awaken. Instead of collecting the bodies of their friends and enemies, many men went exploring to see what they could loot from the fort. One playfully jerked the lanyard of a Confederate cannon. It fired, and the canister still loaded inside narrowly missed some Federals lounging in front of the gun.

A lieutenant colonel who had been ordered to post guards at all of the bombproofs decided he had better double-check the placement of his sentries. He found that almost all of them had been lax in stopping looters from wandering around the fort. Worse, he had somehow missed posting guards at the most important bombproof of all, Fort Fisher's main magazine. Inside were more than six tons of black powder.

Before the colonel could post sentries at the magazine, a lieutenant from another regiment passed its door. He noticed several men standing around, one of whom called, "Have you got it all out?" A voice replied, "Perhaps not. They've got a light in there now." The curious lieutenant asked what was inside. "Boxes of powder" was the reply. The unruffled lieutenant suggested that the men might not want to be carrying an open torch around powder. The men, marines who may have had a touch of liquor for breakfast, didn't listen.

At seven-thirty that morning, one of the leathernecks raised his torch high inside the magazine and set off more than thirteen thousand pounds of gunpowder. More than 250 Federal soldiers disappeared in the flash. The marines were atomized. Soldiers and sailors were killed by flying pieces of wood, and dozens were buried under the tons of sand that flew up in the air and then settled back down.

Many Federals, unwilling to blame their comrades for their own deaths, theorized that the Confederates had rigged a time bomb to blow up the fort. An electrical wire was found running from the fort, and it was theorized that the Confederates may have set off the blast by remote control. The fort's Confederate commander laid the rumors to rest when he explained that the wire was a telegraph line. The official Federal board of inquiry placed responsibility for the fatal blunder squarely on the drunken men, who should have been under the control of their officers.

"IN HIS NETHER GARMENTS": GENERALS CAUGHT IN THEIR UNDERWEAR

Civil War generals on both sides must have had a recurring nightmare in which they slept late, woke up, and discovered they were late for battle. They rushed to the front and were standing in front of their superiors and subordinates about to give a status report on the enemy when they noticed everyone was laughing and pointing fingers. They looked down to see what was so funny.

They were in their underwear.

It happened several times in the war.

Union brigadier general Joseph Jackson Bartlett was a brilliant twenty-one-year-old attorney from Elmira, New York, when he entered service as major in the Twenty-seventh New York. Though he didn't have a day of military training, he handled himself well at First Manassas. At the end of the battle, when most of the Union army was fleeing to the rear in panic, Bartlett calmly, slowly sent his men back in an orderly rear-guard action. He was one of a small number of officers credited with saving the bulk of the Union army from capture. For his skill at controlling his men, he was rewarded with a promotion to colonel.

He fought well in other battles and was named a brigadier general in October 1862. His superiors praised his calm in battle in report after report.

Only once was Brigadier General Bartlett rattled. That was when Confederate major general J. E. B. Stuart came looking for him. In

November 1863, during the campaign at Mine Run, Virginia, Stuart's intelligence told him that Bartlett was staying at New Baltimore, a between-the-lines outpost. Stuart rode up to Bartlett's headquarters just in time to see the general running into the woods "in his nether garments," according to Stuart's official report. Stuart did not send troopers into the woods looking for him.

This near-capture did not diminish the Federal high command's respect for Bartlett. He was one of the generals who accepted the Confederate stacking of arms at Appomattox Courthouse on April 12, 1865, three days after Lee had formally surrendered the Army of Northern Virginia.

Bartlett became a politician and lawyer after the war and served as United States minister to Sweden in President Grant's administration. He was always well dressed for formal occasions.

Bartlett escaped capture in his underwear. Brigadier General Edwin Henry Stoughton did not.

Stoughton seemed to get promoted for no reasons other than that his Yankee family was descended from early settlers and his uncle was a successful politician. He did not display any outstanding talents at West Point, graduating seventeenth among the twenty-two students in the 1859 class. Once commissioned, he was assigned routine garrison duty in New York Harbor. On March 4, 1861, as the nation was on the brink of war, Stoughton resigned his commission, which he was allowed to do since there were no rules at that date about having to serve a certain amount of time in the army in exchange for the education.

Stoughton's family may have pressured him to return to service. In September 1861, he was appointed colonel of a regiment raised in Vermont. The regiment was assigned to garrison duty around Washington that winter.

In the spring of 1862, Stoughton was finally forced into combat when Union major general George McClellan tried invading Virginia from its peninsula. After this hard-fought campaign, Stoughton took a five-month leave of absence, apparently to rest from the rigors of the field. McClellan had him appointed a brigadier general in his absence, much to the consternation of older, more experienced officers. Stoughton was only twenty-four. At the time, he was the youngest general in the Union army. He had served in only one campaign.

When Stoughton returned to the field, he was given command of the outer ring of defenses around Washington. One of his charges was to capture Captain John Singleton Mosby, a partisan raider whose local presence was so pervasive that several Union-occupied counties in northern Virginia were called "Mosby's Confederacy." Though Mosby rarely commanded more than two hundred men, he was a thorn in the side of the Union, raiding picket posts, wagon supply trains, storehouses, and even steam trains.

Mosby loved the attention he was getting from the Federals. In early March 1863, Sergeant Ames, a deserter from a New York cavalry regiment, found his way to Mosby's camp and convinced the partisan that he, Ames, would help lead a raid on his former headquarters. Though suspicious of the New Yorker, Mosby and twenty-nine men threaded their way through Union picket lines and rode into Fairfax Court House, Virginia, in the dead of night on March 8, 1863.

Ames captured his former captain and brought him to Mosby. The raiders then stopped at the house of the lieutenant colonel of the New Yorkers, who had heard the riders come into town and figured out who they were. Dressed only in his nightshirt, he rushed out the back door of his house and wiggled down the hole of the outhouse, where he hid until morning. He left his wife to meet Mosby. She was, in Mosby's description, "like a lioness at the door." When the Yankee emerged the next morning, his wife forced him into a cold bath and burned his nightshirt.

A prisoner agreed to point the Confederates to Stoughton's headquarters. When they arrived, they pretended they were Union soldiers, calling out that they had a dispatch for the general. An officer came to the door and had a pistol shoved into his stomach. He led Mosby himself to the general's upstairs bedroom.

Stoughton did not wake when Mosby entered the room. According to legend, Mosby pulled down the covers and lifted the general's nightshirt to reveal his bare buttocks—which he soundly slapped. (Mosby mentions the slap in some accounts and ignores it in others.)

"General, did you ever hear of Mosby?" Mosby asked.

"Yes, have you captured him?" the groggy general asked, apparently unconcerned that someone other than the mistress he had brought with him from Massachusetts had slapped his buttocks.

"No, he has captured you. I am Mosby and Stuart's cavalry has possession of Fairfax Court House. Be quick and dress," Mosby ordered.

Stoughton slowly dressed in front of a mirror until an amused Mosby ordered his men to help him finish in quicker fashion. One of the raiders handed the general his watch. Stoughton was impressed that the Confederate did not confiscate it.

Though he had only twenty-nine men with him and didn't fire a single shot, Mosby captured one general, two captains, thirty enlisted men, and fifty-eight horses, once again living up to the nickname "the Gray Ghost." For weeks, the planks of bridges leading to Washington would be pulled up at night lest Mosby try to steal into the city to kidnap the president.

President Lincoln wasn't worried. In fact, he was amused at Mosby's feat. "I don't mind the loss of the brigadier as much as the horses. I can make a much better general in five minutes, but the horses cost $125 a piece!" Lincoln said.

Stoughton was exchanged by the Confederates within a few months, but the boy general's career was over. He was now the laughingstock of the Union, the general captured in his underwear by the man he was supposed to be capturing himself. When Stoughton tried to report back to the army, he discovered that it had no plans of giving him any sort of command. He resigned and moved back to New York City, where he entered law practice with his uncle. Stoughton did not have to live long with his embarrassment. He died in 1868 at age thirty.

Mosby lived to be eighty-two, long enough to make friends with his old enemies. He even became a Republican and served as counsel to Hong Kong in the administration of his friend U. S. Grant, another general he almost captured on one of his raids, though Grant was fully clothed at the time.

Another set of Confederate partisan rangers operated mostly in western Virginia and Maryland, leaving the eastern part of Virginia to Mosby. One night, it managed to double Mosby's pleasure, bagging two generals in one night.

Early in 1862, Union brigadier general Benjamin Franklin Kelley captured the wife, daughter, and four-year-old son of John Hanson "Hanse" McNeill in an effort to smoke him out of hiding. Kelley even sent the family to a prisoner-of-war camp in Ohio. It did not work. McNeill and his son Jesse continued their raiding. The innocents were eventually released, but the McNeill family held a grudge against Kelley for making war on wives and children.

In December 1864, not long after his father had died leading a raid against the Federals, Jesse McNeill started forming an idea. His father had always wanted to capture Kelley in retaliation for the shabby treatment his family had received. Jesse realized that the war would end soon. If he was going to get his revenge, it would have to be now.

Kelley was not exactly a great prize. A West Virginia merchant who stayed loyal to the Union, he had raised a Federal cavalry regiment and been wounded in one of the first actions in the region. Union commanders kept him on local duty in West Virginia, mainly guarding the railroad lines in that state and Maryland. After one bungled counterattack on Confederate raiders, Kelley was severely criticized by Union major general Phil Sheridan, who said wryly, "I respectfully present the name of Brevet Major General Kelley for being exceedingly cautious when there is no danger and not remarkably so when there is."

As McNeill thought about capturing Kelley, he realized he would have the same opportunity to capture Kelley's commander, Major General George Crook. Crook was a much better general than Kelley. He was an 1852 West Point graduate, though he had ranked far down the rolls. Book learning was not Crook's strong point. On-field command was. He quickly rose through the ranks and became a division commander cited for bravery in four different battles. In October 1864, he was given command of the Department of West Virginia, though he made his headquarters in Cumberland, Maryland.

On the snowy, bitterly cold night of February 21, 1865, McNeill and sixty-three raiders, including at least one as young as sixteen, rode quietly into Cumberland. They had already sent scouts into the city to establish that the two generals were in their headquarters. They captured one outpost of five pickets by saying that the town was surrounded and telling the pickets to wait in their shed until morning. The men meekly promised to comply.

The raiders rode into the middle of town at three in the morning. The few Federal soldiers who were awake among the hundreds stationed there barely paid them any attention. If the Federals had studied the situation, they would have noticed that the raiders moved in four squads—two to kidnap the generals, one to steal horses, and one to destroy the telegraph office.

The squad assigned to capture Kelley in his hotel room found him guarded by only a single sentry, who gave up without a word. The Confederates walked in and found the general softly snoring away. They shook him awake and ordered him to dress.

The squad sent to capture Crook knew exactly where to go. One Confederate was the son of the man who owned the building. Another was the son of the hotel keeper. They, too, captured their general without incident. Both men were sound asleep and had to be ordered from their nightshirts into their uniforms. The raiders were so quiet and the generals so compliant that their aides sleeping in adjoining rooms were not awakened.

While the generals were getting dressed, the horse-stealing squad gathered all the mounts in the street. A policeman asked what they were doing.

"McNeill's Rangers are coming. We are moving the horses to safety," came the answer.

"Good idea," said the cop, who then went on his way.

Twenty-five minutes after entering town, the raiders were on their way out again with two fully dressed Union generals in tow. They had missed one. Brigadier General James A. Garfield was also staying in the hotel. Also missed was Captain William McKinley. Both men would parlay their Civil War experience into terms as president of the United States, and both would be assassinated.

It was almost daylight before the generals were missed. Since the telegraph squad had destroyed the office and equipment, there was no way to wire ahead to try to catch the raiders. The generals were eventually sent to Staunton, Virginia, a 154-mile, three-day trip. When they arrived, an impressed Crook had to admit, "This is the most brilliant exploit of the war!"

After being treated to a dinner hosted by Confederate major general Jubal Early, the two Union generals were put on board a train bound for Richmond. By chance, one of the other riders was Colonel John Singleton Mosby, who had captured Union brigadier general Stoughton two years earlier. Mosby was highly entertained when he heard the story. He grasped the hands of each of McNeill's raiders and joked, "You boys have beaten me badly! The only way I can equal this will be to go to Washington and bring out Lincoln!"

Crook was missed, but observers said the Confederates might just have well have kept Kelley. At a musical show back in Cumberland, Mary Clara Bruce, daughter of the hotel keeper, was to sing a song called "He Kissed Me When He Left." It was well known that Miss Bruce and General Crook had been seeing each other. After the title of the song was announced but before she could start singing, a Union soldier shouted, "No he didn't. McNeill didn't give him time!"

Crook was paroled within a month. He later helped chase down Lee and was present at Appomattox. He returned after the war and made good on his promise to Mary. They were married. Crook held no grudges against Mary's brother, the man who had captured him and who was now his brother-in-law. Crook spent the next twenty years fighting Plains Indians.

Kelley, too, was exchanged, but the fifty-eight-year-old shopkeeper was too old to fight Indians. He held a number of bureaucratic positions the rest of his life.

Both generals were careful to keep their pants on for the rest of the war.

Getting surprised in one's underwear—or worse—was not purely a Federal foible. It also happened to one of the most capable generals of the Confederate cavalry.

Major General Matthew Calbraith Butler was one of the true aristocrats of South Carolina. He was a member of the South Carolina legislature. His uncle was United States senator Andrew P. Butler. His cousin was Congressman Preston S. Brooks. His wife was the daughter of Governor Andrew Pickens. Butler could have sat out the war as other wealthy men did, but the twenty-five-year-old joined a cavalry regiment as its captain. He worked his way up through the ranks, fighting well in the early battles of the war before being severely wounded at Brandy Station, Virginia, on June 9, 1863, when a Federal cannonball took off his right foot.

The next year, Butler returned to action with his old friend and cavalry mentor, Major General Wade Hampton. When Hampton was sent to the Carolinas to resist Sherman's advance, Butler went, too. In early March 1865, the exhausted Butler was asleep in a house in Fayetteville, North Carolina, when a Federal patrol found an unguarded road into town. Not expecting trouble so soon, Butler had asked a slave to wash the dust from the only uniform he had left. Seeing the Federals out front, Butler and his lieutenant threw on the only clothes they had—boots, hats, and overcoats—and rushed for their horses. They got away but were more than a little embarrassed.

The Union army forgave Butler for his Confederate service. During the Spanish-American War, he was called into the United States Army to fight in Cuba. He died in 1909. His tombstone says he was the "knightliest of the knightly." It makes no mention about his escape from the Yankees in his birthday suit.

Of all the soldiers on either side who captured or almost captured generals while they were sleeping, only John Singleton Mosby, a world traveler, could make the claim, "I've seen England. I've seen France. I've seen a general in his underpants."

A "Black Powder Jollification" Goes Bad

If a soldier faces death, he wants it to be on the battlefield with his face toward the enemy. He does not want to be shot in the back, to end his life as a coward running from danger. He does not want to die in camp, felled by a fever he can't see or dysentery he can't control. Nor does he want to die in a prison camp, wasting away from lack of food or freezing to death from lack of blankets. Most of all, he does not want to die a needless death caused by his own stupidity.

An uncounted number of Civil War soldiers blew themselves up by the careless handling of gunpowder. In two well-documented cases during Sherman's campaign in the Carolinas, at least twenty Yankees blew themselves to bits without an armed Confederate within miles. Sherman lost more men in South Carolina to their own carelessness than to enemy fire.

He reached Columbia, South Carolina, by February 17, 1865. After viewing the city through a spyglass and seeing that it was free of soldiers, he entered the town with only one of his four corps. As they marched across a pontoon bridge, the men of the Fifteenth Corps sang, "Hail Columbia, Happy Land. If I don't burn you, I'll be damned!" Sherman, riding a few paces in front, pretended not to hear.

That afternoon, the Fifteenth Corps started looting the city's homes. By dark, the men had set at least twenty fires around the city, though Sherman later claimed fleeing Confederates who had set cotton bales afire were responsible. By the morning of February 18, nearly a third of the city's buildings had burned to the ground.

Sherman ordered that all the black powder and ammunition left by the Confederates be thrown into the Saluda River so it would be useless to any roving rebels who might still be operating behind the Union army. One Federal was carrying powder and chemicals toward a wagon when he somehow broke open either a chemical bottle or a keg of powder, leaving a trail of combustible material that made a very effective long fuse. No one will ever know if the man was smoking. Regardless, the accidental fuse somehow caught fire. The fire spread to the wagons loaded with munitions. In a flash, sixteen Federal soldiers disappeared in an explosion that rocked the city.

A female diarist, spreading the false rumor that more than two hundred drunken Federals lost their lives in the fires they set, wrote that she wished the whole army had been roasted alive. The deaths from the explosion thrilled her: "How I rejoice to think of any of them being killed!"

Sherman reacted to the accident by saying that the life of one of his soldiers was of more value than any Confederate arsenal, of more value than Columbia itself. If that were true, he should have brought his sixty-three thousand men together, told them the details of the accident, and reiterated how dangerous black powder could be. He didn't, the accident was repeated within two weeks, and more Federal soldiers died.

From Columbia, Sherman's army marched north to burn the town of Winnsboro before swinging northeast to capture Camden and move toward the pretty town of Cheraw on the Pee Dee River. Confederates scurried out of the way of Sherman's fast-moving army. Most of them headed for Cheraw.

The train tracks from Charleston ended in Cheraw. Thus, the little town suddenly found itself a military depot as Confederate lieutenant general William J. Hardee and the Charleston garrison flowed into town before escaping over the Pee Dee and into North Carolina. With Hardee came tons of powder and artillery ammunition, far more than he had time to move across the river before Sherman arrived. Hardee put at least some of the munitions in a ravine near the Pee Dee, perhaps in anticipation of rescuing some of it or blowing all of it up before he fled.

Sherman did not give Hardee that luxury. Outlying Federal regiments surprised the last of the fleeing Confederates on March 3. There had not been time to destroy all the military goods. The Federals captured twenty-four cannons, two thousand muskets, thirty-six hundred barrels of gunpowder, five thousand rounds of artillery ammunition, and twenty thousand rounds of infantry ammunition. It is not clear from Union records if this counted the material in the ravine, or even if the ammunition dump's existence was undiscovered by the Federals.

On March 6, some Federal soldiers were goofing off near the ravine by lighting small piles of black powder. Exposed to open air and a flame when not under pressure, black powder disappears in a cloud of white smoke with a *whifpt* sound that can be pretty amusing. The soldiers were conducting what they called a "black powder jollification" when one of their piles ignited a line of powder leading into the ravine.

When the soldiers allowed the trail to burn into the ravine, they signed their death warrant. The ravine exploded with a deafening roar that broke every window in every house and building on the street closest to the accident. "Several" soldiers were reported killed and others wounded. Sherman again suspected sabotage. He threatened to hang the mayor and burn the town in retaliation. Once again, he had to back down when a sheepish officer told him that the men had killed themselves because of their carelessness.

Sherman was glad to leave South Carolina for North Carolina. He had lost more than a dozen soldiers to Confederate cavalrymen in retaliation for the rape of South Carolina women. He had also lost twenty to thirty men who blew themselves to smithereens in carelessly handling captured ammunition. He had to get out of the state before his army killed itself.

Lieutenant Rambo and the Fighting Seminarians

The third-largest battle in Florida, the Battle of Natural Bridge, on March 6, 1865, involved only about 550 men on each side. How it came to be fought is one of the sadder blunders in a sorry Civil War saga of how military insiders treated those out of favor.

Union brigadier general John Newton proposed late in the war that he lead an attack on St. Marks, Florida, a small town on the Gulf of

Mexico about thirty miles south of Tallahassee. Newton's written explanation of the expedition cited a February attack on Fort Myers by the Confederates. He suggested that the Union attack the Confederates as a means of drawing them off from trying Fort Myers again.

That explanation does not make much sense, as the distance between St. Marks and Fort Myers is several hundred miles. Newton's true purpose in attacking St. Marks may have been to get some glory and regain a measure of military respect before the war ended.

Newton was a Virginian who graduated second in the 1842 class of West Point, a ranking that almost sentenced him to service as a civil engineer, rather than service in the infantry or cavalry, as lower-ranked graduates were always assigned. When the Civil War started, Newton defied his Virginia family and stayed loyal to the Union, which rewarded him with the commission of a brigadier general. He served credibly for the first year and a half of the war, working his way up to a divisional command at Fredericksburg in December 1862.

It was after watching Major General Ambrose Burnside launch his disastrous, bloody assaults against entrenched Confederates that Newton made his career-damaging mistake. Newton and another brigadier visited President Lincoln and asked that Burnside be replaced for incompetence. Lincoln did replace Burnside, but the senior general swore revenge on the men who had crossed him.

For a while, Newton escaped Burnside's wrath. He was promoted to major general and took over command of the First Corps at Gettysburg upon the death of Major General John Reynolds. Then the army bureaucracy went to work on him. First, Newton's major generalship was revoked. Then he was transferred west to a division under Sherman, who seemed not to like him. In the fall of 1864, Newton was transferred to the Siberia of the Civil War, the Department of Key West and the Dry Tortugas, a command where absolutely nothing worthwhile was happening at a time when Grant was closing in on Lee and Sherman on Johnston.

Sitting in Key West, Newton must have realized that the war would soon be over and he would have nothing to show for it, all because he had accused his commanding general of incompetence. He knew that when the war was over he would not even be allowed to return home. His family had rejected him.

The Confederate raid on Fort Myers, unsuccessful though it was, gave Newton an opportunity. Though his written request to launch a counterattack specifically targeted St. Marks, he could not have missed reading the map. Less than two days' march above St. Marks was Tallahassee, one of the last uncaptured capitals of the Confederacy. The opportunity was clear. If Newton could sweep up from St. Marks to capture Tallahassee, his honor might be restored, as might that revoked major generalship.

He gathered the only infantry forces available to him (two black regiments commanded by white officers) and the Second Florida Cavalry (a mounted regiment of Floridians who had stayed loyal to the Union) and set sail. Bad weather forced the Federals to stay off St. Marks for several days, long enough for the alarm to scatter across northern Florida for all Confederate militia units to gather to repel the invaders.

When Newton and his men finally landed, they first tried to capture a bridge at Newport. But since the Confederates had pulled up the planking and dug in across from the bridge, no Federal could even come close. After hiring a local guide, the Yankees learned of a natural bridge several miles north where the St. Marks River plunged underground for about fifty yards before surfacing again. Newton left the Second Florida Cavalry at Newport and marched north with his black soldiers.

The Confederates had anticipated that move and were already digging a semicircular set of trenches so all their fire could converge on the narrow Natural Bridge. Militia units—including a detachment of badly frightened teenage boys from West Florida Seminary in Tallahassee (now Florida State University)—were coming from all over the northern part of the state. Only a handful of the Confederates had military experience. A few had been discharged from the army for wounds suffered on distant battlefields. One battery of artillery was commanded by a strong, soft-spoken man everyone trusted to put his cannonballs where he wanted them. His name was Rambo, Lieutenant Drury Rambo.

In overall command was Major General Sam Jones, a hard-drinking 1841 West Point graduate who had been shifted from post to post, an indication that no one in the Confederate high command had much confidence in him. Jones set up his command post several miles in the rear of Natural Bridge, far enough away that no one would shoot at him. Command on the field fell to Brigadier General William Miller, an Ithaca, New York, native who had moved south as an infant. Though he had no formal military training, Miller had bravely and ably led the First Florida Regiment at Shiloh and Stones River before being seriously wounded. For the past eight months, he had been in charge of the reserve forces of Florida.

When Newton arrived at Natural Bridge, he was surprised to see it defended. All day long, he sniped at the trenches. Scouting north and south of the river told him that there was simply no other way to cross the swampy land and the deep river. It would be necessary to cross Natural Bridge in order to gain the road behind it. That road led to Tallahassee. Three times, Newton sent charges to try to cross the narrow strip of land. The concentrated fire from the dug-in Confederates was deadly. Almost all the officers of the two black regiments were hit, as were a large number of soldiers.

Some Federals were killed by backwoods trickery. One Confederate crawled to an extreme flank of the Federals and hid behind a tree. He would load, generally aim his weapon, and then raise a shout. Whenever he saw a curious Federal head move from behind a tree to see where the noise was originating, he would shoot it. "Then coolly reloading, he would yell again, and the operation would be repeated, and at every shot down would go a black or white Yankee with a bullet through his skull—a most advantageous mode of fighting and worthy of imitation," wrote a witness to the battle.

General Miller put his young seminarians, ages fourteen to seventeen, in the center of the line, normally a position occupied by combat-tested units. In this case, the protective Miller must have wanted to keep his eye on them. A diarist later said one of the excited boys told her, "We stayed right behind General Miller the whole time to protect him!" One witness wondered just how effective the seminarians were in the battle:

> The boys were armed with old smoothbore muskets, shooting a ball and three buck shots. I was amused at four of these boys behind a small tree. The front one with one of these muskets along side of the tree and the other three playing tag at his back. He fired the musket, which kicked him back, knocking those behind him down backward. All arose astonished, two of them ran off, and the other two stayed to reload the musket. They did not attempt to fire it again. It was hot for us there with small arms fire and a six-pounder howitzer that the Federals brought with them. If I had put my hat out, I could have caught a hatful of bullets, but I managed to escape every one.

Newton's single cannon couldn't dislodge any of the Confederates' nine guns, nor could he frighten their infantry into running. As night fell, he finally retreated. Seeing the Federals leave the field, one excited Confederate captain leaped atop his breastworks to urge his men forward. A lagging Federal was waiting for the first stupid rebel to reveal himself. The captain was shot down in the middle of waving his sword, one of only three Confederates killed on the field. Twenty-one were wounded.

The Battle of Natural Bridge was a disaster for the Federals. Twenty-one men were officially counted as dead, eighty-nine were wounded, and thirty-eight were missing and presumed dead. The 27 percent casualty rate at Natural Bridge ranks it among the bloodiest Federal defeats of the war.

Writing his official report on March 7, Newton knew where to place the blame: "The navy was unable to cooperate in any manner; the ammunition was nearly expended, and our communications, owing to the failure to land a force of seaman at Port Leon as agreed upon."

After mailing that report, he must have thought about what had happened to him the last time he criticized a Union officer. On March 19, more than two weeks after the battle, Newton filed a more detailed report in which he claimed complete victory. In retrospect, it seemed he had even driven the Confederates from the field at Natural Bridge.

He now praised the same admiral he had criticized in his first report: "I cannot close this communication without expressing the obligation I am under to Rear Admiral Stribling for the hearty cooperation which he ordered his officers to afford, and his own endeavors to make the expedition a complete success."

Brigadier General John Newton, the man who hoped to regain the esteem of his colleagues by capturing Tallahassee, never won that permanent promotion back to major general. His postwar letters to the War Department lamented how his old colleagues, most of them junior to his service, had been promoted while he had not. (Newton did win a brevet, or honorary, major general's commission.)

Though Newton suspected the War Department held his whistle-blowing against him, he did not allow his mistake to sour him on service to his country. He later became chief of engineers for the army and took on responsibility for clearing obstructions to the port of New York. Much of New York City's reputation as a fine port can be traced to his unselfishness. Newton died in 1895. He is buried at West Point.

KILPATRICK'S SHIRTTAIL SKEDADDLE

Union major general Judson Kilpatrick captured attention when he became the first Union officer wounded in the war upon being hit at the Battle of Big Bethel, Virginia, in June 1861. He secured his place in history when he became the first Civil War general to win a battle by fleeing in his long johns.

───────────

Kilpatrick graduated from West Point in May 1861 and moved almost immediately into the fighting with an appointment as captain of the Fifth New York Regiment. Wounded at Bethel, he was forced into a hospital until September, when he rejoined the army. Though he was a veteran of only one battle, his wound had made him a minor hero in the North. Thus, at age twenty-five, he was appointed a lieutenant colonel of the Second New York Cavalry Regiment.

Kilpatrick loved the cavalry, though it cannot be said that the cavalry loved him. He saw horses as something to be ridden until they dropped and his men as something to be used until they stopped bullets. Behind his back, his troopers began to call him "Kill-cavalry." But while his men may have doubted his command skills, his superiors did not. By fall 1862, he was a colonel. By mid-June 1863, just before Gettysburg, he was a brigadier general at age twenty-seven.

Kilpatrick's lack of caution on the field made him a brave but foolhardy commander. He had a habit of rushing into enemy fire, though cavalry generals were supposed to think more about strategy and tactics than how glorious their charges looked.

On the third day of Gettysburg, Brigadier General Kilpatrick, who had been a general a little over two weeks, ordered Brigadier General Elon John Farnsworth, who had been a general four days, to make a charge to draw Confederate attention away from a possible Federal counterattack once the Pettigrew-Pickett-Trimble Assault was repulsed. Kilpatrick had not been ordered by his superiors to make such a maneuver. It was something he had thought of on his own.

Farnsworth looked at the field. It was rocky. The charge would be uphill. At the top of the hill were Confederates behind a wooden fence who would be shooting at Union cavalry picking their way around boulders. Farnsworth turned to Kilpatrick and protested: "Shall I throw my handful of men over rough ground, through timber, against a brigade of infantry?"

"If you are afraid to lead this charge, I will lead it," Kilpatrick said.

Farnsworth should have let Kilpatrick do just that, but his manhood had been questioned. He lost more than a quarter of his men before they ever reached the fence. Farnsworth himself was shot several times. Some Confederates claimed he was in such agony that he took his own life to ease his pain. Just as Farnsworth had predicted, the charge was a failure.

Kilpatrick was not brought up on charges for initiating the fighting without orders, but some of his superiors questioned the waste of lives. As he would do throughout his career, Kilpatrick denied responsibility.

In February 1864, Kilpatrick was involved in another ill-fated cavalry expedition. He took Colonel Ulric Dahlgren, the young, one-legged son of Union admiral John Dahlgren, into his command. Together, they planned a two-direction raid on Richmond designed to demoralize Virginians more than win any military advantage. Kilpatrick and his fifteen hundred men ran into opposition in attempting to enter the city and retreated before Dahlgren had a chance to get into position with his five hundred men. When Dahlgren realized Kilpatrick had left him, he tried to ride around Richmond to safety. Dahlgren ran into Confederate pickets and tried to bluff them into surrendering. They responded by shooting him five times.

The true nature of the Kilpatrick-Dahlgren Raid is a mystery. On Dahlgren's body were papers that suggested his mission was to kill Confederate president Jefferson Davis and his cabinet. Robert E. Lee sent the papers to Union major general George Meade and asked if the plot was real. Meade, who had not approved the raid, asked Kilpatrick. True to form, Kilpatrick denied knowledge of the assassination plot. Meade publicly backed Kilpatrick's innocence but privately told his wife that he thought Kilpatrick was guilty.

Kilpatrick's abandonment of Dahlgren and his suspected involvement in an assassination plot were apparently the last straws for the Union army. He was shipped west in hopes that Major General Sherman could bring him under control.

Wounded again at the Battle of Resaca, Kilpatrick was around for the fall of Atlanta and was in on the planning of Sherman's next bold move. That was the March to the Sea, during which Sherman was to take sixty-three thousand men cross-country to the Georgia coast without a supply line. He picked four corps of infantry and one corps of cavalry to go with him. "Kilpatrick is a hell of a damn fool, but that is just the sort of man I want leading my cavalry on this expedition," Sherman said.

Through Georgia and into South Carolina, Kilpatrick and his

mounted corps shielded Sherman's two marching wings. And just as he had always done, Kilpatrick allowed himself to be surprised. At the Battle of Aiken, South Carolina, on February 11, 1865, Kilpatrick ignored warnings that Confederates were in the area and led his men into an ambush. Wheeling his horse and fleeing, he became an object of capture for the Confederates. The best they could do was grab his hat. Dozens of Union troopers were killed and captured. Kilpatrick later denied that leading his men into an ambush was his fault.

Four days later, Kilpatrick and the rest of Sherman's army were on the outskirts of Columbia, South Carolina. Sometime over the next four days, Sherman made the acquaintance of a young woman historians of the day described as "the most beautiful woman in all of Columbia." She was the twenty-year-old Marie Boozer. Something about the big-nosed, mutton-chopped, thin-lipped, cruel-eyed, twenty-nine-year-old Kilpatrick appealed to the comely Marie. It was not his shyness. Women were among Kilpatrick's few vices. He did not drink, but he always opened his camp to less-than-virtuous women.

Whatever Kilpatrick had that won Marie, she fell in a big way. When Sherman's army marched north from Columbia, her carriage went rolling along also. Confederate prisoners tied to the carriage reported that Kilpatrick frequently made his way back to her carriage, climbed in, and rode with his head in her lap, his legs dangling over the carriage's sides.

Though Sherman had been virtually unopposed by Confederate forces since Aiken, that changed once he reached North Carolina. Kilpatrick thought he could block the three roads leading from the southwest into Fayetteville. If the Confederate cavalry under Lieutenant General Wade Hampton wanted to get to the city to defend it, it would have to ride right through him. He camped his corps so his men could watch all three roads.

What Kilpatrick didn't know was that one of his officers had been captured by Hampton and had revealed not only Kilpatrick's plan to trap the Confederate cavalry but the exact location at Monroe's Crossroads where Kilpatrick was spending the night with Marie Boozer. Hampton decided to spring his own trap.

As dawn broke on March 10, the Confederate cavalry swooped down on Monroe's Crossroads. A Confederate soldier jumped from his horse onto the porch of the house where Kilpatrick was staying. An unarmed man in his underwear came running out. The Confederate grabbed him by the arm and demanded, "Where is the general?" The long-johned fellow pointed to a Federal officer riding away into the night. The Confederate dropped his grip, jumped on his horse, and took off in pursuit.

He went after the wrong officer. The man standing in his underwear was Kilpatrick. The general ran to a horse, swung aboard, and rode into the darkness. Behind him in the house lay his shirt, pants, coat, boots, hat, sword, pistols, and mistress.

In Kilpatrick's official report, he claimed he had been almost dressed—though in carpet slippers—and going to check the feed of his horses when the attack came. He said he ran into the woods at the time of the attack—not that he fled on his horse. Since Kilpatrick did not make a habit of personally checking his horses, and since wearing carpet slippers on cold, wet ground does not ring true, his claims appear to be another excuse for getting caught—literally, this time—with his pants down.

Marie Boozer came downstairs when she heard shooting. A considerate Confederate rode up to her, threw his military overcoat around her bare shoulders, and took her to a nearby ditch where she was safe. Kilpatrick's love nest was now a target of bullets, which whomped into the boards with regularity.

Though they had the element of surprise, Hampton's Confederates were beaten back at Monroe's Crossroads. The problem was that one entire wing of the assault, bogged down in a nearby swamp, was unable to attack the Union support camp at the same time the others were attacking Kilpatrick's headquarters. Within a couple of hours, Kilpatrick's other brigades and several infantry regiments came up to drive off the Confederates.

Technically, the Confederates lost the Battle of Monroe's Crossroads, but they took more than 300 Federal prisoners and released more than 150 Confederates. They killed over 20 Federals while leaving at least that many of their own dead. The road to Fayetteville was opened, and Hampton's Confederate cavalry was able to advance to the city unmolested.

Famous for his wound in one of the first battles of the war, Kilpatrick had now advanced his fame in one of the last battles. Amused Union infantrymen, no friends of the cavalry, dubbed it "Kilpatrick's Shirttail Skedaddle." Kilpatrick and Marie never even got to share another embrace. When Sherman learned the circumstances of the battle, he sent Marie south on the first steamboat from Fayetteville to Wilmington. Sherman did not care how she got home to Columbia from there.

Kilpatrick was not through being surprised by gunshots. While he was at the head of his column riding into Raleigh, North Carolina, several weeks later, a lone Confederate cavalrymen popped off a few rounds at him. An enraged Kilpatrick had the captured man hanged after giving him five minutes to write his wife a goodbye letter.

Kilpatrick survived the war and his embarrassment about getting caught in his underwear. Strangely, for a man who loved the army, he resigned not long after the war. He became a minister to Chile and died at his post in 1881. His remains were moved to West Point, where he was reburied—presumably wearing a uniform.

"A Devil in Human Shape": Alfred Rhett Fails to Impress the Yankees with His Excellent Breeding

Here's a word of advice if you are the son of a fire-breathing newspaper editor who played a prominent role in taking South Carolina out of the Union, creating the Confederacy, and starting a war that killed more than three hundred thousand Northerners. It is not a good idea to ride up to some Yankee cavalrymen, condemn them for cursing, threaten to put them on report, and then tell them your name.

Robert Barnwell Rhett, Sr., the father of Colonel Alfred Rhett, must have come out complaining in Beaufort, South Carolina, in 1800. Born in the heart of sea-island cotton country, he was elected to the state legislature at the age of twenty-six. At that time, John C. Calhoun, the state's most prominent politician, was beginning to develop his theories on nullification. He held that any state had the right to nullify federal laws with which the state did not agree. Further, if the federal government did not agree to withdraw the offending law, the state could leave the union. It was a theory that rested on the idea that the nation was a collection of states joined by common interests but not forever bound. In the view of Calhoun, the Constitution allowed states to leave the union.

Rhett not only embraced Calhoun's ideas, he thought Calhoun was too liberal on the issue of states' rights. Rhett, who kept climbing the political ladder until he reached the United States House, wanted South Carolina to leave the United States as early as 1850. He took over Calhoun's Senate seat upon the old statesman's death in 1850 and demanded that the state immediately secede.

The issue revolved around slavery. The success of cotton cultivation depended on the continuation of slavery, in the view of planters and their supporters. Any movement by the federal government to restrict the spread of slavery threatened their way of life. When he got little support for secession even from his own state, Rhett resigned his seat in protest.

That did not mean he intended to fade into obscurity. He and his son Robert Jr. started using their bully pulpit—the *Charleston Mercury*, which Junior edited while Senior acted as publisher—to call for secession. The two wrote countless editorials in the 1850s and early 1860s calling for the South to secede. One article titled "Address to the Slave Holding States" called for a "confederation" of states to set up its own government.

Finally, the years of agitation between North and South came to a head when Lincoln was elected. The slave-holding states decided that no matter what Lincoln said, he intended to free the slaves. South Carolina seceded on December 20, 1860, fulfilling a thirty-five-year-old dream for Rhett. Within minutes of the passage of the Ordinance of Secession, Rhett's newspaper boys were on the streets of Charleston with a one-page extra edition featuring the entire short text of the ordinance. The bottom of the page contained a huge headline that came to symbolize the broken country: "The Union Is Dissolved!"

While six other slave-holding states held secession conventions, Rhett prepared to take over as president of the new Confederacy. After all, he had coined the term and was the chief (if unappointed) spokesman for secession. When the new Confederate States met in Montgomery, Alabama, early in 1861 to select a president and cabinet, Rhett fully expected to return with the mantle of leadership. However, Southern politicians saw him not as a potential leader but as a radical who would not come across well with either a moderate Southern public or a North that might be convinced to let the South go its own way. Virtually no one supported him for the office. Rhett then figured he would at least get a cabinet position. But Jefferson Davis was wary of Rhett, too. Davis offered him no political office.

An embittered Rhett returned home to Charleston and started wielding the only weapon he had, his newspaper. For the rest of the war, he wrote anti-Davis editorials accusing the president of everything from being corrupt to being secretly pro-Union.

Alfred Rhett did not join his brother and father in denouncing Davis. Instead, he joined the Confederate army. He was present at the firing on Fort Sumter, the start of the war his father always expected but never really wanted. Being hotheaded and carrying a grudge apparently ran in the family. During the attack on Fort Sumter, Rhett found himself at odds with another officer, W. Ransom Calhoun, a West Pointer who ignored Rhett when issuing orders to Rhett's regiment. This slight of honor drove Rhett to challenge Calhoun to a duel. The two men fought it out with pistols. Calhoun came out on the short end. Though dueling was supposed to be on its way out and its participants were often disciplined, Rhett never suffered any consequences from killing his fellow officer. In fact, he was promoted to colonel and given command of Fort Sumter during a time when the fort was under constant threat of attack by Federal forces.

After Sherman captured Columbia toward the end of the war, it became obvious to the Confederates in Charleston that they could no longer hold the city. Quietly, on the night of February 17, 1865, they abandoned the fort they had held against all odds for four years and evacuated the city.

Rhett marched north into upper South Carolina with Lieutenant General William J. Hardee and what remained of the Fort Sumter garrison. They knew they would soon meet the greatest challenge of their service, an attempt to stop Sherman's sixty-three-thousand-man army, now headed toward North Carolina.

Hardee and General Joseph Johnston decided the only way to defeat Sherman was to meet parts of his army. Sherman's men were marching north in two wings that were usually separated by several miles and sometimes by up to a day's march. Johnston hoped he could surprise and defeat one wing before the other could turn and attack him. To do that, he had to set up an ambush from a heavily fortified position. And to determine where to set the trap, Johnston had to know the destination of Sherman's army. To find that information, he needed some sacrificial lambs. He had to slow one wing of Sherman's army and watch what direction the other turned. The only men available for the job were Hardee's men coming up from Charleston. That included Colonel Alfred Rhett.

Johnston ordered Hardee to strike Sherman's left wing at the small community of Averasboro, North Carolina, about ten miles north of Fayetteville. Johnston reasoned that the right wing would not bother stopping to help the left if the resistance was light. If the right wing continued marching straight, it would be obvious that Sherman was heading for Goldsboro. If it swung left, Raleigh would be his destination. Johnston must have grimly considered the third possibility. If the right wing swung left in support of its left wing, Hardee and his eight thousand men would be wiped out.

On March 15, skirmishing started. Rhett was in command of a brigade of soldiers dug in along a road. Hardee intended for Rhett to do little more than harass the Federals. The whole idea was not to do fierce battle but to continually fall back and slow Sherman's left wing so scouts could watch the right wing.

A battlefield is always a confusing place, with infantry deploying to and fro and cavalry riding back and forth. During the first Averasboro skirmish, a force of mounted men rode up to Rhett and ordered him to surrender. They also cursed him. Rhett, who must not have heard the order to surrender, did not recognize the men insulting him. Perhaps dust and the wear and tear of going four months without new clothing obscured the uniforms.

"I will put you men on report to General Hampton for using such disrespectful language to me!" Rhett shouted. Hampton was the Confederate lieutenant general in charge of cavalry.

The threat did not mean much to these men. Their commander was Union major general Judson Kilpatrick, and they had just captured a Confederate colonel, Rhett, wearing a nice pair of Russian-made riding boots and a dress uniform covered in gold braid.

Rhett was a proud Southerner but not necessarily a smart one. He did not keep his identity a secret. Whether he had identification papers on him or whether he verbally declared who he was is not known, but the word soon swept through the Union army that the son of the man who had started the whole idea of secession had been captured.

Neither did Rhett act humble in front of his captors, some of whom had thoughts of hanging him from the nearest tree. "From the conversation of this Rebel Colonel, I judge him to be quite as impractical a person as any of his class," wrote one Union officer who interrogated Rhett. Another wrote that Rhett was "incarnate, selfish, and a devil in human shape, who is but a type of his class and whose polished manners and easy assurance made him only more hideous to me and utterly heartless. Selfish ambition and pride of class gave tone to his whole discourse."

Rhett's boots, which attracted attention from everyone he saw, were taken from him. They were eventually returned when it was discovered that the secessionist had such small feet that no officer in the Union army could wear them.

Rhett was sent to Sherman, who greeted him warmly and asked about mutual friends in Charleston. Sherman's officers were taken aback by the general's casual treatment of the man whose family had played such a prominent role in starting the war.

Rhett survived his few months in prison camp and later went on to South Carolina politics. Like his father, he never bowed, never scraped, never apologized. After the war, he wrote a lengthy article defending dueling as a reasonable means of settling disputes.

THE FIVE FORKS SHAD BAKE

Generals should be asked the following question: "If you know the enemy is all around you, that your position is weak, and that you have been ordered to hold it at all costs by a commander locked in his own life-and-death struggle, would you leave your headquarters without telling subordinates where you are going and attend a fish broil?"

Any general who answers, "Sure, why not?" should be drummed out of the army after being sentenced to studying the Battle of Five Forks.

Five Forks is the crossroads meeting of five roads about ten miles southwest of Petersburg, Virginia. In late March 1865, as Lee realized that Union cavalry forces were moving south in an attempt to gain his flank, he sent Major General George Pickett and ten thousand men to secure Five Forks and protect the Southside Railroad. Pickett moved from quiet Five Forks and advanced several miles to Dinwiddie Court House, where he attacked cavalry under Union major general Phil Sheridan. Determining that the cavalry was strong, Pickett pulled back to Five Forks. He then discovered that his force was virtually isolated from the rest of Lee's army to the northeast. Pickett telegraphed Lee asking that some diversion be made along his line and that reenforcements be sent before the Federals discovered the break in the lines.

Lee replied that "Five Forks must be held at all hazards," because Pickett's force was the only thing that stood between Sheridan and the railroad. If Pickett withdrew, the Federals would have access to the Confederate trenches defending Petersburg.

Pickett did not act like a general who had essentially been told to fight to the last man. He ordered his soldiers to throw up some earthworks, but he did not put any urgency into those orders by instructing that the earthworks be developed into full-fledged trenches or redoubts (small forts). Neither did he put much effort into cutting down trees, which would have served to clear fields of fire and to supply logs for use as breastworks. Pickett and his cavalry commander, Major General Fitzhugh Lee, Robert E. Lee's nephew, later wrote that they "did not expect an attack that afternoon," and so did not make feverish preparations for one. They apparently ignored an attack made the day before into the gap between them and Lee's flank, which had demonstrated to the Federals how weak the Confederates were growing.

Pickett and Fitz Lee were not the two smartest generals Robert E. Lee had in his command. Pickett had graduated fifty-ninth and last in the West Point class of 1846, Fitz Lee forty-fifth out of forty-nine in 1856. Up to and including his last battle, Pickett rarely showed much initiative on the battlefield. When given the chance for independent command, such as an important mission in February 1864 to capture New Bern, North Carolina, he failed in overall execution, though his better subordinates succeeded in their portions of the plan. Fitz Lee fared better, learning cavalry tactics at the right hand of J. E. B. Stuart. Still, he was a little rusty coming into the engagement at Five Forks. Severely wounded the previous September, he had been out of action the preceding months.

Pickett and Fitz Lee, both combat veterans of the entire war, did not believe the Federals were going to attack them at Five Forks. All the Yankees they could possibly count were just out of sight, but they somehow convinced themselves that nothing was going to happen.

As noon approached on April 1, the two generals received an invitation to lunch from Major General Tom Rosser, a Confederate cavalry general. Two days before, Rosser, an avid net fisherman, had caught a quantity of shad in the Nottaway River. He was now broiling them over an open fire and needed help eating them.

Fresh fish was something the two generals were not about to turn down. Just that morning, they had sadly watched the spectacle of their hungry men stealing a breakfast of roasted corn from their horses' rations.

Fitz Lee was so hungry that he ignored a message from the left flank reporting that the Federals had placed themselves between Five Forks and Robert E. Lee's trenches. If the message was accurate, Five Forks was now cut off from the rest of the Confederate army, a grave condition. To the shocked surprise of the colonel delivering the message, Fitz Lee told him to go see what the matter was and, if necessary, to order the cavalry division over to help. In the face of the enemy, a major general had just casually turned over command of the cavalry to an aide.

Worse than that, Fitz Lee rode away without telling that colonel where he was going. Pickett did the same thing. Both of the commanding generals on the field, warned that they were about to come under attack, left their posts to pick fish bones and pop hush puppies. The next most senior general on the field, Major General William Henry "Rooney" Lee, Robert E. Lee's son, did not even know he was now in effective command of the troops at Five Forks. His cousin Fitz and Pickett had not told him.

Around four o'clock that afternoon, the fish-stuffed Pickett casually asked Rosser for a couple of couriers he could send the two miles to Five Forks to make sure he was not needed. Pickett watched as the two men rode away. He was still watching when a force of bluecoats snatched one of the couriers right off his horse.

Seeing an armed force of Federals within a few hundred feet of their cookout was cause for alarm. Pickett and Lee mounted their horses and galloped for what they assumed were the front lines, the crossroads of Five Forks. Pickett ran past a gauntlet of Federals firing at him so accurately that he felt compelled to lean down on his horse on the opposite side of the incoming musket balls. Lee, following, was cut off. He wheeled around and looked for another route.

Neither man should have bothered. The Battle of Five Forks was almost over. The outcome had been sealed the moment the Federals advanced in midafternoon. They had thirty thousand men to Pickett's ten thousand. The Federal infantry charged straight ahead, overpowering Pickett's men by sheer numbers. More than half his force was captured, as were all six guns at the crossroads. The guns' brave young commander, Colonel Willie Pegram, was mortally wounded, just two months after his brigadier general brother, John, had been killed in a nearby battle. Pickett made it back just in time to flee with his shattered command. Fitz Lee and Rosser headed for Robert E. Lee's trenches.

Robert E. Lee was angry with Pickett and let it show when he saw the general from a distance, asking an aide, "Is that man still with the army?"

The three generals were never able to mount much of a defense for themselves, though it would be twenty years before the story of the shad bake emerged. Until then, whispers were that one or more of them were drunk and unable to perform their duties.

Modern historians speculate that the generals might have been victims of an "acoustical shadow" that hid the sounds of fighting just two miles away. This phenomenon occurs when sound waves bounce up and away into the atmosphere, instead of fanning out in all directions. It can be caused by thick woods between points or temperature inversions that create layers of air with varying sound-bearing capabilities.

There might be some merit to that argument. When generals could not get together to synchronize their pocket watches, orders were often based on vague directions, such as "Attack when you hear the sound of my guns opening the battle." Even generals expecting attacks depended on the sound of their pickets' firing to alert them to action on their fronts and flanks. That was the purpose of pickets, to be an early-warning system.

While there is no good excuse for three generals who left their posts without informing their subordinates where they could be found, they probably thought they would hear any shooting in time to get back to direct the defense of their lines. Mounted and galloping, they could have reached Five Forks in less than eight minutes.

The lesson is plain. Never eat fish when a superior enemy lurks in the woods.

CAPTURED AFTER APPOMATTOX: BAD-LUCK BRIGADIER GENERAL WILLIAM PAYNE

Confederate brigadier general William Henry Fitzhugh Payne wasn't a blunderer. He was just plain unlucky. Though he had a distinguished field record, Payne was probably on a first-name basis with the guards at the Johnson's Island, Ohio, prisoner-of-war camp for Confederate officers. He spent more than a quarter of the war in prison. He also got to know his surgeons well.

Payne was born wealthy and intelligent, a combination that almost assured a gentleman success in the antebellum South. He graduated from Virginia Military Institute in 1849 and immediately enrolled in the University of Virginia's law school. Payne was a natural politician. At age twenty-six, he was elected commonwealth attorney. When the war started, he was living in Warrenton, where he competed for clients with another young lawyer, John Singleton Mosby.

For some reason, Payne did not use his V.M.I. degree and political power to secure an officer's rank. He joined as a private, but his leadership skill was quickly recognized. Before First Manassas, he was named captain of J. E. B. Stuart's First Virginia Cavalry, the famed "Black Horse Cavalry." His company participated in the charge that broke the Federal line, which helped start the stream of frightened men back toward Washington.

By May 1862, Payne was a major in the Fourth Virginia Cavalry. During the Peninsula Campaign, he was among the Confederates retreating slowly northward in the face of McClellan's overwhelming forces. On May 5, Major Payne was shot in the mouth and left for dead on the field during the Battle of Williamsburg. Captured, he was one of the first Confederate officers sent to Johnson's Island, a prison camp on an island in Lake Erie near Sandusky, Ohio. He did not have to stay long before an exchange brought him back south. By September, still nursing his mouth wound, he was back in the saddle with a promotion to lieutenant colonel. He got back in time to fight at Antietam.

Payne tried to ignore his wound, but it put him back in the hospital for several months. It was February 1863 before he returned to full combat duty. Riding with J. E. B. Stuart on the Pennsylvania Campaign, Payne was involved in a heavy fight at Hanover, where his horse was killed and he suffered a deep cut on the leg from a Yankee saber. Stuart's men were unable to pull Payne to safety before having to abandon the field. Once again, Payne was captured. Once again, he was shipped to Johnson's Island, just over a year after his first stay there.

Payne's second prison stint lasted almost a year. These were not pleasant months. He spent much of his time in the prison hospital fighting severe diarrhea. It could not have helped the health of the man from the sunny South when Lake Erie sometimes froze over.

Finally, in August 1864, Payne was exchanged back south. He was made a brigadier general on his return and given a cavalry brigade. He was active in the Shenandoah Valley, where he waged a losing battle against Sheridan's campaign of private-property destruction. He fought at Third Winchester and Cedar Creek.

By the spring of 1865, Lee's army was forced into the trenches of Petersburg. Payne was with him. Lee assigned Payne's men to Major General George Pickett during the abortive attempt to disrupt Union activities near Five Forks, an important crossroads south of Petersburg. Payne was wounded for the third time on March 31 when Pickett pushed toward Dinwiddie Court House. His arm shattered by a bullet, Payne was determined not to be captured again.

He successfully made his way home to Warrenton, a small town southwest of Washington, and took to his bed to heal. More than two weeks later, on April 14, five days after Appomattox, Payne was captured a third time. It is unclear why he was taken into custody from his home after Grant had approved a surrender of Lee's forces that allowed all officers to return home. This last time, Payne remained in Federal custody for more than six weeks. He was finally released on May 29.

Payne's return to civilized life apparently agreed with him. Though he was bothered by his mouth wound for the rest of his life, he resumed his successful law practice. He even moved to the heart of Yankeedom, Washington. He lived until 1904, dying at the age of sixty-four. The shattered mouth, the slashed leg, the shattered arm, the loss of body fluids from diarrhea, the chill of Johnson's Island in the winter, and sixteen months in a Federal prison camp never combined to kill this unlucky general.

THE HOME GUARD'S RUNAWAY CANNON

Home guards never were meant to be front-line soldiers. They were a county or city's last line of defense in case enemy raiders made a dash behind lines to attack civilians, factories, or infrastructure. Generally made up of men too old, too young, too infirm, too wounded, too rich, or too stupid to defend their country, home guards were sometimes without uniforms, training, and even military arms. After the war, one man described his father's home-guard unit as "prehistoric" and commented that his father had been armed with a pair of flintlock pistols and a saber rusted solidly in the scabbard.

Still, home guards saw their share of action. Home-guard units in Indiana and Ohio were the first to challenge Confederate brigadier general John Hunt Morgan's two-thousand-man mounted raid across the Ohio River. In Marianna, Florida, a Confederate home-guard unit threw up what it thought was an effective barricade against a mounted Union raid. The Federals laughed at how feeble it was before blasting it down with one cannon shell.

On other occasions, home guards decided discretion was the better part of valor. Most home-guard units in Pennsylvania wisely decided not to muster when they encountered Robert E. Lee's Army of Northern Virginia marching to Gettysburg. Like other civilians, they watched from a safe distance.

The Burke County Home Guard, based in Morganton, North Carolina, had a particularly rough time during the war. On two occasions, it tangled with, and lost to, better-trained Federal soldiers.

The first battle came in June 1864 at the hands of Colonel George W. Kirk, a Tennessee native who had stayed loyal to the Union. Kirk led a 150-man raid of the Third North Carolina Mounted Volunteers (Union) out of the Tennessee mountains into the North Carolina foothills. His objective was Camp Vance, set up near Morganton for the training of conscripts and the North Carolina Junior Reserves, sixteen- and seventeen-year-old boys who were being pressed into service late in the war.

Kirk could not have timed his raid better. The boys were at the beginning of their training and had not even been issued muskets. Kirk walked in under a white flag and demanded the training camp's surrender. After encountering some resistance, Kirk burned the camp save for its hospital and started marching back to Tennessee, prisoners in tow.

The Burke County Home Guard was called out, and the chase was on. During a skirmish with another militia unit, Kirk proved what type of fighter he was when he forced the prisoners to act as human shields. After one of the captured Confederates was killed, Kirk shouted to the militia unit that it was shooting its own men. The confused Confederates let Kirk slip away for another few miles.

The Burke County Home Guard caught up with Kirk's force about fourteen miles outside Morganton at Winding Stairs Knob, named after the twisting trail that led to the top of the mountain. Kirk had the high ground, giving him an advantage. The terrain was so steep that the only way to advance was right up the road. That's what the home guard did. Its leader, W. W. Avery, one of Burke County's leading citizens, led the way and was one of the first to fall mortally wounded. After losing several more men in what was an impossible situation, the Burke County Home Guard turned around and went home, carrying its casualties.

The next encounter the Burke County Home Guard had with Federal soldiers came ten months later, on April 17, 1865, when it faced an even larger, better-trained, and better-armed force of Tennessee Unionists. The Tennessee men were under the overall command of Major General George Stoneman and the direct command of Brigadier General Alvan Cullem Gillem, a Tennessee native and 1851 West Point graduate who had stayed loyal to the Union. Gillem had served much of his Civil War career in Tennessee until joining Stoneman's month-long mounted raid into North Carolina and Virginia in March.

Stoneman and Gillem's instructions were to avoid military conflicts as much as possible. Instead, they were to destroy factories, crops, and barns. Their purpose was not to fight Confederate soldiers but to discourage the civilian population. At that point of the war, there was suspicion on the part of Union military leaders that the remnants of the Confederate armies might try to make it into the North Carolina mountains, where they could continue guerrilla action for years. The Union wanted the civilians of the region to know they would suffer if that happened.

Gillem was good at this sort of war. His main claim to fame had come the previous September, when he led a surprise raid on the Greeneville, Tennessee, house where Confederate brigadier general John Hunt Morgan was staying. After surrendering, Morgan had been shot down by one of Gillem's men. On this North Carolina raid, Gillem ignored the complaints of Confederate townspeople when they said that his men were ransacking their houses and stealing private property instead of looking for military goods.

After Gillem and his mounted force of several thousand soldiers left Lenoir, North Carolina, they turned southwest to attack Morganton. To reach the town, they had to cross the Catawba River at Rocky Ford. Waiting for them was the Burke County Home Guard. Leading the guard this time, however, was a real soldier. He was Major General John Peter McCown, a man who had graduated high in his 1840 West Point class and who had spent twenty years with the United States artillery branch before joining the Confederacy. McCown had given fair service early in the war, but like many other generals, he had run afoul of General Braxton Bragg. McCown was court-martialed for not following Bragg's orders at the Battle of Stone's River in December 1862. That experience cost him any further major assignments. McCown now commanded a home-guard unit of fewer than a hundred men who had scrounged up one small cannon.

The Burke County Home Guard did itself proud—at least at first. It had the high ground, a bluff looking down on Rocky Ford several hundred feet below. When Gillem foolishly sent his troops directly across the ford, he directed them into a death trap. Confederate accounts say that twenty or more troopers were dropped into the Catawba.

Though a professional artillerist, McCown must not have had much time to train the home guard on the proper method of loading and firing a cannon. At least, he apparently hadn't had time to show his men how to secure a cannon on the edge of a cliff. Local stories say the home guard got off one good round, then reloaded and fired again. This time, the recoil dislodged the cannon, which went rolling its merry way downhill.

Gillem figured out that he was wasting the lives of his men trying to ford the river right in front of the Confederates. He sent his men upriver, out of range of the muskets, to find an unprotected crossing. Seeing this, and peering over the bluff to establish that their cannon was beyond retrieval, the Burke County Home Guard decided to withdraw. Rather than heading into Morganton, where they would face the wrath of angry Federals, many of them melted into the hills west of town.

From Morganton, Gillem's Union men moved west in an attempt to get out of the state before regular Confederate troops could mount a defense against them. Turned back at Swannanoa Gap near Asheville, they marched through Rutherfordton.

An officer from Pennsylvania summarized the opinion many Union soldiers held about Gillem and his Tennessee Unionists: "They stole everything they could carry off, put pistols to the heads of the citizens, persuaded them to give up their pocketbooks, and even took the rings from ladies' fingers. The sympathy we used to feel for the loyal

Tennesseeans is being rapidly transferred to their enemy [Confederate civilians]."

The Burke County Home Guard had done its best against the brutes from Tennessee, but it wasn't quite enough. If someone had only thought to chock the wheels of that cannon . . .

CONFEDERATE CHEROKEES SURRENDER TO DEFEATED FEDERALS

Historians still debate whether the Cherokee Indians serving in Thomas's Legion scalped many Union soldiers. Some of the Indians claimed they had, but most researchers believe the Cherokees were pulling gullible listeners' legs.

It is known that, in May 1865, Thomas's Legion scored the last Confederate victory in North Carolina, and that the Indians couldn't pass up one last opportunity to intimidate white men by playing the role of "savages" to the hilt. Oddly enough, the Indians used the victory as an opportunity to surrender their superior force to the numerically inferior Federals. In the context of the times, this was no blunder. It made perfect sense.

Raised in the mountains of western North Carolina with Cherokees as his neighbors, William Holland Thomas came to identify with them. He became a clerk in an Indian trading store and prospered through his business acumen. He never abandoned his Indian friendships. During the late 1830s, when white settlers eager for Indian lands were pushing for their expulsion, Thomas convinced President Andrew Jackson to allow some of the tribe to stay in the mountains. For years, he was their de facto lawyer in disputes large and small.

When the war erupted, the fifty-six-year-old white state senator saw an opportunity for the Indians to prove their loyalty to the Confederacy—and perhaps win more concessions than had been possible from the Union. Thomas signed up at least 130 Cherokees in one company and sent them to Knoxville, Tennessee, for drill. Their arrival created quite a stir, as the citizens trooped out to the Indian camp to get a look at soldiers who went by names like Astoogatogeh, Ahmactogeh, Cah hah, Cahtoquaskee, and Chunollegah. Within months, the ranks of the regiment swelled as some of the Indians' white mountaineer neighbors joined. Over the history of Thomas's Legion, more than a thousand mountaineers and Indians served, the mix generally running 50 percent of each race.

The Indians' reputation was greatly enhanced—or diminished, depending on one's point of view—by an engagement near Cumberland Gap in September 1862. Fired on from ambush, the Indians charged their attackers. Some reports claim they scalped a large number of men before their officers could rein them in. Supposedly, those scalps were returned to the Federals with an apology and a promise not to do it again.

It is known that Western Cherokees fighting in the Indian territories and Arkansas scalped hundreds of Federals. Whether Thomas's Legion scalped again is debatable. One thing is sure—the Cherokees' reputation for fierceness spread like wildfire. One letter writer near one of their early camps at Strawberry Plains, Tennessee, thirteen miles from Knoxville, claimed that as long as the Indians were there, all stealing from civilians ended. The thieves were too afraid of running into an Indian in the dead of night.

Though they wore Confederate uniforms like their white compatriots, the Cherokees were still Indians. Before raids, each man consulted an oracle stone to see if he would return. Successful raids were often celebrated with war dances. Feathers were often part of their uniforms.

Thomas was successful in keeping his Cherokees close to their mountain homes. He knew that if the Indians joined regular Confederate units, they would find themselves in camps where death could claim them because of unsanitary conditions and the Indians' susceptibility to diseases carried by white men. By keeping his Cherokees in the mountains,

Thomas enabled them to visit their homes and sometimes live there. He wanted them used as a type of roving home guard, protecting mountain passes and bridges from invasion from eastern Tennessee, which fell under Union domination early in the war.

The Confederacy compromised with Thomas. It took his white men and left his Indians. The whites of Thomas's Legion served in the Shenandoah Valley under Major General Jubal Early. Meanwhile, the Indians performed the type of duty Thomas imagined. Though the North Carolina mountains were never major battlegrounds, they were constantly being probed by small bands of Unionists from eastern Tennessee. Chief among these was a Tennessee native, Colonel George W. Kirk, who recruited Unionists to fight against their Confederate neighbors.

On one occasion, Kirk was almost caught by the Indians. On February 1, 1865, he raided Waynesville, North Carolina, with four hundred cavalry and two hundred infantry. Before he could pull back over the mountains, a home-guard unit caught up to Kirk and captured a pass he intended to use. Kirk changed direction and moved southwest to Soco Creek. That was a mistake. During the War of 1812, Tecumseh, the Indian who tried to unite all the tribes against white westward expansion, had held a council of war there. It was holy ground.

Thomas's men descended on the Yankees from all sides and fought a fierce, if brief, skirmish. Because the war was winding down, it was hard to get ammunition to the Confederates in the mountains. Witnesses said some Indians went into battle with fewer than five musket cartridges, hardly enough to keep up a telling fire. Still, Kirk got the message. He evacuated Soco Creek as fast as he could, but not before leaving behind plenty of Union blood to consecrate the sacred Indian ground.

In a few more months, the war was over for most of the Confederacy, but not for the soldiers in the mountains. Rumors of the surrender of the armies under Lee and Joseph Johnston filtered back to the mountains, but Brigadier General James Martin, the commander of all Confederate forces there, received no official word that he, too, should surrender.

On April 29, 1865, Martin conferred with his officers at Waynesville, about thirty miles west of Asheville. They suspected that surviving Confederate forces were planning to assemble in the North Carolina mountains to fight a guerrilla action. Martin believed he should keep Thomas's Legion in the field, as the Indians' scouting skills would be valuable if such a change in Confederate tactics came about. Martin had fewer than five hundred soldiers left, but he felt confident they could hold off a division. His men knew the mountains. Until ordered otherwise, he intended to fight.

Martin saw a chance to win one more Confederate victory on May 6, 1865, when one of his scouts discovered a small force of Federals occupying Waynesville. Martin ordered a group of his cavalry to the town. While scouting on the outskirts of Waynesville, they ran into the Federal regiment they were seeking. A small firefight ensued. One Federal soldier died, probably the last man killed in the Civil War east of the Mississippi. The Confederate patrol rode back to report on finding the Yankees.

That night, Martin decided to play mind games with the Federals. His Cherokees ringed the town's hills and built large fires that they knew would be seen by the Yankees below. As the fires grew in intensity, so did the war whoops of the Cherokees. They danced and beat drums. The Indians wanted to have a little more fun before the Federals forced them back into the mountains.

The next morning, the Federal colonel sent out a flag of truce and asked for a conference. Colonel Thomas and General Martin agreed and came into town. Along with the two white officers came twenty of the largest, fiercest-looking Cherokees, stripped to the waist and painted for war. The Federals nervously eyed the strong, silent warriors. Thomas played the moment for all it was worth. He told the Federal colonel to surrender and leave Waynesville. The Federal colonel asked for time to think things over.

Martin and his officers also took time to confer. Someone pointed out that Lee and Johnston had already surrendered, so it would only be a matter of time before more Union troops turned to mop-up operations in the mountains. Though the Confederates had the Federals surrounded and frightened and had just demanded their surrender, the Confederate officers agreed that the best bet was for them to surrender.

The proposed deal was that the Confederates would officially surrender, keep their arms, and allow the Federals to leave Waynesville with no further bloodshed. The Federal colonel demanded that the arms be turned over to him. Martin finally agreed to the terms.

At least some of the Indians and mountaineers did not see any reason why they should comply with the agreement. While the bulk of Thomas's Legion went through formal surrender processing and gave up their arms, others did not. They simply went home, keeping their rifles, shotguns, pistols, and ammunition.

Thomas's Legion, one of the Confederacy's most unusual fighting units, thus disbanded.

BIBLIOGRAPHY

Axelrod, Alan. *The War between the Spies*. New York: Atlantic Monthly Press, 1992.

Barrett, John. *The Civil War in North Carolina*. Chapel Hill: University of North Carolina Press, 1963.

————. *Sherman's March through the Carolinas*. Chapel Hill: University of North Carolina Press, 1956.

Bastain, David F. *Grant's Canal: The Union's Attempt to Bypass Vicksburg*. Shippensburg, Pa.: Burd Street Press, 1995.

Boatner, Mark M., III. *The Civil War Dictionary*. New York: David McKay Company, 1959.

Botkin, B. A. *A Civil War Treasury of Tales, Legends and Folklore*. New York: Promontory Press, 1960.

Brown, Dee Alexander. *Morgan's Raiders*. New York: Konecky & Konecky, 1959.

Brownlee, Richard S. *Gray Ghosts of the Confederacy: Guerrilla Warfare in the West, 1861–1865*. Baton Rouge: Louisiana State University Press, 1958.

Catton, Bruce. *The Army of the Potomac: Mr. Lincoln's Army*. Garden City, N.Y.: Doubleday & Company, 1951.

———. *Grant Moves South*. New York: Little, Brown & Company, 1960.

———. *Grant Takes Command*. New York: Little, Brown & Company, 1968.

The Civil War Book of Lists. Conshohocken, Pa.: Combined Books, 1993.

Cooling, Benjamin. "Forts Henry and Donelson: Union Victory on the Twin Rivers." *Blue & Gray* 9 (February 1992): 45, 49.

Crowe, Vernon H. *Storm in the Mountains*. Cherokee, N.C.: Museum of the Cherokee, 1982.

Current, Richard N., ed. *Encyclopedia of the Confederacy*. 6 vols. New York: Simon & Schuster, 1993.

Cussler, Clive. *The Sea Hunters*. New York: Simon & Schuster, 1996.

Davis, Burke. *J. E. B. Stuart: The Last Cavalier*. New York, Bonanza Books, 1957.

———. *Sherman's March*. New York: Random House, 1980.

Davis, William C. *Battle at Bull Run*. Garden City, N.Y.: Doubleday & Company, 1977.

Dickison, Jonathan J. *Confederate Military History: Florida*. Secaucus, N.J.: Blue & Gray Press, 1899.

Edwards, William B. *Civil War Guns*. Secaucus, N.J.: Castle Books, 1962.

Elliott, Robert G. *Ironclad of the Roanoke*. Shippensburg, Pa.: White Mane Publishing, 1994.

Faust, Patricia, ed. Historical Times Illustrated *Encyclopedia of the Civil War*. New York: Harper & Row, 1986.

Fishel, Edwin C. *The Secret War for the Union: The Untold Story of Military Intelligence in the Civil War*. Boston: Houghton Mifflin, 1996.

Foote, Shelby, *The Civil War: A Narrative*. 3 vols. New York: Random House, 1958, 1963, 1974.

Freeman, Douglas Southall. *Lee's Lieutenants*. 3 vols. New York: Charles Scribner's Sons, 1942–44.

———. *R. E. Lee*. 4 vols. New York: Charles Scribner's Sons, 1961.

Furgurson, Ernest B. *Chancellorsville 1863: The Souls of the Brave*. New York: Alfred A. Knopf, 1992.

Gerrell, Allen, Jr. *The Civil War in and around St. Marks, Florida*. Self-published, 1993.

Gragg, Rod. *Confederate Goliath*. New York: HarperCollins, 1991.

Grant, U. S. *Personal Memoirs of U. S. Grant*. 1886. Reprint, New York: Literary Classics of the United States, 1990.

Hartje, Robert. *Van Dorn: The Life and Times of a Confederate General*. Nashville, Tenn.: Vanderbilt University Press, 1967.

Henry, Robert Stelph. *Nathan Bedford Forrest: First with the Most*. New York: Mallard Press, 1991.

Hoehling, A. A. *Damn the Torpedoes! Naval Incidents of the Civil War*. Winston-Salem, N.C.: John F. Blair, Publisher, 1989.

————. *Thunder at Hampton Roads*. Engelwood Cliffs, N.J.: Prentice-Hall, 1976.

Holien, Kim B. "The Battle of Ball's Bluff." *Blue & Gray* 7 (February 1990): 9–18.

Johns, John E. *Florida during the Civil War*. Gainesville: University of Florida Press, 1963.

Johnson, Charles F. *The Long Roll*. East Aurora, N.Y.: The Roycrofters, 1911.

Johnson, Ludwell H. *Red River Campaign: Politics and Cotton in the Civil War*. Baltimore, Md.: Johns Hopkins Press, 1958.

Johnson, Robert Underwood, and Clarence Clough Buel, eds. *Battles and Leaders of the Civil War*. 4 vols. Reprint, New York: Thomas Yoseloff, Inc., 1956.

Josephy, Alvin M., Jr. *The Civil War in the American West*. New York: Alfred A. Knopf, 1991.

Keller, Allan. *Morgan's Raid*, Indianapolis, Ind.: Bobbs-Merrill, 1961.

Longstreet, James A. *From Manassas to Appomattox*. Reprint, New York: Mallard Press, 1991.

McBride, Robert. *Civil War Ironclads: The Dawn of Naval Armor*. Philadelphia, Pa.: Chilton Books, 1962.

McFeely, William S. *Grant*. New York: W. W. Norton & Company, 1981.

Miller, Edward A., Jr. *Gullah Statesman*. Columbia: University of South Carolina Press, 1995.

Musicant, Ivan. *Divided Waters: The Naval History of the Civil War*. New York: HarperCollins, 1995.

Nesbitt, Mark. *Rebel Rivers*. Mechanicsburg, Pa.: Stackpole Books, 1993.

Paludan, Phillip Shaw. *Victims*. Knoxville: University of Tennessee Press, 1981.

Proctor, Samuel. *Florida 100 Years Ago*. Gainesville: University of Florida Press, 1960.

Robertson, James I. *General A. P. Hill: The Story of a Confederate Warrior*. New York: Random House, 1987.

Roland, Charles. *Albert Sidney Johnston: Soldier of Three Republics*. Austin: University of Texas Press, 1964.

Rosen, Robert N. *Confederate Charleston*. Columbia: University of South Carolina Press, 1994.

Sears, Stephen. *To the Gates of Richmond: The Peninsula Campaign*. New York: Ticknor & Fields, 1992.

Semmes, Raphael. *Memoirs of Service Afloat*. Secaucus, N.J.: Blue & Gray Press, 1987.

Sifakis, Stewart. *Who Was Who in the Civil War*. New York: Facts on File Publications, 1988.

Sommers, Richard J. *Richmond Redeemed: The Siege at Petersburg*. Garden City, N.Y.: Doubleday & Company, 1981.

Sterling, Dorothy. *Captain of the* Planter. Garden City, N.Y.: Doubleday & Company, 1958.

Stern, Philip Van Doren. *The Confederate Navy: A Pictorial History*. New York: Da Capo Press, 1992.

Still, William N., Jr. *Iron Afloat*. Columbia: University of South Carolina Press, 1971.

Sword, Wiley. *Shiloh: Bloody April*. New York: William Morrow & Company, 1974.

Trotter, William R. *The Civil War in North Carolina.* 3 vols. Greensboro, N.C.: Signal Research, 1988–89.

Tucker, Glenn. *Front Rank.* Raleigh: North Carolina Confederate Centennial Commission, 1962.

Wakeman, Sarah Rosetta. *An Uncommon Soldier: The Civil War Letters of Sarah Rosetta Wakeman.* Edited by Lauren Cook Burgess. Pasadena, Md.: The Minerva Center, 1994.

Warner, Ezra. *Generals in Blue: Lives of the Union Commanders.* Baton Rouge: Louisiana State University Press, 1964.

———. *Generals in Gray: Lives of the Confederate Commanders.* Baton Rouge: Louisiana State University Press, 1964.

Welsh, Jack D. *Medical Histories of Confederate Generals.* Kent, Ohio: Kent State University Press, 1995.

Wert, Jeffry D. *General James Longstreet: The Confederacy's Most Controversial Soldier.* New York: Simon & Schuster, 1993.

———. *Mosby's Rangers.* New York: Simon & Schuster, 1990.

INDEX

Guard, 307–10
Burnside, Ambrose P.: at Antietam, 113–14, 115, 116; at Battle of the Crater, 250; fires Pinkerton, 95; at Fredericksburg, 121, 127–33, 134, 135, 138, 139, 286; as inventor, 49; at Knoxville, 190; at New Bern, 66; replaces McClellan, 244
Butler, Benjamin, 136, 137, 232; at Big Bethel, 21; at Dutch Gap Canal, 147, 148; at Fort Fisher, 268, 269, 270; at New Orleans, 102, 216; at Outer Banks, 139
Butler, Matthew, 34, 282

Cairo, USS, 62–63, 64
Calhoun, John C., 296
Calhoun, W. Ransom, 297
Call, Richard K., 4
Camden, S.C., 284
Camp Vance, N.C., 307
Cape Fear River, 267, 272, 277
Carrick's Ford, Va., Battle of, 23
Casco class of monitors, 100
Cashier, Albert. See Hodgers, Jennie
Cashtown, Pa., 1121
Catawba River, 308, 309
Catlett's Station, Va., 196
Cedar Creek, Va., Battle of, 257, 305
Cedar Mountain, Va., Battle of, 216
Centralia, Mo., 260–61
Chalmers, James, 119
Chancellorsville, Va., Battle of, 159, 230, 236

Chantilly, Va., 104–5
Charleston Mercury, 296
Charleston, S.C.: compared to Pensacola, 4, 5; and Fort Sumter, 10, 11, 298, 300; port of CSS Hunley, 208, 209, 210; port of CSS Planter, 85; saved at Secessionville, 31; shelled by Greek fire, 53; "Stone Fleet," 46, 47
Chattanooga, Tenn., 192–94, 200, 204
Cheraw, S.C., 284–85
Cherbourg, France, 240
Cherokee Indians, 310–13
Chesnut Hill, Va., 198
Chickamauga, Ga., Battle of, 164, 190, 202
Chimo, USS, 100
Chowan River, 186
Cincinnati, Ohio, 184
City Point, Va., 194–95
Cleburne, Patrick, 202
Clingman, Thomas, 121
"Clotheslines, Battle of the," Fla., 150
Cochrane, John, 134, 135, 137
Colt repeating rifle, 49–50
Columbia, S.C., 283, 293
Columbia, Tenn., 153
Committee on the Conduct of the War, 45
Conestoga, USS, 63
Confederate uniforms, 29
Connally, John, 154
Corcoran, Michael, 233
Corinth, Miss., 75, 123, 173
Craig, Henry, 47–48, 49
Crater, Battle of the, Va., 195, 247, 249, 252, 269
Crittenden, George, 58–59, 60

Crook, George, 279–81
Cross Keys, Va., Battle of, 234
Cumberland Gap, 190, 191, 311
Cumberland, Md., 279, 280
Cumberland River, 58, 60, 183, 184, 188
Cumberland, USS, 16, 17–18, 61–62
Curtis, Samuel, 173
Cussler, Clive, 211
Cussons, John, 154
Custer, George Armstrong, 51, 198, 199

Dahlgren, John, 214
Dahlgren, Ulric, 214, 292
Davis, Benjamin, 116–18
Davis, Jefferson: and A. S. Johnston, 75; defends the South, 20; and Edward Rhett, 29; employs Union spies, 212; at First Manassas, 28–29; follows construction of ironclads, 227; and Henry Heth, 176; and John Dunovant, 32; and Kilpatrick-Dahlgren plot, 214, 292; and Leonidas Polk, 237; upgrades muskets, 214; and Zeb Vance, 68
Davis, Jefferson Columbus (Union general), 152–53
Davis, Varina, 212, 213
Department of East Tennessee, 176
Department of Key West and the Dry Tortugas, 137
Department of Texas, 7–8
DeSoto Point Canal, Miss., 145–47, 148
Dinwiddie Court House, Va., 300, 305